Diego Gambetta is a Fellow of King's College, University of Cambridge. He has worked in the Italian Public Administration as a researcher and labour market policy advisor. His interests include the theory and the empirical analysis of individual decision mechanisms. He is the author of *Were They Pushed or Did They Jump? Individual Decision Mechanisms in Education*.

Trust

Making and Breaking Cooperative Relations

Edited by

DIEGO GAMBETTA

Basil Blackwell

HM
132
.T783
1988

First published 1988

Basil Blackwell Inc.
432 Park Avenue South, Suite 1503
New York, NY 10016, USA

Basil Blackwell Ltd
108 Cowley Road, Oxford OX4 1JF, UK

Library of Congress Cataloging in Publication Data

Trust: making and breaking cooperative relations.
Includes index.
  1. Interpersonal relations. 2. Trust (Psychology)
3. Cooperativeness. I. Gambetta, Diego, 1952–
HM132.T783 1988   302.3′4   87-25691
ISBN 0–631–15506–6

British Library Cataloguing in Publication Data

Trust: making and breaking cooperative
relations.
  1. Social interaction 2. Trust (Psychology)
I. Gambetta, Diego
302.14   HM291

ISBN 0–631–15506–6

Typeset in 10 on 12pt Times
by DMB (Typesetting), Abingdon, Oxon.
Printed in Great Britain by T. J. Press Ltd, Padstow, Cornwall

Contents

Contents

Contributors

BERNARD WILLIAMS, Professor of Philosophy, University of California, Berkeley.

PATRICK BATESON, Provost of King's College, Cambridge, and Professor of Ethology, University of Cambridge.

DAVID GOOD, Lecturer in Social Psychology, University of Cambridge.

PARTHA DASGUPTA, Professor of Economics, University of Cambridge, and Fellow of St John's College, Cambridge.

JOHN DUNN, Professor of Political Theory, University of Cambridge, and Fellow of King's College, Cambridge.

NIKLAS LUHMANN, Professor of Sociology, University of Bielefeld.

GEOFFREY HAWTHORN, Reader in Sociology and Politics, University of Cambridge, and Fellow of Clare Hall, Cambridge.

ANTHONY PAGDEN, Lecturer in History, University of Cambridge, and Fellow of King's College, Cambridge.

ERNEST GELLNER, William Wyse Professor of Social Anthropology, University of Cambridge, and Fellow of King's College, Cambridge.

KEITH HART, Lecturer in Social Anthropology, University of Cambridge.

EDWARD LORENZ, Assistant Professor in Economics, University of Notre Dame.

DIEGO GAMBETTA, Fellow of King's College, Cambridge.

Foreword

The essays which make up this collection are the individual results of a cooperative enterprise. During 1985–86 a number of scholars from all quarters of the social sciences met in a series of seminars – held in King's College, Cambridge – to discuss the elusive notion of trust. The origin of these seminars can be traced back to my own struggle to make sense of the persistent and apparently insoluble political and economic problem Italy has faced over the century since it became a politically united nation: the underdevelopment of most of her southern regions which, in spite of multifaceted and protracted endeavours, shows no sign of coming to an end. The explanations offered for this, whether structural or cultural, appeared inadequate from both a theoretical and a political perspective; and the need for a more effective understanding was directly proportional to the growing pessimism. It is paradoxical that in a country where Vico was among the first of philosophers to demolish forcibly a metaphysical view of history and place the latter firmly in human hands, the inhabitants seem to wander in darkness and blame, for the lack of progress, *la fortuna*.

Except for two essays – Anthony Pagden's on eighteenth-century Naples and mine on the mafia – this volume diverges from that point of departure, and in a mixture of theoretical and historical contributions tries to address the underlying problems, shared by many other political and economic areas where cooperation fails to emerge irrespective of the collective interest. It explores the causality of cooperation from the perspective of the belief on which cooperation is predicated, namely *trust*.

The importance of trust pervades the most diverse situations where cooperation is at one and the same time a vital and a fragile commodity: from marriage to economic development, from buying a second-hand car to international affairs, from the minutiae of social life to the continuation of life on earth. But this very pervasiveness seems to have generated less analysis than paralysis: in the social sciences the importance of trust is often acknowledged but seldom examined, and scholars tend to mention it in passing, to allude to it as a fundamental ingredient or lubricant, an unavoidable dimension of social interaction, only to move on to deal with less intractable matters. This is clearly a case where the increasing specialization of the social sciences militates against thoroughgoing enquiry. A solo grand synthesis, on the other hand, though tempting, is hardly conceivable given the standards of conceptual and methodological rigour set by each of the constituent disciplines. This volume therefore seeks to avoid both parsimonious narrowness and insubstantial comprehensiveness, and to combine instead the wide-ranging perspective demanded by trust with some degree of disciplinary incisiveness.

The number of disciplines represented in the seminar, and likewise in this volume, is virtually exhaustive of the field, including anthropology, economics, history, philosophy, political science, socio-biology, sociology, and socio-psychology. The preparation of this interdisciplinary dish, with so many ingredients, has not proved a success in any naïvely utopian sense: the sense of discomfort and isolation that scholars in the social sciences sometimes feel in connection with the limitations of their subject – especially when it comes to questions concerning humans other than academics – does not imply that they are ready to embrace each other fraternally as soon as they are given the chance. On the contrary, if they think *their* subject is narrow, they are often inclined to think that those of others are at least equally – but even less agreeably – so. This, in conjunction with other idiosyncrasies in language, tradition, and methods – separating, for instance, those who dislike formal thought and those who dislike the lack of it – often makes for lively debate, which as far as any progress in the common interest goes, however, is often distracting if not detrimental. The seminars in which these papers were first presented were not short of such debate.

Yet there were many points of convergence, and some genuine progress was made towards a better understanding of a crucial but underexplored concept. Thus in spite of the heterogeneity of their authors, these essays can be read as a fairly integrated set, at least as integrated as one could realistically expect, *rebus sic stantibus*, in the social sciences today. A tangible sign of this integration is the large number of internal cross-references, frugal traces of longer discussion.

Before proceeding to a brief outline of the contents, I would like to thank all those who participated in the seminar. In particular, among those who did not deliver papers but made frequent and illuminating contributions to the discussion, I would like to express my appreciation

Foreword

to Frank Hahn, Ugo Pagano, and Tony Tanner. My gratitude goes also to King's College and to the Social and Political Science Committee of the University of Cambridge for the provision of funds. In addition, the College was the donor of something immeasurably more valuable than cash: a unique environment where an interdisciplinary exchange is encouraged and facilitated by daily proximity.

The volume is divided into three parts. While all the papers address, in varying combinations, the questions of what generates, maintains, substitutes, or collapses trusting relations, those in the first part do so through a range of theoretical perspectives and those in the second focus on a series of historical examples. The opening essay, by Bernard Williams, considers the general and realistic options available to society to motivate cooperation and avoid the sub-optimal outcomes generated by the Prisoner's Dilemma. A particular stress is laid upon the limits of each option. The second essay, by Patrick Bateson, discusses the general mechanisms of evolution which can realize stable cooperative equilibria among animals without postulating the need for trust; at the same time, Bateson traces an evolutionary path through which trust may have emerged as an aspect of awareness and an essential element of human cooperation.

The following two papers deal with the micro-mechanisms that produce and sustain trust. David Good analyses the implications of a wide spectrum of socio-psychological evidence for the notion of trust and for the rationality of its manifestations, and reviews the conditions which make cooperation variably dependent on trust. Partha Dasgupta explores the role of trust in economic transactions, shows how rational agents may be expected to search actively for it, and demonstrates that trust is a peculiar resource which is increased, rather than depleted, through use. The remaining two papers in the first part of the book are concerned with the relevance as well as the fragility of trust in the context of social and political life. John Dunn criticizes the weakness of those political theories which marginalize trust and makes a forceful case for its centrality in any adequate understanding of politics. Niklas Luhmann draws a conceptual map in which trust is differentiated from related concepts, and tries to capture the specificity of its importance for modern societies. Both Dunn and Luhmann share the view that a rational exploration of other people's interests can hardly serve as an adequate substitute for trust.

The essays in the second part refer back to the issues raised in the first by building on specific historical cases. Geoffrey Hawthorn, with reference to India and South Korea, deals with the question of whether and how vicious circles unconducive to economic development can be broken and overriden. Anthony Pagden, focusing on Spanish rule in eighteenth-century Naples, describes the ways in which trust can be intentionally destroyed for the purpose of domination. Ernest Gellner – drawing on the Islamic world and the Soviet Union – argues that anarchy, the absence of a centralized authority, can be productive rather than destructive of trust and cohesion. My paper on the mafia indicates how a society based on mutual distrust can develop into a stable social structure and reproduce itself over a long period. Keith Hart looks at the attempts of migrants in Ghana to identify the mutual relations – somewhere between trusting and self-enforcing agreements – most appropriate to safe economic transaction. Edward Lorenz reports on similar, if more successful, experiments on the part of French firms and their subcontractors.

My own general reflections, in the light of an overview of the papers contained in this volume and the problems they raise, will be found in the conclusion.

Diego Gambetta
King's College, Cambridge

Part I

Trust Considered

1

Formal Structures and Social Reality

Bernard Williams

In the first part of this paper, I take up some analytical questions about the theory of games and its application to social reality. I emphasize the importance of thinking, not in terms of one-off games or even of repeated trials, but in terms of the general motivations or dispositions that exist in a society. In the second part, I consider some complications in the idea of a 'motivation to cooperate', and the relation of that idea to the idea of trust. In the third part, I offer some very general speculations about the motivations that might be necessary or sufficient to sustain a social framework of cooperation.

I

I start from some points about the classical Prisoner's Dilemma. If x_1 represents the situation in which a player X confesses, and x_0 that in which X does not confess, then the preference schedule of each player, A and B, in the standard game (PD) is as follows:

A: $a_1b_0 > a_0b_0 > a_1b_1 > a_0b_1$

B: $a_0b_1 > a_0b_0 > a_1b_1 > a_1b_0$

(PD)

These preferences, of course, lead to the well-known result: since for each player 1 strictly dominates 0, they both confess and each player gets no better than his third preference.

However, other preference schedules are possible, and some of these have been discussed by Sen (1974). Consider those that define what Sen calls the *assurance game* (AG):

A: $a_0b_0 > a_1b_0 > a_1b_1 > a_0b_1$

B: $a_0b_0 > a_0b_1 > a_1b_1 > a_1b_0$

(AG)

Sen (1974: 78) writes: 'A contract of mutual non-confession does not need any enforcement in the AG, whereas it is the crux of the matter in the PD.' However, this is a little misleading. It is true that in AG the players share a first preference for a_0b_0. But, as indeed Sen says, they do both need assurance, and the prospect of the enforcement of a contract might be how the assurance was secured. This points up an important difference in the possible role of sanctions, a difference relevant to political theory. The addition of sanctions may change the utilities for a basically egoistic agent, or they may provide assurance for an agent who is basically cooperative. The latter, a very important possibility, is connected to a point I shall consider later: that the disposition to cooperation is typically cost sensitive.

There are other routes to assurance as well. The assurance needed is notoriously complex. Each needs to know that the other has the AG preference schedule. Moreover, each needs to know that the other knows that he (the first) has that preference schedule. If that is not so, each can conduct, and can replicate, reasoning that will lead him to believe that there is a risk that the other will defect, and hence he will defect himself, since each still has the preference

$$\text{self}_1 \text{ other}_1 >> \text{self}_0 \text{ other}_1$$

Without this knowledge, or something that will stand in for it, the cooperation will unravel. In the standard theory of games, such knowledge is given *a priori*, since everyone is assumed to have complete relevant information and also the capacity to apply it with complete rationality.

Recent work has been more willing to weaken these assumptions. In real life there are several types of limitation, for instance:

(R1) (a) People are imperfectly informed, both about other people's preferences and about their assessment of probabilities.
      (b) Limitation (a) itself may be imperfectly understood.
      (c) The acquisition of such knowledge may be variously impossible, expensive, and so on. One particular difficulty is that any actual process of inquiry may itself change preferences, destroy information, raise more questions, and generally confuse the issue.
      (d) There is a very significant limit, for social as well as cognitive reasons, on the recursive complexity of possible calculations.

These real-life truths about the cognitive limitations of real agents I have labelled collectively (R1).

An impressive illustration of limitation (d), and of the way in which it can go beyond purely cognitive limitations, is provided by the history of conspiracy in post-war France (Williams 1970). The baroque structure of these intrigues, in which an agent might act to create the impression that a second agent was acting so as to create the impression that the first agent was engaged in a conspiracy (for instance, that one), must surely have resulted in a situation in which no one really understood what anyone was doing; and this lack of understanding will also have affected the situation to be understood. Since such a situation is structured by the agents' intentions, and their intentions are conditioned by their increasingly confused grasp of others' intentions, there comes a point at which there is no truth of the matter about what they are doing.

Sen refers to a third preference schedule, which he calls *other-regarding* (OR):

$$A: a_0b_0 > a_0b_1 > a_1b_0 > a_1b_1$$
$$B: a_0b_0 > a_1b_0 > a_0b_1 > a_1b_1$$

(OR)

As Sen remarks, with these preference schedules no player even needs assurance, since a_0 and b_0 are strictly dominant strategies for A and B respectively. But this helps us to see another kind of artificiality in the classical theory: that the structure implies either the one-off expression of a preference, or the repeated expression of one preference unaffected by learning. A second real-life truth is:

(R2) Preferences relevant to cooperation change, in particular under the impact of information about the reliability of different kinds of assurance.

Thus someone might start with the OR preference schedule and, finding that he frequently got his second preference, become discouraged.

When, in the classical theory of non-repeated (or only trivially repeated) games, we see the transactions as expressions of preferences, we are licensed to understand the preferences simply in terms of utilities attached to the outcomes. The outcomes are preferred simply as such, and while the preference schedules that characterize games such as PD, AG, and OR can be described as 'egoistic', 'cooperative', 'altruistic' or whatever, those descriptions merely provide some psychological scenery: the operative element is preference defined over a class of outcomes. In reality, however, preferences are expressions of actual psychological attitudes, notably of dispositions; and a given choice, such as the choice on a given occasion whether to cooperate with another agent, will be a function of several dispositions and attitudes – to risk, to cooperation, to this kind of enterprise, to this agent, to some group to which this agent belongs, and so on. These assorted facts about agents' dispositions will feature in other agents' beliefs, and affect their own decisions.

In these respects, Axelrod's (1984) competition between different strategies over repeated trials, important and interesting though it is, relates only indirectly to the question of human cooperation in society. All the competitors were playing PD, so they all had the same preference schedule. What differed were the strategies, aimed at maximizing their scores as determined by that preference schedule. Moreover, the players were the strategies themselves, and the scores were allocated to those strategies. What the system therefore models is the survival or success of a conditional behaviour pattern, and the most natural interpretation of it is the intended one, in terms of evolutionary theory.[1] In the case of a human agent in social interaction, both his strategies and his preference schedule – the desire he has, for instance, for cooperation as such – may have conditional features, and also be modified by experience.

If an agent cooperates on a given occasion, this is not of course necessarily because he has an altruistic disposition to cooperate; as we have already noticed, and the literature only too often reminds us, a threat of sanctions applied to an egoistic agent can produce the same result. Besides that possibility, however, there are motives to cooperation that are not egoistic, but are more restricted than the kind of thing represented by the simplest psychological generalization of the preference schedule OR. There are general dispositions to cooperate which are conditional, and in particular are sensitive to costs: an agent will cooperate if it does not cost too much, but beyond this threshold he will not. The threshold may itself change over time. Moreover, failing perfect knowledge of the other agents' dispositions, he may take a risk on a cooperative initiative if the cost of being deceived falls below a certain threshold. In these various senses we have a third real-life truth:

(R3) A disposition to cooperate is cost sensitive.

It is very important that the costs do not have to be egoistic. Indeed, an agent who had had some disappointing experiences might come to reject, for egoistic reasons, the simplest psychological generalization of OR (that is to say, the disposition that consists merely in the fact that he always orders such outcomes in the OR way.) But a rejection of it could be expressed in terms of reasons that are not simply egoistic: by appealing to a right of self-defence, for instance (particularly when it is a matter of the kind of costs that are found unacceptable), or in the name of obligations to other groups, of family, friends, or whatever.

II

The previous discussion has referred often to motives (or, again, dispositions) to cooperate. Before moving on to consider, in the third

---

[1]   See P. Bateson, this volume. It has reasonably been found a reassuring feature of Axelrod's results that the successful strategies were all 'nice', in the sense that they never defected first.

part of this paper, different sorts of motivations to cooperation, we should examine more closely what cooperation, and motives to cooperate, are. This will bring out some assumptions on which the discussion rests. I shall take it that:

> Two agents *cooperate* when they engage in a joint venture for the outcome of which the actions of each are necessary, and where a necessary action by at least one of them is not under the immediate control of the other.

(The description can of course be generalized to cover cooperation by more than two agents; and one agent is said to cooperate, or to engage in cooperation, when there is someone with whom he cooperates.)

Under this definition, a situation in which two agents cooperate necessarily involves at least one of them *depending on* the other, or being, as I shall also put it, a *dependent party*. There are, of course, ventures that would naturally be called 'cooperation' but do not fall under this definition, because everyone in them is under the immediate control of everyone: if a party does not do his bit, this can be immediately detected. These are of no interest to the present discussion, which entirely concerns cases in which one party depends on another. (One important example of this is, of course, that in which one agent makes his essential contribution *before* the other makes his, but this need not be so, as the traditional PD itself illustrates.) They are the cases that lead us – though not quite directly – to the notion of trust.

Cooperation is a symmetrical relation: if X cooperates with Y, Y cooperates with X (if that seems unnatural, read 'cooperates' as 'engages in a cooperative venture with'). *Depends on*, however, is a non-symmetrical relation: if X depends on Y – in the sense that his getting what he wants out of the venture[2] depends on Y doing his part – it may or may not be the case that Y depends on X.

Within these definitions, we can distinguish significantly different kinds of motive that may be called 'motives to cooperate'. The phrase covers, most generally, any motive to enter a joint venture – that is to say, a situation in which one will be cooperating. But not all motives that lead agents to cooperate, on various occasions and in different circumstances, will produce the same results. In particular, some motives permit one to be a dependent party in some situations of cooperation, whereas others – though they are indeed motives to cooperate – will lead

---

[2] 'Getting what he wants' rather than the standard reference to his 'pay-off', to emphasize that an agent's aims in taking part in a cooperative venture need not be egoistic. An important case is that in which the agent's satisfaction from the venture necessarily implies the success of the venture – for instance, because what he wanted was *the venture to succeed*, not what he could get out of the situation if it did not succeed. If all the participants want that kind of satisfaction, then indeed they all depend on each other. The existence of a society involves there being many situations of that kind.

the agent to join in only if he is not the dependent party. One source of the Prisoner's Dilemma and similar problems of course lies in the fact that these various motives need not coincide.

The question for social theory is: what motivations do there need to be for there to be cooperation? That is the question to which the remarks in the third section are meant to contribute. One thing is immediately obvious: there will not be any cooperation if the only general motives there are for joining cooperative ventures are such that no one can (knowingly) be the dependent party.

This proposition, which is self-evident and about society, needs to be distinguished from another claim which is about individuals, and is true only under special circumstances. This is the claim that no *individual* agent can hope to enter cooperative ventures if he will not take a dependent position, or, again, if he usually defects when in a non-dependent position. This is no doubt often true in communities where agents and their dispositions are well known, but it need not be true in others. My question concerns what kinds of structure, in general, might serve to support cooperation. One possible *answer* to the question is that the only way to produce practices of cooperation is by confining them to persons whose dispositions and character are individually known to one another (they rely on what might be called 'thick trust'). This is a discouraging answer for modern life; the present point, however, is merely that it is one answer, among other possible answers, to the question of what motivations need to exist in society if people are to cooperate.

The obvious proposition was that if there are to be continuing practices of cooperation, then people must be motivated, one way or another, to enter into dependent positions. It is natural then to take two further steps. The first is to say that, in general, people will not do this unless they have some assurance that the other, non-dependent, party will not defect. This point, in a very abstract form, is of course central to the game-theoretical structures I have already discussed. This is also the place for the notion of trust. Cooperation requires trust in the sense that dependent parties need some degree of assurance that non-dependent parties will not defect: as I have already said, this need not take the form of 'thick' trust, individually based belief, but it must take some form or other. The next step after this is to claim that, in general, people will not trust others enough to bring about cooperation unless their assurance is to some extent well based: that is to say, unless people are also in general motivated, one way or another, not to defect if they are in a non-dependent position.

Both these steps involve empirical claims, and there are surely cases in which one or both of them might turn out false. But in their heavily qualified, 'for the most part', form, it is reasonable to take them as a basis for the discussion of trust and cooperation. I shall take these claims for granted in the way that I shall from now on discuss motivations to cooperate. I shall speak of motivations to cooperate, and their possible sources, sometimes to refer to motivations someone might have to become a dependent party, and sometimes to mean the motivations of non-dependent parties not to defect. They are two different sorts of thing. But once we leave the one-off case, and consider properly the implications of social practices of cooperation, and if we grant the empirical assumptions I have just mentioned, we are entitled to treat these two different things together, because they will, usually and for the most part, exist together – where 'together' means (as we have already seen) 'together in the same society', not necessarily 'together in the same person'.

The variety of dispositions that can lead an agent to cooperate or to withhold cooperation is very important in considering how various kinds of motivation and, correspondingly, various kinds of institution, may be effective or may unravel. In the second section of the paper I turn to some speculations on that question. They are extremely schematic, and designed to encourage lines of enquiry rather than to close the question.

III

I start with an axiom, which may be called *Hume's axiom*:

Only motivations motivate.

This might be thought to be a tautology, and that is, just about, what I take it to be. Its content, relative to the question under discussion, is that if someone acts to further some collectively desirable outcome, then his doing so must be explained by some disposition or desire that he has (for instance, to do just that). His so acting cannot be explained merely by the fact that it furthers that outcome, or merely by his knowing that it does. It follows from this that if one wants people to pursue such outcomes, one will have to see that appropriate motivations do actually exist to produce that result. What kinds of motivation might serve to stabilize the possibility of cooperation?

It will be useful to introduce, firstly, a distinction between *macro-motivations* and *micro-motivations*. A general account of this distinction would involve a good deal of elaboration and qualification: I hope that what follows will be adequate to the present discussion. Suppose an agent regularly performs acts of cooperation, and that the cooperative aspect of the acts is an intentional feature of them (he has not, for instance, carried out his side of a bargain by accident). We can explain

these acts at various levels of generality. With some agents, this pattern
of explanation will refer to a general motive to cooperate; the description
of the acts as cooperative enters into the characterization of a
motivation which he displays on all these occasions. This agent possesses
a *macro-motivation* towards cooperation.

A cooperative macro-motivation does not have to be altruistic or
ethical. There can be an *egoistic macro-motivation* to cooperation. This
is the situation inside a Hobbesian structure. The motivation to cooperation is egoistic, since it lies essentially in the fear of the sanctions of the
sovereign. However, the motivation to cooperation is also a macro-
motivation, because what the sovereign's sanctions are designed to bring
about (among other things) is a motivation, in general, to cooperate. It is
not an accident that, from egoistic considerations, the agent on these
various occasions cooperated: he knew that what he had egoistic reason
to do was, precisely, to cooperate.

A *non-egoistic macro-motivation* will characteristically be found in
some moral or ethical disposition, such as the recognition of a general
duty of fidelity, or a duty to a state which requires cooperation. It could
lie in the agent's relations to religious norms; though some crude
religious moralities, couched purely in terms of reward and punishment,
would return us to the egoistic option – the Hobbesian system with a
divine sovereign.

A *micro-motivation* to cooperation is a motive to cooperate, on a
given occasion or occasions, which does not imply any general motive to
cooperate as such. A *non-egoistic micro-motivation* might consist in
friendly relations towards a given person, the natural expression of
which includes a willingness to cooperate with her. I may have, further, a
disposition to enter into such friendly relations, and then I shall, in all
those cases, be disposed to cooperate; but still I shall not have, in virtue
of that, a macro-motivation towards cooperation, as opposed to a
disposition to enter relationships in which I am motivated to cooperate.

An *egoistic micro-motivation*, lastly, is fairly self-explanatory: I have
such a motivation to cooperate when, in those circumstances, I see it as
in my egoistic interest to do so, but this is not because I am generally
motivated, as in the Hobbesian system, to cooperate as such. This does
not rule out the possibility that I may regularly find myself in such
situations, or even that there may be some structure as a result of which I
regularly find myself in such situations: to produce such a structure
might be a triumph of the Invisible Hand. It will be a mark of this kind
of motivation, however, in a pure form, that there will be no motivational momentum from one case of cooperation to the next. I may
readily cooperate with X the next time, because I readily believe that it
will suit my interest to cooperate with X next time, but there is no general
disposition to cooperate, or even to cooperate with X, as such, and if the

particular features of a given occasion do not make it in my interest to cooperate, I shall not do so.

If we now ask, in terms of these types of motivations, what a society needs in order to sustain structures of cooperation, a number of speculative conclusions seem to be plausible.

1 *No macro-motivation by itself will do.*

(a) No egoistic macro-motivation by itself will do: it will be ineffective, or detestable, or both.

Since under this option the general motivation to cooperate is directly linked to the perception of self-interest, it is extremely sensitive to such things as the expectation of detection, and since this fact is itself common knowledge, there is (as in the classical PD case) a constant temptation to pre-emptive action. For such reasons, the system tends to unravel, and is prone to instability. The religious version might be thought to be more effective (though scarcely less detestable), if people could be brought to believe it, but the observed level of behaviour in societies which allegedly have believed it seems notably not to bear this out. It may be that the certainty of a 100 per cent detection rate was offset by uncertainties about the practice of the court.

(b) No non-egoistic macro-motivation by itself will do.

The purest form of such a disposition will be what I called earlier the simplest psychological generalization of the OR preference schedule, and this is unstable, particularly because of (R2) and (R3). As I have already remarked, that disposition can be conditionalized and made more complex: someone may think it right to cooperate if certain conditions are fulfilled, and not if not. But the need for these defences implies that the agent has other, in particular egoistic, motivations. Unless cooperation also, to some extent, serves those interests as well, the practices of cooperation will be unstable in the face of those other motivations. Another reason for the conclusion concerns not the potential enemies of cooperation, but the kinds of rewards it offers. Many cases of cooperation are satisfactory to the participants for reasons that imply cooperation but do not focus on it, and unless there are quite a lot of such cases, cooperation will not acquire much general attraction, and is likely to unravel in resentment. This is a particular danger for social arrangements based simply on egoism modified by a few moral principles such as the requirement to keep promises.

2 *Egoistic micro-motivation by itself will not do.*

Without some general structure, egoistic micro-motivation merely returns us to the Prisoner's Dilemma. So if this kind of motivation is to do all the work, we need an Invisible Hand structure that will bring it about that a tendency to defect is offset by some other egoistic micro-motivation (and will also allow this to be adequately known, etc.) But one needs extraordinarily strong and implausible functionalist assumptions to believe that such structures could be self-regulating and self-preserving, and there is abundant evidence to hand, generated by a body of relentless social experiment, to show that they are not.

Conclusions 1(a) and 2 together imply:

3 *No egoistic motivation by itself will do.*

Conclusions 1, 2, and 3 together imply that if anything will do by itself it will have to be non-egoistic micro-motivation. This will presumably have to be something like 'thick trust' – reliance on and between a group of persons in terms of their known dispositions, personal relations, and so on. It is not easy to see how this could be extended beyond a very small society. The only apparent way of taking it beyond that is to identify a particular set of people, a government or elite group, in whom thick trust is invested, and whose activities, example, or regulation serve to sustain cooperative activities throughout the society; but if this is conceivable at all, I find it impossible to see how such a structure could be the basis of our arrangements without an arrant degree of traditionalist or charismatic mystification. In fact, it seems to be obvious that

4 *Non-egoistic micro-motivation will not do by itself, for us.*

'We' are inhabitants of the modern world, involving vastly complex and complexly interrelated societies, which achieve an immense amount through impersonal relations. In particular, we do a great deal by relying on egoistic micro-motivations, and it is a remarkable achievement of the modern world to have brought this about. Indeed, it is obvious beyond a certain level of social size and complexity that we must rely a lot on such motivations, because of (R1): the kinds of mutual knowledge needed to stabilize egoistic micro-systems is easier to bring about in such circumstances than the kinds of knowledge involved in 'thick trust'. Moreover, this impersonality of modernity brings with it some well-known positive values that depend on mutual personal ignorance: freedom and the benefits of privacy – privacy not merely for the ego but for shared personal life which is genuinely personal.

If all of conclusions 1 to 4 are correct, then none of these kinds of motivation will do by itself. So should we look to some combination of them? Granted what has been said, the most promising combination, and one that has found favour, is one between egoistic micro- and non-egoistic macro-motivations. One version of this, the combination of egoism and a few moral principles, I have already mentioned. But the non-egoistic element might take some other, perhaps richer, form (this might, very recklessly, be called Durkheim's solution.) But there is a notorious problem of how the non-egoistic motivation is to be encouraged and legitimated, when people are constantly and professedly expressing egoistic micro-motivations in much of their life; and there is a tendency for the required ideology to become ineffective humbug.

If that is right – and obviously each of these points needs proper discussion, which I cannot try to give them here – then in these terms there is no solution. But all that means is that there is no solution *at this level of generality*. The problem of cooperation cannot be solved merely at the level of decision theory, social psychology, or the general theory of social institutions. In fact, that there is no one problem of cooperation: the problem is always how a given set of people are to cooperate.

In a modern state, people are motivated by some version or degree of each of the sorts of motivations that have been distinguished, and their actions are often overdetermined, quite often by all four. The right question to ask, at this level of generality, is not which of these simple models could be made to do all the work, but rather what combinations of such motivations make sense. How are they disposed to undermine one another? It will be particularly important here to ask what kinds of non-egoistic micro-motivation there are, and which of them might relate coherently (more coherently than national-level thick trust could) to both the egoistic micro-motivations and the large impersonal structures of a modern state. Asking such questions, we may be able to get some general perspective on the problems of cooperation in a given historically shaped society.

REFERENCES

Axelrod, R. 1984: *The Evolution of Co-operation*. New York: Basic Books.
Sen, A. K. 1974: Choice, orderings and morality. In S. Körner (ed.), *Practical Reason*, Oxford: Basil Blackwell. Reprinted in his *Choice, Welfare and Measurement*, Oxford: Basil Blackwell, 1982.
Williams, P. M. 1970: *Wars, Plots and Scandals in Post-war France*. Cambridge: Cambridge University Press.

2

The Biological Evolution of Cooperation and Trust

Patrick Bateson

We do not know whether animals trust each other, but we may ask whether the conditions of their social life favoured the evolution of what we understand to be trust in humans. More directly, we can discover whether they behave in ways that benefit others. Since they often do so, we may also ask what favoured the evolution of such behaviour and under what conditions cooperation is likely to occur in those animals that show it. The answers to such questions are important because so many non-biologists believe that the social behaviour of animals consists of nothing but strife and manipulation. If animal nature is the result of the competitive process of Darwinian evolution, then surely it must also be ruthlessly competitive. Such a conclusion does not follow from an acceptance of Darwinism. It is also a travesty of what biologists have observed and what most now believe.

In this chapter I discuss how the observed cooperation between animals may be interpreted in terms of the most widely accepted explanations for biological evolution.[1] I shall begin with a description of the character of neo-Darwinian explanations and then deal with three ways in which the observed cooperation might have arisen. The first explanation is that, at least in the past, the aided individuals were relatives; cooperation is like parental care and has evolved for similar reasons. The second is that the cooperative behaviour generated characteristics in a collection of individuals that, under special conditions, favoured such groups over those that did not cooperate so effectively. Finally, cooperating individuals jointly benefited even though they were not related; the cooperative behaviour has evolved because those who did it were more likely

[1] I am grateful to Nick Davies, Diego Gambetta, Philip Kitcher and Bernard Williams for their comments on an earlier version of this chapter.

to survive as individuals and reproduce than those who did not. The three evolutionary explanations are not mutually exclusive.

These questions about the evolution of cooperation do not bear directly on the issue of trust, though they may give pause to anyone who supposes that trust is required for effective cooperation (defined simply in terms of working with and assisting others). To maintain such a position it would be necessary to argue that, for example, honey bees trust each other. Even though the study of cooperation in animals seems irrelevant to an understanding of trust in humans, careful analysis of the conditions in which cooperative behaviour is expressed suggests that many animals are exquisitely sensitive to the behaviour of others. This observation suggests an explanation for the evolution of the mental state that we recognize as trust in outselves. Discussions about evolution also draw attention to the explicit distinctions which biologists are forced to make between what animals do and the immediate and long-term consequences of their behaviour. In such discussions the meaning of 'interest' is not in much doubt.[2] I shall amplify this point since it is so easy to conflate the consequences of a dynamic process with the way in which those consequences are generated. I am going to start, though, with a simple description of Darwin's explanation, because opportunities for confusion abound and even those who are supposedly expert in the area are sometimes responsible for a great deal of muddle.

MODERN EVOLUTIONARY THEORY

Virtually every biologist who cares to think about the subject believes that all living matter has evolved. Existing species were not created in their present form at the beginning of life on this planet. The modern scientific debates are about how the changes came about, not about whether or not they happened. Increasingly, theorists agree that the evolution of life requires several distinctly different explanations. Stable forms may often arise by chance, for instance; and extinctions and opportunities for further change may result from environmental catastrophe. However, chance and catastrophe are unsatisfying and inadequate as explanations when we try to understand the numerous and exquisite examples of correlations between the characters of organisms and their physical and social environments. For instance, carnivorous and herbivorous mammals have strikingly different types of teeth and the differences are readily related to methods of feeding. To take another

---

[2] The presumption is usually that the single currency of evolution is the genetic endowment that is required to build the bodies and behaviour patterns and which was effective in doing so in the past. It certainly does not follow that the expression of the genes in any one individual is inevitable or independent of other conditions (see Bateson 1986).

dental example, the large canine teeth found in carnivorous animals are also seen in non-carnivorous animals, which use them as weapons in fights with members of their own species. Male polygynous primates that fight with other males for females have much larger canines than male primates that are characteristically monogamous (Harvey, Kavanagh, and Clutton-Brock 1978). Character–environment correlations of this type are known as adaptations. They catch our attention because they seem so well designed for the job they perform. Much the most coherent explanation for the evolution of such phenomena is still Darwin's. Indeed, Darwin's proposal is much better seen as a theory about the origin of adaptations than as a theory about the origin of species.

Darwin's proposed mechanism depends crucially on two conditions. Firstly, variation in a character must exist at the outset of the evolutionary process. Secondly, offspring must resemble their parents with respect to such a character.[3] The short-term steps in the process involve some individuals surviving or breeding more readily than others. If the ones that survive or breed most easily carry a particular version of the character, that character will be more strongly represented in future generations. If the character enabled them to survive or breed more readily, then the long-term consequence is that the character will generally be correlated with the conditions in which it worked. If differences between individuals depend on differences in their genes, Darwinian evolution results in changes in the frequencies of genes.

Darwin used the metaphor of selection to describe the evolutionary process of adaptation because he had in mind the activities of human plant and animal breeders. If people want to produce a strain of pigeons with longer tail feathers than usual, they pick from their flock those birds that have the longest feathers and exclusively use them for breeding purposes. This is artificial selection of the long-tailed pigeon by animal breeders. By analogy, Darwin referred to the differential survival of the characters that adapt an organism to its environment as *natural* selection. The Darwinian formulation emphasizes that the precise way in which a character enables an individual to survive or breed better is part of the process.[4] The way in which the character works is not the same as the long-term changes in the frequencies of genes that are required for the expression of the character. Moreover, the evolutionary process does

---

[3] In modern versions of Darwin's theory, the correlation in the character may exist between collateral genetic relatives such as siblings or uncles and nephews. Usually, the correlates will exist because genetic relatives are more likely to share copies of the same rare genes, but the similarities may arise for other reasons. Genetic inheritance is not a requirement for Darwinian evolution to work.

[4] It is because an explanation for the evolution of a particular character has to refer to the specific way in which it has worked (and by implication has done better than other characters) that the formulation is non-circular. 'Survival of the survivors' is, of course, vacuous.

not require the postulation of an unconscious motive for propagating genes (let alone a conscious one).[5] Gene propagation is merely the result of a character, such as a particular form of behaviour, that works better than another version.

I should locate a potential source of confusion before going any further. To state that a gene makes the difference between a character that works (and is thereby transmitted to the next generation) and one that does not says nothing about the other conditions that are required for the expression of that character. It certainly does not mean that the expression of the character is inevitable; nor does it imply that its form is predictable if the conditions in which it evolved change.

If motives are unimportant, what about the 'selfishness' that is sometimes claimed for genes? Richard Dawkins (1976; 1982) has argued vividly that individual organisms do not survive from one generation to the next, while on the whole their genes do. He proposed that therefore Darwinian evolution has acted on the genes. Dawkins's approach to evolution was presented in characteristically entertaining form when he suggesteed that the organism is 'a robot vehicle blindly programmed to preserve its selfish genes'.

In order to understand Dawkins's particular brand of teleology, it may be helpful to forget biology for a moment and think about the spread of a new brand of biscuit in supermarkets. Consider it from the perspective of the recipe. While shoppers select biscuits and eat them, it is the recipe for making desirable biscuits that survives and spreads in the long run. A word in the recipe might specify the amount of sugar to be added and make the difference between a good and a bad biscuit. Because it serves to perpetuate itself, that word is selfish in Dawkins's sense.[6] This novel way of looking at things is unlikely to mislead anyone into believing that what shoppers really do in supermarkets, when they pick a particular brand of biscuit off the shelves, is select a word in the recipe used for making the biscuits. It is odd, then, that the selfish gene approach has encouraged people to run together the crucial differences between individuals that survive and those that do not with the genetic consequences of differential survival in later generations. It has been a muddling conflation.

[5] It is unfortunate that, in many of the writings about evolutionary biology, intention is allowed to intrude – as in the sentence: 'Animals attempt to maximize their inclusive fitness.' Biologists who do this will claim that they use a shorthand for: 'Animals behave *as if* they were attempting to maximize their reproductive success.' Nonetheless, the phraseology does cause confusion – even in the minds of its authors.

[6] In my analogy, a word in the recipe corresponds to a gene in biology; the biscuit to the individual organism; the supermarket to the environment; and the shoppers' choices to natural selection. Biscuits do not carry the recipes within them and do not participate in recipe replication, so the analogy is inexact. Nevertheless, the distinction between what shoppers do and the long-term effect on words in recipes is relevant to biology.

We should return to the strict meaning of Darwin's metaphor and make an explicit distinction between the short-term causes of differential survival and the long-term effects of differential survival on the frequency of the genetic replicators, as indeed Dawkins (1982) himself has done. Once made, the distinction saves much muddle in modern discussions of evolution. It also serves a valuable role in drawing attention back from a preoccupation with single genes to the ways in which genes work together. Each gene depends for its survival on the outcome characteristics of the whole gene 'team'. Furthermore, special combinations of genes work particularly well together, and the gene that fits into one combination may not fit into another. The concept of the coadaptation of genes is helpful in re-establishing that organisms do, indeed, exist as entities in their own right.

THE EVOLUTION OF COOPERATION

If, as seems likely, a great deal of biological evolution involved differential survival, the outcome of the competitive evolutionary process is often social cooperation. Emperor penguins huddle to conserve warmth. Cattle press tightly together to reduce the surface exposed to biting insects. In many species, individuals clean each other. Male lions cooperate to defend females from other males. Mutual assistance may be offered in hunting; for instance, cooperating members of a wolf pack will split into those that drive reindeer and those that lie in ambush. As a result all of them are believed to get more to eat.[7] In highly complex animals aid may be reciprocated on a subsequent occasion (Trivers 1971; 1985). So, if one male baboon helps another to fend off competition for a female today, the favour will be returned at a later date (Packer 1977). What is usually obvious about such cases is that all the participating individuals benefit by working together.[8]

Three evolutionary explanations have been proposed for non-manipulative social cooperation: (1) the individuals are closely related; (2) the surviving character is the property of many individuals; and (3) the individuals mutually benefit. These explanations do not exclude

[7] The belief that cooperating predators obtain more food than those that hunt on their own is attractive. However, Packer (1986) argues that the evidence does not stand up to careful scrutiny. There may be benefits in this respect, but they remain to be convincingly demonstrated. Meanwhile, biologists need to keep their minds open to alternative explanations for hunting in groups.

[8] Sometimes behaviour may be successfully manipulated, as when a nestling cuckoo is able to obtain care from a hapless pair of reed warblers. Alexander (1974) has suggested that, even within a species, offspring may not operate in their own best interests and may have been manipulated by their parents in such a way as to further the long-term interests of their parents.

each other, but it is helpful to deal with them separately. The first explanation has been the domain of the subject called sociobiology by E. O. Wilson (1975), and has been extensively and critically discussed (for example Kitcher 1985). The idea of 'kin selection' is an extension of the intuitively obvious point that animals will often put themselves at risk and do things that are bad for their health in the production and care of offspring.[9]

The use of the term 'altruism' in sociobiological discussions was unfortunate because of its moral connotations. The evolutionary principle can be perceived more clearly, perhaps, when a non-behavioural example is used. Consider those insects, like wasps, that are conspicuously marked and unpalatable to their predators. Birds that eat wasps are unlikely to repeat the experience, since birds learn quickly. This does not help the wasps that died. However, in the ancestral condition, the few wasps that were conspicuously marked were likely to be closely related. Those that died provided protection for those that survived by making them less prone to predation. As a consequence, conspicuous yellow and black abdomens may have spread until all wasps were marked in the same way. It is not difficult to see how a precisely similar argument can be mounted for care directed towards close relatives. The point is that the giving of aid to a relative may evolve simply because the expression of that character increases the probability that it will recur in later generations.

BEHAVIOUR OF GROUPS

The second evolutionary explanation for cooperation is the most contro-versial, largely because a good argument has been confused with a bad one. The bad argument is that animals ought to be nice to each other for the good of the species.[10] This idea is inadequate because any individual

[9] After a calculation made in a London pub, J. B. S. Haldane declared that he would lay down his life for two brothers or eight first cousins. However, it would have only been sensible for him to lay down his life if he especially wanted to perpetuate the habit of self-sacrifice. And even if he had wanted to do that, he would have needed to be sure that the difference between the presence and the absence of the self-sacrificial tendency was associated with a difference in a single gene. If it was two genes, presumably he would have needed to save at least four brothers or 64 first cousins (and also assume that they would all breed as much as he would have done himself). In general, Hamilton's (1964) formalization of inclusive fitness applies to whole organisms when the difference between two types is that one type helps other individuals and the other does not, and the behavioural difference is due to a difference in only one gene.

[10] 'Good for the species' arguments have a long history and can even be found in some of Darwin's writing (e.g. Darwin 1871). They were clearly present in Kropotokin's (1902) famous book on mutual aid and recurred in another celebrated book by Allee (1951). More recently, Lorenz (1966) explained the restraint on aggression within a species in the same terms.

that breaks the rule and behaves in a way that benefits itself at the expense of other members of its species will eventually populate the world with individuals that behave in the same self-serving way. The good argument is that some assemblages of individuals may, through their concerted efforts, generate an outcome that puts their group at an advantage over other groups. This argument becomes more obvious once observed characters are separated conceptually from their effects on gene frequencies found in individuals in subsequent generations. The well-adapted character that survives from one generation to the next is not the same as the necessary conditions for its expression. Once these distinctions are made, we can ask: to what does that character belong? The character, which the metaphorical hand has supposedly selected, may be formed by more than one individual. The characteristics of the whole entity provide the adaptations to the environment. One assemblage of individuals, acting as an organized system, can compete with another in the strict Darwinian sense of differential survival.

The possibility of group characters changing in Darwinian fashion is not in question among serious evolutionary biologists. However, the consensus in the last ten years has been that the conditions for such evolution were too stringent, since groups are usually much slower to die off than individuals and individuals can readily move from one group to another (see Maynard Smith 1976). That consensus was probably formed too readily and has been under attack in recent years.[11]

The essential point is that the outcome of the joint action of individuals could become a character in its own right. The nature of this argument may be perceived most clearly in the arrangements of different species that are obliged to live together in symbiotic partnership. A good example is provided by the lichens which are found on virtually every stable surface throughout the world, from rocks and tree trunks to paving stones and old roofs. While they look like single organisms, lichens are composed of algae and fungi fused together in obligatory partnership. In Darwinian terms, though, the overall features of a lichen might enable it to survive better in a given environment than a lichen with other characteristics. Even though the character is replicated in an 'offspring' lichen by the independent reproduction of the component

---

[11] See for example D. S. Wilson (1980). Grafen (1984) suggests, that the 'new group selection' stems from a paper by Hamilton (1975), and argues that the logic applied to kin selection applies to the changes in the frequencies of genes within the successful groups. In one sense he is certainly right, in that cooperating groups are likely to be much more closely related to each other than they are to membrs of groups that do not cooperate so effectively. In another sense, though, he misses the point that the character that makes one group more likely to survive than another is a property of the whole assemblage and not of the component individuals. In addition, Boyd and Richerson (1985) argued that group selection would have been particularly potent in animals that readily copied the behaviour of the majority in their social group.

algae and fungi, the mechanism of inheritance is irrelevant to the evolutionary process. As long as offspring characteristics are correlated with parental characteristics, it does not matter how they came to be that way.

To take a specific example, suppose that in one 'individual' lichen algal and fungal mutations have products that combine to make the lichen less tasty to reindeer. The less palatable lichens will survive better than those without the mutants. This is not because of competition between components, but because of the effects they have on the entity of which they are a part. In terms of my supermarket analogy, different recipes might be used for the biscuit and its chocolate coating, but the customers select the whole package and by doing so increase the numbers of copies of both types of recipe. The general point is that the methodology of focusing on the genetics of individuals merely serves to muddle the issue of what is necessary for differential survival with what is required for replication. Once liberated from this confusion we can, with easier minds, examine the characters generated by the cooperative behaviour of social groups of animals.

The emergent properties of social life might have been important in evolution when cheating individuals were penalized by adversely affecting the group in which they lived (see Crook 1980). Clearly, a cheat could sometimes reap the benefits of the others' cooperation without joining in itself. However, such actions would not be evolutionarily stable if the cheat's social group was less likely to survive than a group without a cheat and the cheat could not survive if it left its own social group.

If the conditions were right, the outcome of the joint actions of individuals in the social group would have changed as the result of Darwinian evolution. It is important to appreciate that this perfectly straightforward Darwinian argument does not undermine what we know about genetics or return to muddled good-for-the-species thinking. It merely draws attention to a higher level of adaptation. This requires acceptance that the characteristics of social groups are the emergent properties of the participating members and that the logic of Darwinian theory applies as much to these characters as to those of individual organisms. Providing examples is never easy, because evolutionary history cannot be replayed, but the conditions necessary for its occurrence are particularly likely to have operated in hominoid evolution. I should add, none the less, that such a view of the differential survival of groups is still heterodox among biologists, mainly because they do not want to lose the ground that was won by examining the evolutionary effects of manipulation and reciprocity at the level of the individual.

MUTUAL BENEFITS

The third explanation for cooperation is sometimes known as 'mutualism within a species' (see for example West-Eberhardt 1975; Wrangham 1982). Two cooperating individuals are not necessarily related, but they are both more likely to survive and reproduce themselves if they help each other. This category includes examples of types like the iterated Prisoner's Dilemma, dealt with so interestingly by Axelrod (1984). For a specified set of pay-offs, everybody benefits by cooperating at the outset. I shall focus here on joint parental care of the offspring.

Every type of parental care is found in animals. Maynard Smith (1977) proposed a useful scheme which suggests how such diversity might have evolved. A simplified (and slightly modified) version of it is given in table 2.1. Consider the bottom right-hand case where neither parent cares for the young; herrings are like this. If a mutant male enters the population and by caring for his young is able to have greater reproductive success than deserting males, male parental care should spread through the population. In many fish, such as the stickleback, males do care for the young and females do not. Exactly the same argument applies if a mutant female has a comparable advantage over other females or enters a population where male care has been the usual practice. If such a female does better than the other females, females will eventually care for the young alongside the males. Biparental care is especially common in the birds.

Even when both parents care for young, their interests do not coincide. They certainly have a common interest in their offspring's survival, but they have diverging interests in as much as each one might be able to increase its reproductive success by spending time seeking extra mates elsewhere. In many species of birds, in which both sexes normally care

TABLE 2.1 *Probabilities that offspring will be produced under four arrangements of biparental care (simplified from Maynard Smith 1977).*

| | | | Female | |
			cares	deserts
	cares	Female gets	P_2	$P_1(1+f)$
Male		Male gets	P_2	P_1
	deserts	Female gets	P_1	$P_0(1+f)$
		Male gets	$P_1(1+m)$	$P_0(1+m)$

P_0, P_1, and P_2 are the probabilities of survival of young cared for by 0, 1, or 2 parents respectively

m is the probability that a deserting male will acquire a new mate

f is the probability that a deserting female will acquire a new mate

for the young and one parent dies or disappears, the remaining mate increases the time and energy it devotes to caring for the young. This frequently observed event raises the question of the extent to which an animal can be a 'free-rider' on the efforts of its mate. Micro-economic models have been borrowed to explain what happens when two animals cooperate but do not share identical interests. I shall describe a model originally proposed by Chase (1980) and which I have slightly modified.

Given that each individual can affect its reproductive success in more than one way, if it reduces the effort devoted to one form of reproduction it must increase the effort devoted to the other by a specified amount in order not to reduce its overall reproductive success. Withdrawing care of offspring must be matched by stepping up the search for an additional mate. If the two forms of achieving reproductive success are taken as separate axes, it is possible to draw lines of equal success. These are comparable with economists' lines of indifference, expressing the same level of satisfaction with different combinations of goods (see figure 2.1). Such lines have three features.

1 Higher levels of reproductive success are achieved as the joint amounts of the incompatible activities are raised.
2 The contours joining points of equal reproductive success never cross each other.
3 The shape of the contours will depend on how much help is received in caring for offspring.[12]

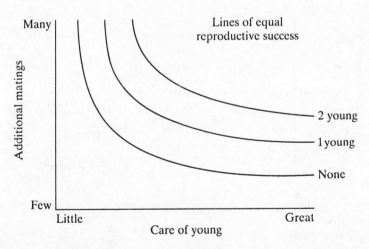

FIGURE 2.1 *Hypothetical lines of equal reproductive success, when an animal can increase its reproductive success by additional matings or by parental care but the two activities tend to be mutually exclusive (from Chase 1980)*

12 This is where I depart from Chase's (1980) formulation of the problem.

We now need to calculate what economists would call a 'resource budget line'. This is the line indicating the maximum amounts of all possible combinations of behaviour of which the animal is capable. If the animal has a fixed amount of energy available, it might use all of that energy on caring for the young which it has had with a single mate. At the other extreme, it might spend all of it on looking for other mates. Those two points should be joined by a straight line (see figure 2.2), which may be drawn across the contours of equal reproductive success. It enables us to ask what is the best response in terms of producing the largest number of young. The best response, and therefore the one that is most likely to evolve, is where the resource budget line touches the contour of highest value in that set of conditions.

Since the pattern of contours changes with the amount of help the animal gets in caring for its young, the best response would also be expected to depend on conditions. Therefore, animals capable of taking note of conditions should evolve so that they change the amount of time they allocate to care of the young in response to changes in those conditions. The model is simple, but the expectation is matched by many observations of birds increasing the parental care devoted to their offspring when their mate deserts or disappears.

Free-riders who leave all parental care to their mates will not evolve if the respective amounts of care given by cooperating parents reach an equilibrium when they both care for the young. Each animal involved in

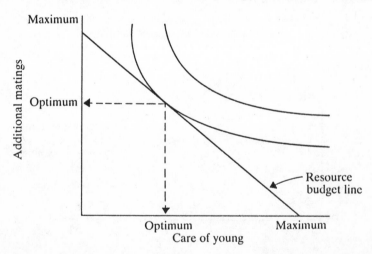

FIGURE 2.2 *The optimal amounts of time devoted to seeking extra matings and to caring for young are found where the resource budget line touches a line of equal reproductive success at a tangent. The animal cannot exceed the maximum time spent searching for extra mates or the maximum amount of time caring for young because of energetic and other restraints*

the cooperative care of young has an independent set of conditional rules about what to do if the help provided by its partner changes. These may not be the same for both sexes and will depend on the opportunities available for getting other matings. The rules will be the product of Darwinian evolution in the sense that the animals that had most off-spring in the past would be those that most nearly found the optimum for a particular set of conditions.

Firstly, consider the female's reaction to the male's contribution, basing it on the optimal response in a particular set of conditions (see figure 2.3). Next consider the male's reaction to the female's contribution. Providing the slopes are right, the two reaction lines generate an equilibrium where they intersect. Note that a stable equilibrium is not an inevitable outcome for all combinations of lines (see Houston and Davies 1985). Similarly, if the two reaction lines do not intersect, the individual with the higher reaction line will do all the work.

Houston and Davies (1985) have provided an illustration of how such postulated rules might work in a common garden bird, the dunnock (or hedge sparrow). Birds are generally supposed to be monogamous, but in the dunnock only some of the breeding arrangements involve a stable relationship between one male and one female. Some are polygynous, some are polyandrous and, even more remarkably, some breed in

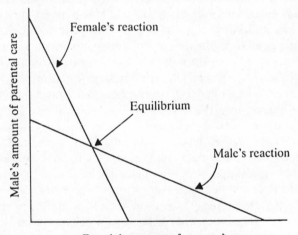

FIGURE 2.3 *The female's reaction to a given amount of parental care by the male and the male's reaction to the female. Both sexes tend to reduce their parental care if the other increases its care, but the nature of each individual's reactions to the other is such that, if both sexes are present and healthy, the value for the amount of parental care given by each sex stabilizes after interplay between the two of them. These values (which need not be the same for the two sexes) represent the separate optima for both of them*

combinations of several males and several females (see Davies 1985). In all breeding arrangements the amount of effort put into feeding the young increases with the number of young. Taking this into account, in monogamous pairs the female is responsible for slightly more than half of feeding. However, the female reduces the number of feeds to the brood when she is helped by two males; her feeding rate is then about 7 per cent less. But although Houston and Davies (1985) found that she does reduce her own rate of feeding the young when she has more help, she certainly does not give up altogether, as might be naïvely expected if she operated on the principle of unenlightened self-interest.

CONDITIONAL EXPRESSION

The example of the dunnocks looking after their young emphasizes how the cooperative behaviour of animals may be exquisitely tuned to current conditions. Even in plants and invertebrate animals, examples of the induction of special responses to special environmental conditions are commonplace. Grasshoppers living on the African savannah are normally greenish-brown. They prefer backgrounds which are the same colour as themselves and they are difficult to see on such backgrounds. Their coloration and behaviour undoubtedly protect them from being eaten. After a savannah fire, offspring of the grasshoppers develop in a different way and black pigment is deposited in their cuticles. Under experimental conditions the developing grasshoppers can be induced to do this simply by placing them on a black substrate (Rowell 1971). Not only do such grasshoppers match their black environment, they prefer to settle on such backgrounds. It is obvious that grasshoppers with a conditional response to the environment in which they are reared are more likely to survive than those that are inflexible. They would also do better than those that go black on a probabilistic basis, matching the likelihood of becoming black to the probability of savannah fires. Clearly, many grasshoppers that go black probabilistically would do so at the wrong time and be highly conspicuous to predators as a result.[13]

It is unfortunate that the emphasis on genes in evolutionary arguments led to the mistaken notion that behaviour which has been shaped by Darwinian processes must be unlearned, inevitable, and unchangeable. One person who fostered this error was the dominant promoter of socio-biology, E. O. Wilson (1975). When challenged about the way he had played down the interaction between the developing individual and its environment, he suggested that the role of developmental processes might usefully be 'decoupled' in the study of social behaviour (Wilson

---

[13] See Caro and Bateson (1986) for a general discussion.

1976). The strong implication was that the development of the individual is merely a complex process by which genes are decoded. Since developmental biologists dismissed this position as naïve (see Bateson 1986), Wilson had to respond to the criticism, particularly when dealing with the obvious plasticity of human behaviour. His solution was to replace genes that prescribe the form of behaviour of an individual by genes that do the same for 'epigenetic rules' (Lumsden and Wilson 1981). The hypothetical rules are supposed to determine how development proceeds and how learning takes place. While the use of such explanatory devices had been commonplace in both biology and psychology, Lumsden and Wilson differed from other theorists of development in proposing that such rules are genetically determined, in the sense that the characteristics of the rules themselves develop independently of the state of external conditions. Such a position does not seem plausible *a priori* and the empirical grounds for doubting it are also substantial (see Bateson 1976; 1983).

What an individual does is highly dependent on circumstances, in terms of both the short-term control of behaviour and the development of an individual's particular style (Hinde 1982; Huntingford 1984). No animal behaves in the same way irrespective of conditions. Nor, of course, do humans. Departures from the norm are not necessarily pathologies generated by abnormal conditions. They may well be highly adaptive responses to particular ecological conditions.

When, in the course of evolution, the form of behaviour became conditional on external circumstances, two things could have happened. Firstly, novel environments were especially likely to generate surprising results. Removal of the buffering against fluctuation would have opened up the behavioural system to short-term change. Secondly, sensitivity to the social environment, as in the case of the cooperating dunnocks, might have set the pattern of long-term change on an evolutionary pathway which led to a state in which trust became an important requirement for cooperation. The mediating step might have been the evolution of self-awareness, an issue that has been explored by Humphrey (1976; 1986) and Crook (1980). If what A does depends on what B has done and likewise B's behaviour is conditional on A's, then they are locked into a game to which it pays both of them to look ahead and calculate the consequences of particular actions.[14] Once self-awareness had evolved, trust might then have become one of the requirements for effective cooperation (see also Axelrod 1984).

In conclusion, it is obvious that social life may sometimes involve conflict and intense competition. It may also involve real benefits and

---

[14] A similar argument was outlined by Jolly (1966) and played a part in the thinking of Trivers (1971; 1985) when he considered the evolutionary consequences of reciprocated aid.

active cooperation. The balance between these conflicting pressures often changes so that, if conditions become really difficult, the cooperative arrangements break down. Or if members of a group are not familiar with each other, no mutual aid occurs until they have been together for some time. As familiarity grows, individuals come to sense the reliability of each other. Furthermore, the expectation of an indefinite number of future meetings means that deception is a much less attractive option. The major message is this: in cooperative behaviour, conditions matter a lot.

CONCLUSION

In this chapter I have described three explanations for the evolution of cooperation. My own view is that all three types of process have been important and may all have been involved in the evolution of some forms of cooperation. Once evolutionary stability of cooperative behaviour was achieved by one or more of the Darwinian processes I have discussed, features that maintained and enhanced the coherence of the highly functional cooperative behaviour would then have tended to evolve. Signals that predicted what one individual was about to do and mechanisms for responding appropriately to them, would have become mutually beneficial. Furthermore, the maintenance of social systems that promoted quick interpretation of the actions of familiar individuals would have become important. Finally, when the quality or quantity of cooperation depended on social conditions, increasing sensitivity and self-awareness would have become advantageous.

In ending, I want to reiterate four points. Firstly, evolutionary process must be distinguished from its consequences; differential survival in the past does not necessarily mean social competition now. Secondly, in biology the outcome of differential survival is the 'interest', and no motive is required for that interest to be maximized by a given course of action. Thirdly, at least three explanations for the evolution of cooperation can be offered. Finally, the conditions in which cooperative behaviour occurs, and those in which it does not, need to be properly explored and understood. When that is done we may be able to explain the origins of trust.

REFERENCES

Alexander, R. D. 1974: The evolution of social behaviour. *Annual Review of Ecology and Systematics* 4, 325–83.

Allee, W. C. 1951: *Cooperation among Animals, with Human Implications.* New York: Schuman.

Axelrod, R. 1984: *The Evolution of Cooperation.* New York: Basic Books.

Bateson, P. P. G. 1976: Rules and reciprocity in behavioural development. In P. P. G. Bateson and R. A. Hinde (eds), *Growing Points in Ethology,* Cambridge: Cambridge University Press, 401–21.

Bateson, P. P. G. 1983: Rules for changing the rules. In D. S. Bendall (ed.), *Evolution from Molecules to Men,* Cambridge: Cambridge University Press, 483–507.

Bateson, P. P. G. 1986: Sociobiology and human politics. In S. Rose and L. Appignanesi (eds), *Science and Beyond,* Oxford: Basil Blackwell, 79–99.

Boyd, R. and Richerson, P. J. 1985: *Culture and the Evolutionary Process.* Chicago: University of Chicago Press.

Caro, T. M. and Bateson, P. P. G. 1986: Organisation and ontogeny of alternative tactics. *Animal Behaviour* 34, 1483–99.

Chase, I. D. 1980: Cooperative and non-cooperative behaviour in animals. *American Naturalist* 115, 827–57.

Crook, J. H. 1980: *The Evolution of Consciousness.* Oxford: Oxford University Press.

Darwin, C. 1871: *The Descent of Man, and Selection in Relation to Sex.* London: Murray.

Davies, N. B. 1985: Cooperation and conflict among dunnocks, *Prunella modularis,* in a variable mating system. *Animal Behaviour* 33, 628–48.

Dawkins, R. 1976: *The Selfish Gene.* Oxford: Oxford University Press.

Dawkins, R. 1982: *The Extended Phenotype.* Oxford: Freeman.

Grafen, A. 1984: Natural selection, kin selection and group selection. In J. R. Krebs and N. B. Davies (eds), *Behavioural Ecology: an evolutionary approach,* 2nd edn. Oxford: Basil Blackwell, 62–84.

Hamilton, W. J. 1964: The genetical evolution of social behaviour. I and II. *Journal of Theoretical Biology* 7, 1–52.

Hamilton, W. J. 1975: Innate social aptitudes of man: an approach from evolutionary genetics. In R. Fox (ed.), *Biosocial Anthropology,* New York: Wiley, 133–55.

Harvey, P. H., Kavanagh, M., and Clutton-Brock, T. H. 1978: Sexual dimorphism in human teeth. *Journal of Zoology* 186, 475–86.

Hinde, R. A. 1982: *Ethology.* Oxford: Oxford University Press.

Houston, A. I. and Davies, N. B. 1985: The evolution of cooperation and life history in the dunnock, *Prunella modularis.* In R. M. Sibly and R. H. Smith (eds), *Behavioural Ecology,* Oxford: Basil Blackwell, 471–87.

Humphrey, N. K. 1976: The social function of intellect. In P. P. G. Bateson and R. A. Hinde (eds), *Growing Points in Ethology,* Cambridge: Cambridge University Press, 303–17.

Humphrey, N. K. 1986: *The Inner Eye.* London: Faber and Faber.

Huntingford, F. 1984: *The Study of Animal Behaviour.* London: Chapman and Hall.

Jolly, A. 1966: Lemur social behavior and primate intelligence. *Science* 153, 501–6.

Kitcher, P. 1985: *Vaulting Ambition.* MIT Press, Cambridge, Mass.

Kropotkin, P. 1902: *Mutual Aid: a factor of evolution*. London: Heinemann.

Lorenz, K. 1966: *On Aggression*. London: Methuen.

Lumsden, C. J. and Wilson, E. O. 1981: *Genes, Mind, and Culture*. Cambridge, Mass.: Harvard University Press.

Maynard Smith, J. 1976: Group selection. *Quarterly Review of Biology* 51, 277–83.

Maynard Smith, J. 1977: Parental investment: a prospective analysis. *Animal Behaviour* 25, 1–9.

Packer, C. 1977: Reciprocal altruism in *Papio anubis*. *Nature* 265, 441–3.

Packer, C. 1986: The ecology of sociality in fields. In D. I. Rubenstein and R. W. Wrangham (eds), Princeton: Princeton University Press, 429–51.

Rowell, C. H. F. 1971: The variable coloration of the acridoid grasshoppers. *Advances in Insect Physiology* 8, 145–98.

Trivers, R. 1971: The evolution of reciprocal altruism. *Quarterly Review of Biology* 46, 35–57.

Trivers, R. 1985: *Social Evolution*. Menlo Park, Calif.: Benjamin/Cummings.

West-Eberhardt, M. J. 1975: The evolution of social behavior by kin-selection. *Quarterly Review of Biology* 50, 1–33.

Wilson, D. S. 1980: *The Natural Selection of Populations and Communities*. Menlo Park, Calif.: Benjamin/Cummings.

Wilson, E. O. 1975: *Sociobiology: the new synthesis*. Cambridge, Mass.: Harvard University Press.

Wilson, E. O. 1976: Author's reply to multiple review of *Sociobiology*. *Animal Behaviour* 24, 716–18.

Wrangham, R. W. 1982: Mutualism, kinship and social evolution. In King's College Sociobiology Group (ed.), *Current Problems in Sociobiology*, Cambridge: Cambridge University Press, 269–89.

3

Individuals, Interpersonal Relations, and Trust

David Good

In the analysis of trust, we are inevitably drawn to the complex two-way interrelationships between it, the economic and political fabric of society, and the individuals who constitute that society. On the one hand we may be concerned with its role in the creation of that fabric and its psychological impact on the individual, and on the other we may be concerned with how that fabric and the properties of those individuals can serve to maintain trust and any associated cooperative behaviours. While many of the authors in this volume have examined several aspects of these interrelationship, I will adopt a narrower focus and concentrate on two parts of the psychological literature which can contribute to our understanding of the individual as a trusting agent.[1] The first of these is concerned with the conditions under which individuals are willing to trust one another in novel circumstances. This will be based mainly on laboratory studies of bargaining games in which the players can adopt either competitive or cooperative strategies. The second is concerned with factors which will affect the durability of trust. This will be based on various studies of the conditions under which an individual's ideas become impervious to change and behaviour becomes routinized. Needless to say, the treatment of these two parts of the literature will be highly selective, and will ignore much of the fine detail in the attempt to frame a rather general picture. All of this will be prefaced by a consideration of the psychological consequences of trust for the individual, and a brief discussion of what I am taking trust to be.

[1] Preparation of this chapter was assisted by various discussions following its presentation in the seminar series which gave rise to this volume, and I am grateful to the many people who offered commentary and criticism. I am particularly grateful to Diego Gambetta for his many useful comments on an earlier draft of this paper.

The background to the observations and proposals which follow is the clear and simple fact that, without trust, the everyday social life which we take for granted is simply not possible. Luhmann makes this point in the opening chapter of his *Trust and Power* (1979), and Garfinkel (1963) illustrated the importance of trusting other persons' claims as to the nature of social reality in his (by now infamous) rule-breaching studies. In these, Garfinkel's confederates behaved as if the nature of a social situation was other than that which it might be taken to be by the unwitting subjects with whom they were interacting. The subjects (or, perhaps more appropriately, victims) were thus presented with grounds for not trusting either their own sense of what the actual social reality was, or the reality claims of their interlocutors. The result of this for many of the subjects was bewilderment to the point that some of them even began to doubt their own sanity.

Central to these subjects' experience of rule breaching is the role played by another's reaction to one's own action, in confirming the validity of the prior experience on which that action was based. As many authors have observed, without such confirmation the social world becomes unintelligible and seemingly unknowable (see for example Kelly 1955; Laing 1965; Rogers 1972). The consequences of not having the measure of predictability in one's life which this interrelationship between experience, action, and reaction entails have been demonstrated in a wide variety of studies. To take an extreme example, Seligman, Maier, and Solomon (1971) report that dogs subjected to random and unpredictable shocks of a relatively low intensity suffer much more than those who are receiving higher but predictable charges. Typically, the first group of dogs becomes listless, their physical condition worsens, and their normal interests diminish when compared with the group receiving the greater but predictable punishment.

Apart from these specific and extreme cases, the general level of trust which an individual holds has also been studied. Rotter and his colleagues have examined, in a large number of studies (see Rotter 1980 for details), the characteristics of individuals who are willing to trust others over a wide range of issues, and in a number of different spheres. In general, they have found that those who are more willing to trust other people are likely to be equally trustworthy in that they are less likely to lie, cheat, or steal. They are also less likely to be unhappy or maladjusted, and are typically more liked by their friends and colleagues.

There are probably many reasons why these relationships between trusting, being trustworthy, and psychological well-being exist, but the fact that trust at a basic personal level is psychologically rewarding is unsurprising. The more difficult questions from a psychological point of view concern the mechanisms which permit this desirable and rewarding state of affairs to come about. Such questions will be the focus of this chapter.

The first substantive definition of 'trust' in the *Oxford English Dictionary* is 'confidence in or reliance on some quality or attribute of a person or thing, or the truth of a statement'. A later variant stresses the economic usage, defining it as 'confidence in the ability and intention of a buyer to pay at a future time for goods supplied without present payment'. Under either of these definitions, or the others offered in this volume, trust is based on an individual's theory[2] as to how another person will perform on some future occasion, as a function of that target person's current and previous claims, either implicit or explicit, as to how they will behave. The explicit claims as to the nature of one's future behaviour are clearly very important, but so too are the implicit claims. These arise from an individual's cooperative behaviour, which is a major source of information in our construction of our views of other persons. However, the relationship between cooperative behaviour and trust is not simple.

If A trusts B to take some future action C, then at one simple level it is A who is trusting B, in that the satisfaction of A's goal requires B to do C, and not something else which would be detrimental to A's interests. As such, it is not A who is being cooperative, but B in performing the action C, and by the same token B is not displaying trust in A. However, at another level this asymmetry is reversed. B displays trust in A's representation of the conditions of the request to do C, and similarly A cooperates in the production of that representation. Furthermore, the behaviour of A and B in a single episode can form the basis for future instances of trust and cooperation. Rarely is it the case that exchanges requiring trust are ahistorical single instances.

Cooperative behaviour by itself is not, of course, necessarily a sign of a cooperative mentality. It could be cooperative by chance rather than design. Similarly, a lack of cooperation need not indicate an uncooperative mentality; nor need it represent some deception or breach of trust. Consequently, while cooperation and trust are intimately related in that the former is a central manifestation of the latter, the former cannot provide, for either the actor or the analyst, a simple redefinition of trust. As we shall see below, the looseness in this relationship is important in the psychological processes which increase the durability of trust.

---

[2] The term 'theory' is used very loosely here, and nothing particular rests upon its choice. The terms 'lay theory', 'lay conception', 'set of beliefs', and the like would do just as well if they were as short.

Overall then, the discussion which follows may be strictly thought of as being concerned with an individual's theory as to the likely future performance of other persons, and the relationship of such theories to cooperative behaviour.

II

The laboratory study of strategic interaction has a long tradition in social psychology. It has focused on a wide variety of different games, of which the Prisoner's Dilemma is the best known, and ostensibly these studies provide the basis for a well-controlled examination of the performance of competing agents under different conditions. They have not gone uncriticized, and undoubtedly one cannot take their results as offering an unproblematic reflection of society at large.[3] However, some of them have produced interesting and suggestive results, and there are four general findings which are relevant to the account being developed here. They are findings which are principally concerned with the conditions under which cooperation is fostered, in cases where the net cost of trust being misplaced will be greater than the actual individual gain from trusting.

The first reflects the case where the studies in question overcome by their very design a particular criticism of laboratory work. All laboratory studies suffer from the fact that they are very short, and the subjects are not tied in any way whatsoever to the enduring consequences of their actions as they would be in everyday life. Rarely are experiments scheduled to last more than a couple of hours, and at most they last for no more than a couple of weeks as in, for example, the Haney, Banks, and Zimbardo (1973) study of a simulated prison.[4] This point would obviously be very serious for any generalizations from laboratory studies where an analogue of long-term political or economic activity was being sought. Apart from brief encounters with itinerant merchants, individuals are inevitably concerned with a time scale greater than two hours. Therefore, the variation across studies in the time perspective that subjects are asked to adopt is of some interest.

[3] Many have argued that such laboratory events are irrelevant to the investigation of human action in society. Indeed, some workers in this field have agreed with this view, and have retreated to a position where their only goal is the development of laws applicable to laboratory events (Rapoport 1970). Many of the criticisms are not without substance, but they do not lead to a necessary conclusion that anything which happens in the laboratory is completely unrelated to everyday life. Real events happen in the laboratory, and subjects deal with them using resources they have brought from the outside world. To ignore this fact, and the information or suggestions which such studies can provide, is to deny oneself a valuable resource.

[4] But even this study did not last the scheduled two weeks, owing to the psychological problems which the stresses induced by the study generated in the subjects.

Pruitt and Kimmel (1976) examined the extensive literature on the Prisoner's Dilemma game, and concluded that one important consideration for subjects is whether or not they view the interchange from a short-term or long-term perspective. In particular, if subjects believed that they would need to interact with each other after the study was concluded, and therefore the usual social and temporal isolation of such interactions was removed, their behaviour became considerably more cooperative. This result is, of course, consistent with many other findings and proposals from the economic and game-theoretic literature (see for example Axelrod 1984).

The second and third findings derive principally from the Trucking Game, which is due to Deutsch and Krauss (1960). The original form of the game is based on the map given in Figure 3.1. In this game, each subject is a manufacturer who must transport his or her products to a sales point by road. There are two roads which might be used, but the shortest route, which is the one they do not have independent access to, can only be used by one truck at a time.

Since time is money in this game, it is in the players' interest to collaborate on the use of the shortest route, but such collaboration requires them to trust one another. Deutsch and Krauss have explored a number of variations of this game, and two results are particularly

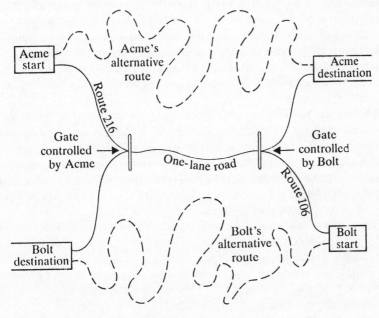

FIGURE 3.1 *Map for Trucking Game*

relevant here. One is that if both gates are removed from the road so that neither player can offer any degree of threat to the other apart from blocking the road with a truck, then there is a much higher degree of cooperation as measured by the total 'wealth' generated by each player (Deutsch and Krauss 1962). Indeed, it is only on this condition that either player makes a profit on their operations at all.

The other is that if the rewards which accrue from each phase of the game are only gradually increased from an initial small sum, then the players are far more likely to achieve cooperation in the production of high personal and aggregate wealth than if the benefit from each phase is initially set at a high value (Deutsch, Canavan, and Rubin 1971).

Confirmation of the importance of gradual change comes from various studies which have explored the 'foot-in-the-door' sales tactic. Freedman and Fraser (1966) had an executive for a road safety campaign ask one group of householders if they would mind having a fairly large and unattractive sign promoting safe driving erected on their front lawn. Only 17 per cent of the group complied with this request. However, a second group were first asked if they would be willing to display a small sign advocating the same position. Almost all of them agreed to this, and when a few days later the request to have the large sign displayed was made, 76 per cent agreed to have it erected.

The fourth finding of interest is common to a very large number of studies. This is simply that the greater the amount of communication there is between the players in a wide variety of games, the greater the likelihood of there being a mutually beneficial outcome. For example, Wichman (1970) reported least cooperation between female subjects when they were in a position where they could neither hear nor see one another, and most when they were in close proximity and could both see and hear one another.

The notion 'amount of communication' is by no means a simple one, and an important qualification concerning its benefit in bargaining or contractual situations concerns the degree of ambiguity potentially present in any communication. While a measure of ambiguity can be of value for the maintenance of any social status quo (for reasons which will be discussed below), and indeed is inevitable, it nevertheless provides a potential for exploitation by the unscrupulous.

The issue of clarity is partly addressed in Christie and Geis's (1970) work on machiavellianism. Over a number of years they developed a personality questionnaire which was designed to rate individuals as either more or less cunning, manipulative, and unscrupulous in their relations with other people. They attempted to validate the scale in a variety of ways, including a laboratory game called the Con Game.[5]

[5] This game is played by three players who must move along a numbered board, and the first one to the end receives a prize. A player's movement is determined by the number

The finding of interest from this work for the argument here is that the most machiavellian of the players were most able to exploit the situation to their greatest advantage, and do much better than chance would predict when the situation was most ambiguous. However, when the game was played such that each player knew exactly what resources the others had, and there was a minimum of ambiguity, this advantage disappeared.

To briefly summarize the content of this section, then, we may propose that in conditions where the long-term interests of the participants are stressed, where only small initial or additional rewards are at stake, where there is no potential for threat and great potential for successful communication in that the ambiguity of the situation is reduced, and where the participants are in free and easy contact, then cooperation and, one might suggest, a certain level of trust can develop. In some respects, the result concerning small initial rewards or small increments, and that concerning the consequences of the absence of threat, might seem counter-intuitive. If there is so little at stake, why should one bother with all the difficulties associated with trusting someone else, and why should the absence of an ability to penalize a defaulter lead to greater apparent trust? To provide answers to these questions, to understand the basis for the set of findings cited in this section, and to understand what factors might make trust robust, it is necessary to examine the cognitive operations which underlie an individual's perceptions and beliefs as to the nature of the social world.

III

A number of papers in this volume (for example those of Lorenz and Dasgupta) make observations on the way in which actual human performance in the economic and political sphere differs markedly from that often assumed. In particular, they draw attention to the fact that the assumption of unbounded cost-free rationality is rarely satisfied, and that often the deviations from the model person are great. The idealist may say that departures from this assumption in the descent to irrationality merely introduce noise into the system, and are therefore incon-

---

thrown on a dice multiplied by the value of one of a set of cards with which he or she is provided at the start of the game. Players are allowed to make coalitions in which they can combine the value of their moves so they can move far faster together than alone. If coalitions are maintained, two players could arrive at the end point together, and would have to negotiate how the reward is to be divided. The most successful players in this game are those who can readily make and break coalitions to their own personal advantage, and drive the hardest bargains over the division of the spoils. The experimenter, in running this game, can vary the value of the cards each player has, and the combinations of types of player, as defined by the machiavellianism index, in each triad.

sequential. While it may be true that any assumption other than that of limitless rationality is extremely difficult for the theoretician to handle, this should not blind us to the fact that such departures exist, and, as I shall argue, that they can play a significant role in the maintenance of trust.

As Dasgupta (this volume) points out, decisions about whether or not one should trust another person depend on that person's reputation, and a favourable reputation is something which economic agents will be concerned to establish. Therefore, the ways in which a reputation for trustworthiness or its opposite is established or destroyed are important. The person whose reputation is at stake will obviously try to influence these processes, but that influence is only limited. Not only will the perceivers of a reputation usually have access to information which the reputation holder does not control, but also the manner in which both types of information are interpreted is not straightforward. Such information will often be ambiguous and open to many readings, and, even when it is not, it is not necessarily the case that all people will accord any particular item the same significance. The interpretation of a reputation will be a function of the interpreter and, therefore, it is necessary to consider how new information is handled and is related to existing views.[6]

This topic, with respect to events and entities in both the social and the physical world, is something in which psychologists have long been interested. The conclusion from this work is that the life expectancy of a theory or view is intimately related not only to the target of the theory, but also to the activity of the lay theorist, and that such theorists act in a way which is quite removed from the stereotypical Popperian falsificationist. Rarely do they seek disconfirmation, and often they do their best to avoid it. The basis for this claim lies in a wide variety of research from a number of different fields.

In a well-known study, Wason (1960; 1968) presented subjects with a sequence of numbers 2 4 6. They were then told that this sequence conformed to a simple rule, and that their task was to discover this rule by generating further three-number sequences which the experimenter would classify as being in accord with it or not. For each sequence, the

---

[6] Obviously, the information which is available to the individual, and is relevant to a reputation, will be a powerful factor, and nothing which follows below should be read as denying this. The sources of this information will range from the beliefs generally held in a society about individuals as members of certain categories, to the particular experiences which any individual has had of other people through various kinds of personal contact. While the analysis here is concerned with how the interpretation of this information is a function of the individual's cognitive processes, the way in which society at large can function as an information processor should not be ignored. Arguably, on this larger scale, society-wide preconceptions can have the same impact as the confirmation biases displayed by the individual.

subjects were required to give the hypothesis they were entertaining about the rule at that point. When they believed they were certain they they had discovered the rule, they were to announce it. A typical exchange (adapted from Wason 1968) between experimenter and subject is given below; the subject took 17 minutes to discover the rule, which was simply 'any three numbers in increasing order of magnitude'.

Sequence	Reason for offering	Feedback
8 10 12	Added 2 each time	Yes
14 16 18	Even numbers in order of magnitude	Yes
20 22 24	Same reason	Yes
1 3 5	Added 2 to preceding number	Yes
	Rule announcement Starting with any number, 2 is added each time to form the next number	Wrong
2 6 10	Middle number is the arithmetic mean of the other two	Yes
1 50 99	Same reason	Yes
	Rule announcement The middle number is the arithmetic mean of the other two	Wrong
3 10 17	Same number, 7, added each time	Yes
0 3 6	Added 3 each time	Yes
	Rule announcement The difference between two numbers next to each other is the same	Wrong
12 8 4	The same number is subtracted each time to form the next number	No
	Rule announcement Add a number, always the same number, to form the next number	Wrong
1 4 9	Any three numbers in order of magnitude	Yes
	Rule announcement Any three numbers in ascending order to magnitude	Right

As can be seen from this protocol, the subject consistently generated sequences which were in accord with the putative rule under test, and this is typical of subjects in such a study. Rarely is evidence which could falsify a rule sought, and often available disconfirming evidence is ignored, as is the case for the seventh sequence 3 10 17. Here the subject offers as the reason for generating the sequence a putative rule 'add 7 each time', when clearly this rule is inadequate to account for the previous acceptable sequences. This might not be an unquestionable interpretation of this subject's particular performance, but it is a tendency which has been well documented elsewhere, for example in Bruner, Goodnow, and Austin's (1956) work on concept formation.

By itself, a study such as Wason's might be dismissed on the grounds that it represents a fairly artificial laboratory task in which the subjects have little interest, but similar failures to seek disconfirmation have been observed in a number of different spheres. For example, Mitroff (1974) indicates that NASA scientists have a strong confirmation-seeking bias in their work, and Mynatt, Doherty and Tweeney (1977) report a similar bias amongst subjects attempting to discover the laws of an artificial universe simulated on a computer. Snyder and Swann (1978) conclude that subjects seek evidence of extroverted behaviour rather than its opposite when trying to evaluate a description of someone who has been described as extroverted. Tajfel (1969) makes the case that such a failure to seek disconfirmation, and an inability to recognize disconfirmation for what it is when it is presented to the individual by chance, are important factors in the maintenance of racial prejudice. Indeed, apart from such evidence, most of us can think of instances where we have sought to maintain our view of something, and it does not require much insight to recognize when we are doing this, and why we do so blinker ourselves. As Tajfel and many others have argued in the case of social categories, being able to reduce a welter of information to a manageable size has attractions even if we know that the basis of that reduction is flawed. Most of us prefer to develop a basis for action, rather than simply to contemplate the many-splendoured diversity of the world around us. Rushing fools may often make mistakes, but the virtues of angelic caution are not very appealing to most.

An important additional element in Tajfel's argument is that the initial interpretation of social events is not fully specified by those events. Thus even events which might offer disconfirmation of one's views, and which are simply made available by chance, can yield to this confirmation bias by being interpreted in a way which hides or denies their potential as counter-example to a view. A wealth of evidence supports this point, and some good examples are provided by experimental studies of inter-personal attributions, especially those who have focused on self-serving biases (see Fiske and Taylor 1984 for an overview). For example, Chaiken and Darley (1973) had subjects watch a film of a production line worker and a supervisor as part of a training exercise. At the end of the film, an event involving both supervisor and worker resulted in the worker's production being lost. The two groups of subjects in this study were watching as either potential workers or potential supervisors. On being asked to report what had happened in the film, the two groups varied greatly in their interpretations. Typically, potential supervisors blamed the worker, and potential workers the supervisor. In a more general way, Kahneman and Tversky (see Kahneman and Tversky 1973; and Kahneman, Slovic, and Tversky 1982) have examined the strategies that individuals employ when confronted by uncertainty and ambiguity in a variety of situations. They provide much evidence that there is a strong tendency for ambiguous or incomplete information to be interpreted in line with the individual's preconceptions. Such interpretations will, of course, serve to reinforce those preconceptions.[7]

This bias towards the preservation of a theory is also reflected in the way that a particular set of actions developed in response to a specific problem can come to dominate an individual's actions even when it is entirely inappropriate. This phenomenon is often referred to as the 'set effect' or *Einstellung*, and was strikingly demonstrated in an experiment by Luchins (1942). In this study, subjects had access to a tap, a sink, and three jugs A, B, and C of given capacities, and were only allowed to fill and empty jugs and to pour them into one another. Their task was to measure out a specified quantity of water into any one of the jugs. Table 3.1 gives a set of trials which some of the subjects followed.

On all of these trials except trial 8, the desired quantity can be achieved by removing from B the volume of A once and the volume of C twice. For trials 1–5 this is the simplest way to achieve the desired quantity, but for trials 6, 7, 9, and 10 simpler solutions exist. On trial 8 this procedure will produce the wrong result. However, having used the simplest solution successfully on trials 1–5, the majority of the subjects persevered with it on trials 6–10. This perseverance was so strong that 64 per cent failed to get the desired quantity in trial 8 even though it is a remarkably simple computation by any standard.

The set effect has been noted in many other psychological studies, and simply reflects the fact that computation is not cost-free, and that often individuals will deploy well-tried strategies even though they may not be the most appropriate way to approach a novel problem. To discover whether a strategy is appropriate or not requires expenditure of precisely the type that an individual may be trying to avoid. In some respects, therefore, the set effect reflects the same kind of 'cognitive inertia' as the confirmation bias. In failing to re-evaluate a procedure when its failure

---

[7] Dasgupta makes the point that if we were all thoroughly moral individuals the issue of trust would not arise, but to say this is to ignore the ambiguity of many social scenes and events. Outcomes are often not easily predicted, and there are many reasons why predictions may fail without the good character of the actor being impugned. This, essentially, is the niche in our social ecology which has made the excuse a possible species. Excuses presume a variety of interpretations for any event, and operate to foreground the one which is most desirable for the excuse giver. In certain respects, the variety and ingenuity of excuses that can be offered highlight this point about social ambiguity (see Snyder, Higgins, and Stucky 1983 for some interesting examples and analysis).

could indicate inadequacy, individuals are not giving due weight to the negative evidence provided by experience.

So far, I have briefly examined some evidence which supports the claim that the nature of the information available to individuals, and the way they process it, can serve to maintain an individual's theory or theories about other people and society, even though one might believe that a careful consideration of that information would lead to rejection of those theories. This has been offered in contrast to assumptions of unbounded rationality, but this is not to say that the social and economic agent is an unwitting dupe who never changes his or her views. To be non-rational in this way is decidedly rational as a strategy for coping with limits on one's rationality. In everyday life there is a constant flow of events which require numerous decisions to be made, and which carry a wide variety of implications for our current mentality. One could spend hours analysing the costs and benefits of each situation in order to derive the maximum benefit from it. However, time is valuable too, and clearly the sensible approach to this problem of processing limits is to develop a scheme in which extensive intellectual work is only done under certain circumstances. Often it is wisest to follow the habits we have developed for ourselves, or the routines which are offered by our culture and society, and to save our intellectual resources for those conditions where the peculiarities of a situation provoke their use.

TABLE 3.1

| | Capacities of jug | | | Target |
	A	B	C	quantity
1	21	127	3	100
2	14	163	25	99
3	18	43	10	5
4	9	42	26	21
5	20	59	4	31
6	23	49	3	20
7	15	39	3	18
8	28	76	3	25
9	18	48	4	22
10	14	36	8	6

The conditions under which such provocation will occur are undoubtedly many, and will vary as a function of the particular cognitive task being considered. In terms of the maintenance of a set of social views, the various 'cognitive balance theories' of the 1960s and 1970s made a number of claims about what these conditions are, and the diversity of the experimental conditions under which cognitive imbalance or dissonance could be induced reinforces the point that this is not a simply described set of conditions (see Eiser 1980 for a brief review). Furthermore, the individual is not an isolated processing unit unaffected by the ways in which certain items of information are emphasized or denied in any particular society. For example, it has been shown that if someone is given cause to think in detail about some event or situation, then he or she will assign a much higher subjective probability to that event occurring or situation arising (Ross et al. 1977).[8]

The overall role of the confirmation bias, and a general cognitive inertia, in the preservation of trust would thus appear to be quite straightforward. Neither reputations nor habits are readily changed in the face of the merest challenge to their integrity or viability, as we all know and understand from our day-to-day experiences. If the bank which I use suffers a heavy loss, then I can take this as evidence that trading conditions have been difficult, but that the bank is still sound and that I should do nothing. Or I might take it as reason to transfer my funds elsewhere, possible even to a sock under my bed if I consider it proof that all financial institutions cannot be trusted to return a depositor's cash. Alternatively, I may never bother to enquire about my bank's welfare. In a different vein, if I habitually get my groceries at one store because it claims to be the cheapest and initially it seemed to be so, and the prices increase from week to week, I can take this as evidence that inflation is at a certain level, and continue to shop there. On the other hand, I may take it that they are no longer living up to their claim, that this is a breach of trust, and that I should shop elsewhere. Or I may just pay the bill without giving the matter any consideration at all.

It should be remembered, though, that this cognitive inertia is quite blind. It can support bad habits as well as good ones, and preserve infamy as well as reputed virtue. In fact, as the paranoid demonstrates in always being able to find a reason to believe that everyone is against him or her in everything that they say and do, bad habits and notoriety are the more resistant of the two to change. Indeed, our very definition and understanding of the terms illustrate that there is not a simple symmetry between good and bad here. While we will usually be willing to ignore some lapses from good behaviour after the fashion discussed above, if presented with a clear breach of trust by someone our faith in that person will be fatally undermined. However, if an untrustworthy person behaves well on one occasion, it is not nearly so likely that the converse inference will be made.

These cognitive foibles also provide some understanding of the results discussed in the second section, and thus serve to support the view that those findings are not mere artefacts of the laboratory, but are of wider

[8] A finding which will come as no surprise to any mud-slinging politician.

significance. The deleterious consequences of the players being able to threaten one another in the Trucking Game may partly be accounted for by the way in which the prominent positioning of the gates focuses attention on that potential threat. From Ross et al.'s (1977) results one would infer that this prominence leads each to increase the subjective probability of the threat being implemented. This is turn could lead to a self-fulfilling prophecy as each attempts to get his retaliation in first.

The set effect (*Einstellung*) could be seen as underlying what might be termed the 'small increment effect'. Stated simply, in repeated runs of the Trucking Game, the participants do not bother to re-evaluate a procedure established in one circumstance when applying it to another which is only marginally different. If on one occasion I lent you £100, and you paid it back as you said you would, then I am quite likely to see a loan of £125 as essentially the same transaction.

The consequences of small increments, however, are only going to be of interest if they are repeated often enough to produce a substantially different state of affairs in the final analysis. Such incremental effects could be quite powerful on their own, but repetition gives rise to effects which could provide further support for a level of cooperation which has been established. This could occur through the increased amount of contact and communication which would necessarily result, thereby producing perhaps the same effect which Pruitt and Kimmel (1976) noted. This would not be the greater amount and variety of simultaneous communication which they discuss, but it might be thought to be similar. To assess this possibility, it is necessary to consider why increased contact might be beneficial.

Generally, it might be thought that there are two factors at work. The first is the impact of depersonification. In a number of experiments, it has been noted that subjects who cannot see or hear the person to whom they are reacting tend to inflict far more extreme punishments upon one another. The most famous study demonstrating this is Milgram (1963). In this, most subjects were willing to give electric shocks, which they had some grounds for believing could be dangerous and possibly lethal, to another person when that person was unseen and in another room. Most were not willing to do so when seated right next to the recipient of the shocks. Clearly, anything which increases contact between parties will reduce this tendency.

Secondly, there are the consequences of increased contact for the establishment of a framework within which individuals will have the belief that there is greater certainty as to the intent behind any communication, and, therefore, less likelihood of their being misunderstood or exploited. This framework will centre on the mutual beliefs of the interactants, and the role of this in communication has been stressed by many authors.[9] Within any human society, the context in which a communicative act is offered is critical to its interpretation. This is true for the full range of such acts, from simple conversations to informal and formal contracts: even the most detailed of contracts cannot make explicit everything which must be understood for its interpretation. The beliefs which are held about another person at the time of communication are a significant part of what that context amounts to. Therefore, anything which contributes to a greater sense of knowing the other can contribute to the participants' belief in the possibility of mutual understanding.

As confidence tricksters know, many superficial aspects of personal presentation can quickly lead to conclusions about the nature of another person's beliefs and sentiments. On first seeing someone, we immediately classify that person according to age, sex, and many other social categories. From this, and the briefest of details from our interaction, we rapidly draw inferences about his or her beliefs and the relationship between us. This is as true of the psychological laboratory as anywhere else, and thus it would not be surprising if repeated interactions in the Trucking Game produced a greater sense of mutual awareness of the kind which Pruitt and Kimmel discuss.

The importance of a high level of mutual knowledge for the development of enduring cooperation is revealed by the disasters which can occur when contracts are entered into by parties who are oriented towards radically different sets of background assumptions, but are unaware of this difference. For example, while some of the European settlers of North America may well have intended to force, swindle, or cheat the indigenous population out of its traditional lands, it is highly unlikely that in the first instance they fully realized the extent of the misunderstandings which underlay their less brutal dealings with one another. The Shawnee did not conceive of someone owning land in the sense we normally presume; when they 'sold' land they did not see themselves as giving exclusive access to the buyers, because things of this type could not be sold in this way. As Tecumseh (1768–1813), one of their most important leaders, is reported to have said: 'Sell a country! Why not sell the air, the clouds and the great sea. . . . Did not the Great

---

[9] One part of the psychological literature which might have been considered in this paper is that which has explored the relationship between an individual's professed attitudes and his or her subsequent behaviour. From this one might have concluded that we are all remarkably untrustworthy, because, according to many reports, the correlation between our words and our deeds is remarkably low. However, the fundamental flaw in this work might be described as a failure to realize that expressed attitudes are communicative acts, and that they can only be satisfactorily understood in the appropriate context. This point is reflected in the fact that the most successful contemporary models of the attitude–behaviour relationship (e.g. Fishbein's) are those which try to build the context into the equation which relates one to the other (see Schuman and Johnson 1977).

Spirit make them all for the use of his children?' (Brandon 1961). At a
more mundane level, there are numerous cases of gross misunderstand-
ing between members of different cultures because they are orienting to
different beliefs systems (Gumperz 1982), and clearly anything which
reduces this and increases the sense of mutual understanding can lead to
greater cooperation.

                                    IV

Despite its apparent fragility and our many attempts to do without it, it is
clear that, in many societies where it is well established, trust is
remarkably robust. Fraud is widespread in all the advanced economies,
and is extremely costly to companies and individuals alike, but rarely
does it lead to the conclusion that no one can be trusted. Similarly, the
recent scandals over 'insider dealing' in London and New York have
done little to dent the contemporary enthusiasm for large-scale corporate
take-overs. Indeed, the failure to notice that a fraudulent transaction has
been conducted is so common that a major problem for investigative
work in this area is the discovery of the victim of the crime.[10] The
observations offered in this paper are only a small part of the story of
how cooperation and trust are developed and maintained, but clearly
they represent a significant part of that process.

A serious consideration of these factors would necessarily force the
abandonment of the cleaner and simpler assumption of perfect rationality, but this is an assumption which is plainly wrong and, if pushed, is
less clear than it might at first seem. On the one hand it requires the
additional assumption that computation is cost-free, and thus leads to a
selective treatment of the costs involved in any economic decision. On
the other it must also assume that decisions are made in a world where all
problems have a close set of solutions – because, if it does not, then
unending computation becomes possible. Unfortunately for this assumption, it would appear that many real-world problems are distinctly open
ended. Such an abandonment would obviously mean that a more
complex view of political and economic agents is required, but this in
itself would not be a bad thing, if the experience of attempts in
psychology to provide computational models of cognitive processes is
any guide.

In the early development of artificial intelligence, something like the
perfect rationality assumption was made in the building of machinery for
processes as diverse as playing chess and translating between different

---

[10] As reported by the head of the City of London Police Fraud Squad in an interview on
the BBC World Service, November 1986.

languages. As was quickly discovered, the 'brute force computing' tactic, as the unbounded rationality assumption was known, was a failure because the decision space to be searched for any moderately realistic problem was of unmanageable proportions. For example, even contemporary machines take an inordinate amount of time to examine all possible two-move sequences in the opening stages of a chess game, because the number of branches in the relevant decision tree undergoes a combinatorial explosion. Not surprisingly, this tactic was quickly dropped, and much effort has subsequently been devoted to the development of more sophisticated and realistic alternatives. If we are to understood the development and maintenance of cooperative and trusting relations, similar unrealistic assumptions will have to be abandoned too.

REFERENCES

Axelrod, R. 1984: *The Evolution of Cooperation*. New York: Basic Books.
Brandon, W. 1961: *The American Heritage Book of Indians*. New York: Simon and Schuster.
Bruner, J. S., Goodnow, J., and Austin, G. A. 1956: *A Study of Thinking*. New York: Wiley.
Chaiken, A. L. and Darley, J. M. 1973: Victim or perpetrator? Defensive attribution of responsibility and the need for order and justice. *Journal of Personality and Social Psychology* 25, 268–75.
Christie, R. and Geis, F. 1970: *Studies in Machiavellianism*. New York: Academic Press.
Deutsch, M., Canavan, D., and Rubin, J. 1971: The effects of size of conflict and sex of experimenter upon interpersonal bargaining. *Journal of Experimental Social Psychology* 7, 258–67.
Deutsch, M. and Krauss, R. M. 1960: The effect of threat on interpersonal bargaining. *Journal of Abnormal and Social Psychology* 61, 181–9.
Deutsch, M. and Krauss, R. M. 1962: Studies of interpersonal bargaining. *Journal of Conflict Resolution* 6, 52–76.
Eiser, J. R. 1980: *Cognitive Social Psychology*. Maidenhead: McGraw-Hill.
Fiske, S. T. and Taylor, S. E. 1984: *Social Cognition*. New York: Random House.
Freedman, J. L. and Fraser, S. 1966: Compliance without pressure: the foot in the door technique. *Journal of Personality and Social Psychology* 4, 195–202.
Garfinkel, H. 1963: A conception of and experiments with 'trust' as a condition of stable concerted actions. In O. J. Harvey (ed.), *Motivation and Social Interaction*, New York: Ronald Press.
Gumperz, J. J. 1982: *Discourse Strategies*. Cambridge: Cambridge University Press.
Haney, C., Banks, C., and Zimbardo, P. G. 1973: Interpersonal dynamics in a simulated prison. *International Journal of Criminology and Penology* 1, 69–97.
Kahneman, D., Slovic, P., and Tversky, A. 1982: *Judgement Under Uncertainty*. Cambridge: Cambridge University Press.

Kahneman, D. and Tversky, A. 1973: On the psychology of prediction. *Psychological Review* 80, 237–51.

Kelly, G. A. 1955: *The Psychology of Personal Constructs*. New York: Norton.

Laing, R. D. 1965: *The Divided Self*. Harmondsworth: Penguin.

Luchins, A. S. 1942: Mechanization in problem solving. *Psychological Monographs* 54, whole issue.

Luhmann, N. 1979: *Trust and Power*. Chichester: Wiley.

Milgram, S. 1963: Behavioural study of obedience. *Journal of Abnormal and Social Psychology* 67, 371–8.

Mitroff, I. I. 1974: *The Subjective Side of Science*. Amsterdam: Elsevier.

Mynatt, C. R., Doherty, M. E., and Tweeney, R. D. 1977: Confirmation bias in a simulated research environment. *Quarterly Journal of Experimental Psychology* 29, 85–95.

Pruitt, D. G. and Kimmel, M. J. 1976: Twenty years of experimental gaming: critique, synthesis and suggestions for the future. *Annual Review of Psychology* 28, 363–92.

Rapoport, A. 1970: Conflict resolution in the light of game theory and beyond. In P. G. Swingle (ed), *The Structure of Conflict*, New York: Academic Press.

Rogers 1972

Ross, L., Lepper, M. R., Strack, F., and Steinmetz, J. 1977: Social explanation and social expectation: biased attributional processes in the debriefing paradigm. *Journal of Personality and Social Psychology* 35, 485–94.

Rotter, J. B. 1980: Interpersonal trust, trustworthiness and gullibility. *American Psychologist* 35, 1–7.

Schuman, H. and Johnson, M. P. 1977: Attitudes and behaviour. *Annual Review of Sociology* 2, 161–207.

Seligman, M. E. P., Maier, S. F., and Solomon, R. L. 1971: Unpredictable and uncontrollable aversive events. In R. F. Brush (ed.), *Aversive Conditioning and Learning*, New York: Academic Press.

Snyder, C. R., Higgins, R. L., and Stucky, R. J. 1983: *Excuses*. New York: Wiley.

Snyder, M. and Swann, W. B. 1978: Hypothesis testing processes in social interaction. *Journal of Personality and Social Psychology* 36, 1202–12.

Tajfel, H. 1969: Cognitive aspects of prejudice. *Journal of Social Issues* 25, 79–97.

Wason, P. C. 1960: On the failure to eliminate hypotheses in a conceptual task. *Quarterly Journal of Experimental Psychology* 12, 129–40.

Wason, P. C. 1968: Reasoning about a rule. *Quarterly Journal of Experimental Psychology* 20, 273–81.

Wichman, H. 1970: Effects of isolation and communication on cooperation in a two person game. *Journal of Personality and Social Psychology* 16, 114–20.

4

Trust as a Commodity

Partha Dasgupta

TRUST, CREDIBILITY, AND COMMITMENT

Trust is central to all transactions and yet economists rarely discuss the notion.[1] It is treated rather as background environment, present whenever called upon, a sort of ever-ready lubricant that permits voluntary participation in production and exchange. In the standard model of a market economy it is taken for granted that consumers meet their budget constraints: they are not allowed to spend more than their wealth. Moreover, they always deliver the goods and services they said they would. But the model is silent on the rectitude of such agents. We are not told if they are persons of honour, conditioned by their upbringing always to meet the obligations they have chosen to undertake, or if there is a background agency which enforces contracts, credibly threatening to mete out punishment if obligations are not fulfilled – a punishment sufficiently stiff to deter consumers from ever failing to fulfil them. The same assumptions are made for producers. To be sure, the standard model can be extended to allow for bankruptcy in the face of an uncertain future. One must suppose that there is a special additional loss to becoming bankrupt – a loss of honour when honour matters, social and economic ostracism, a term in a debtors' prison, and so forth. Otherwise, a person may take silly risks or, to make a more subtle point, take insufficient care in managing his affairs, but claim that he ran into genuine bad luck, that it was Mother Nature's fault and not his own lack of ability or zeal.

[1] I am most grateful to Diego Gambetta for suggesting that I write on this topic, and to him, Kenneth Arrow, Paul David, John Hartwick, Dieter Helm, Hugh Mellor, Ugo Pagano, Peter Temin, and Menahem Yaari for illuminating discussions on the subject. I have also benefited greatly from the searching comments made by participants of the trust seminar and those of the seminar of the Sub-Faculty of Economics at Oxford University.

I have given these preliminary examples so as to make seven points, each of which I will elaborate in what follows. Firstly, if there is an absence of suitable punishment, that is incurred loss, for breaking agreements or contracts, individuals will not possess the appropriate *incentives* to fulfil them; and since this will be generally recognized within the population, people will not wish to enter into transactions with one another. Thus, what could in principle be mutually beneficial relationships will not be initiated.

Secondly, the threat of punishment for errant behaviour must be *credible*, else the threat is no threat. To put it another way, the enforcement agency itself must be *trustworthy*: it will do what it says and only what it says. I should add, parenthetically, that the enforcement agency may be society at large. Social ostracism, and the sense of shame that society can invoke, are examples of such punishment. I should also add that at another extreme are cases where the 'enforcement agency' may be the injured party to the transaction. Here, as in game-theoretic models of reciprocal altruism (analysed by Friedman 1971; Trivers 1971; Aumann and Shapley 1976; Rubinstein 1979; Maynard Smith 1982; Axelrod 1984; Fudenberg and Maskin 1986), it is the injured party which punishes the 'defaulter' by ceasing to transact with him (see the fourth section of this chapter, and also Singer 1981, for a fine exploration of the link between ethics and sociobiology).

Thirdly, and this follows from the first and second points, trust among persons and agencies is interconnected. If your trust in the enforcement agency falters, you will not trust persons to fulfil their terms of an agreement and thus will not enter into that agreement. By the same token, you will not trust the enforcement agency – for example, the government – to do on balance what is expected of it if you do not trust that it will be thrown out of power (through the ballot-box or armed rebellion) if it does not do on balance what is expected of it. It is this interconnectedness which makes trust such a fragile commodity. If it erodes in any part of the mosaic it brings down an awful lot with it. This is *one* reason (there are others) why the medical and legal professions had, and in many places still have, such stern codes of conduct instilled into their members; they needed to break this intricate link, as it were, so that vital transactions concerning health and protection could be entered into even if enforcement costs were to rise due to an erosion of trust elsewhere in the economy, through rapidly changing social mores or for whatever other reason (see Arrow 1963).

Fourthly, and this is implicit in the third point, you do not trust a person (or an agency) to do something merely because he says he will do it. You trust him only because, knowing what you know of his disposition, his available options and their consequences, his ability and so forth, you expect that he will *choose* to do it. His promise must be credible. That is why we like to distinguish 'trusting someone' from 'trusting someone blindly', and think the latter to be ill-advised.

Fifthly, and this follows from the fourth point, when you decide whether to enter into an agreement with a person, you need to look at the world from *his* perspective as it is likely to be when it comes to his having to fulfil his part of the agreement. This explains why the mathematician Richard Bellman (1957), and the game theorists Thomas Schelling (1960) and Reinhard Selten (1965; 1975), instructed us always to calculate *backwards, against* time, and *not forwards, with* time (I will elaborate on this point later on).

Sixthly, even though there are no obvious units in which trust can be measured, this does not matter, because in any given context you can measure its value, its worthwhileness (see below). In this respect, trust is not dissimilar to commodities such as knowledge or information.

Seventhly, and for the moment most importantly, I am using the word 'trust' in the sense of correct expectations about the *actions* of other people that have a bearing on one's own choice of action when that action must be chosen before one can *monitor* the actions of those others.

There are other uses of the word 'trust'. When on meeting an acquaintance one says 'I trust your family is well', one is expressing a hope that his family is well. I do not think that anything else is implied. On the other hand, when one says 'trust Frank Hahn to say that one must economize on trust', one is merely saying that one's expectations of his attitude have been confirmed. But this use does not have the potency that the word actually possesses. For whether one is right or wrong about Hahn may have no bearing on one's actions. Trust is of much importance precisely because its presence or absence can have a strong bearing on what we choose to do and in many cases what we *can* do. The clause concerning the inability to *monitor* others' actions in my definition of trust is crucial. If I can monitor what others have done before I choose my own action, the word 'trust' loses its potency. I should emphasize that an inability to monitor the actions of others need not be due to the fact that my choice of action temporally precedes those of others. Certainly in many cases this will be so, such as my lending you a book, trusting that you will return it in five years' time. But there are a great many other cases where what I ought now to do depends on whether you have done what you said you would do and where I cannot *now*, or possibly ever, monitor whether you have actually done it. I will not burden you with examples of this sort. Nothing of analytical importance depends on this particular classification.

I have so far, in defining one's trust in others, talked of the significance of others' unobservable *actions* for choosing one's own course of action. But there is another important class of cases where trust, in the sense that I wish to use the term, comes into play. This is when others *know* something about themselves or the world which I do not, and when what I ought to do depends on the extent of my ignorance of these matters. An agreement between myself and such other people may call upon them to disclose their information. But can I trust them to be truthful; that is, can I trust them to send me the correct signals, those they would send if they were truly trustworthy? (They do not actually have to be *truthful* for me to rely on them. As long as I always know how to interpret their messages correctly I can trust them. Thus the ancient Cretan was as informative as a knowledgeable saint.) Examples of this class abound. When I ask my mother what she would like as a present I hope I can trust her to tell me the truth and not try to save me money. When I go to a second-hand car dealer I worry whether I can trust him not to sell me what Americans call a 'lemon'. The point is not so much whether the car is in fact a lemon (the dealer may not know) but whether the dealer *knowingly* sells me a lemon.[2]

Having distinguished these two broad categories around which the concept of trust revolves, I am going to restrict myself, in what follows, to the second; that is, those circumstances where an individual does not know fully the disposition (or motivation) of the person(s) with whom he is considering a transaction. The reason for this is that at the *analytical* level both categories raise the same issues. There are some derived notions of trust; for example, I trust that the value of the pound will not fall to zero tomorrow. But this *is* a derived notion, since the value of the pound tomorrow depends upon what we all do, what we all expect, what we all know, and so forth. My definition covers such cases automatically.[3]

Talk of 'contracts' and 'agreements' might suggest that I am, in discussing trust, taking an unduly legalistic attitude. I do not intend to do that, and I use 'contracts' and 'agreements' merely as props. A contract can be vague. In fact no contract, even if it is scrutinized by sharp lawyers, can detail every eventuality, if for no other reason than that no

[2] In the insurance literature, resource allocation problems arising from incomplete information on the part of one party regarding other parties' *actions* are called 'moral hazard', and those arising from incomplete information on their part regarding the others' *characteristics* (for example, other parties' disposition, or the knowledge they possess) are called 'adverse selection'. At a very general level, moral hazard and adverse selection raise very much the same sorts of issues (see for example Laffont and Maskin 1981).

[3] Luhmann (this volume) suggests reserving the term 'confidence' for 'trust' in the ability of social institution (e.g. the market) to *function* as is expected of it. Likewise, it seems to me, we show 'confidence' in our doctor's *ability* to cure us of our ailments, in our teacher's *ability* to inspire us, in our civil servants' *ability* to take the correct decisions, and so on. Thus confidence stems from ability, and trust from a person's underlying disposition or motivation.

language can cope with unlimited refinement in distinguishing contingencies. Thus trust covers expectations about what others will do or have done (or what messages they will transmit) in circumstances that are not explicitly covered in the agreement. In many cases there may not even *be* an agreement: can I trust people to come to my rescue if I am about to drown? Towards the end of this article, when I will conclude that trust is based on *reputation* and that reputation has ultimately to be acquired through behaviour over time in well-understood circumstances, it will be seen that none of these distinctions, between actions and message transmission, between legal contracts and implicit understandings, is of any analytical moment for the problem at hand. It is important to realize that when Sam Goldwyn remarked that a verbal contract is not worth the paper it is written on, he was only half right, and that all that is interesting in the concept of trust lies precisely in that half which was wrong.

In defining trust I have spoken of one's expectations regarding others' choice of actions that have a bearing on one's own choice of action. Now, of course, choice need not be based exclusively on self-interest and nothing I have said or will say supposes that it is so based. We are all at once both egoists and altruists, occasionally rising to the moment and doing what is the right thing to do and not what is in our personal interest, and unhappily often failing to so rise. Furthermore, it is often the case that the mere fact that someone has placed his trust in us makes us feel obligated, and this makes it harder to betray that trust. Again, at the general analytical level it does not matter whether we see people – having imposed moral constraints on their available set of options – choosing in the light of self-interest, or whether they explicitly consider trade-offs between self-interest and the interests of others. The problem of trust would of course not arise if we were all hopelessly moral, always doing what we said we would do in the circumstances in which we said we would do it. This is, the problem of trust would not arise if it was common knowledge that we were all trustworthy. A minimal non-congruence between individual and moral values is necessary for the problem of trust to *be* a problem. So of course I shall assume that there *is* non-congruence: all I want to warn you against is the idea that non-congruence necessarily implies undiluted personal greed.

It is nevertheless possible to claim on the one hand that a person is untrustworthy and on the other that he can be trusted to do what he said he would on a given occasion. This is because on this occasion he may have the right incentive. 'Trustworthiness' concentrates on a person's overall disposition, his motivation, the extent to which he awards importance to his own honesty. Being able to trust a person to do what he said he would, on the other hand, requires us to know not only something of his disposition, but also something of the circumstances surrounding the occasion at hand. If the incentives are 'right', even a trustworthy person can be relied upon to be untrustworthy. 'Every man has his price': repugnant though it is to our sensibilities, the cliché captures the view that no one awards an infinite weight to his own honesty. Even Yudhishthira in the epic *Mahabharata*, renowned for his trustworthiness, uttered on one occasion what in effect was a lie so as to throw off his unrighteous enemies. Yudhishthira, as it turned out, was a consequentialist. But the point is that his enemies did not know this. They thought that Yudhishthira could never be motivated to deviate from the path of truth. This is why the lie worked.

We wish to know the sort of person we are dealing with before we deal with him. But we will know it only imperfectly. We form an opinion on the basis of his background, the opportunities he has faced, the courses of action he has taken, and so forth. Our opinion is thus based partly on the theory we hold of the effect of culture, class membership, family line, and the like on a person's motivation (his disposition) and hence his behaviour. The opinion which is publicly formed and held is this person's reputation. Our problem in essence is to infer the person's qualities from such data. This will be the central theme in the remaining sections of this article.

Can one trust oneself? Here I will not address this question at any length. But I will discuss it briefly as a springboard for my central case – trust in others. There is the trivial sense of not trusting oneself to do the right thing in circumstances when one cannot think things through clearly, such as a state of intoxication or great emotional stress. There is not much to discuss here, except to note that in certain cases society commits itself to render invalid any agreements entered into in such states. The important class of cases that needs analysis is where a person does not trust the extent of his own commitment, his *ability* to carry out and see through his own projects. In many such cases he imposes routines on himself, at great inconvenience (to himself and on occasion to others), not merely to stay in mental and physical shape, as it were, but to persuade *himself* of his own commitment. The rituals of Hindu ascetics might usefully be understood in some such terms. An interesting instance of this trust in oneself arises in those all-too-familiar cases where one's values or preferences are expected to change over time. What should one do now if one expects (and in extreme cases knows) that one will acquire values later which are incongruent with one's current values? The right way to attack the problem, as has been shown by a number of economists, is to view it as an intertemporal game between one's temporal selves.[4] The classic example, as noted by Strotz (1955–56), is

[4] The classic article on the subject is Strotz (1955–56). Important subsequent contributions include Phelps and Pollak (1968), Blackorby et al. (1973), and Peleg and

that of Odysseus and the Sirens (for elaborations, see Elster 1979). From our point of view the interesting feature of the story is that Odysseus had the option of (quite literally) binding himself *now* to a future course of action (by excluding the option of trying to get to the Sirens). He exercised that option, and this enabled him to choose a further option (that of listening to the Sirens) which he would not have chosen had he not been able to so bind himself. Of course, it is also the case that Odysseus could trust his fellow wanderers not to hear his pleas during the critical period in which he begged for release. Otherwise he would not have had the option of binding himself. Odysseus's customary self had, as game theorists would call it, a first-mover advantage over his bewitched self.

The suggestion of a link between commitment and trust is made in this volume on several occasions. I think the link is a pretty obvious one. I also think it best not to dwell too long on it, because it tends to distract from trust itself. When one wonders whether to enter into a binding commitment one is really wondering which intertemporal game to play. This can be clearly seen in the case of an exchange of contracts on a house. The penalty (loss of money, honour, and so forth) for breaking a verbal agreement is usually less than the penalty for breaking the legal agreement that is entailed on exchange of contracts. All that commitment does is turn the original game into one in which the explicitly or implicitly agreed-upon courses of action are credible. If they are credible, then the participants can be trusted to carry them out. To use once again the game theorist's terminology, certain types of commitment (for example an exchange of contracts; and to people of honour, a promise) change the initial game into one in which mutually beneficial courses of action become equilibrium strategies when in fact they were not so initially. (I will illustrate this presently.) Such commitments often involve the expenditure of resources, such as lawyers' fees and deposits. But the gain is a mutually beneficial transaction that can be trusted to be carried out. Presumably, each participant calculates the cost of such commitment and compares it to the 'gains' to him emanating from it. The cost of commitment is then the price that has to be paid for each party to trust the other to fulfil the terms of the agreement. We are now solidly in the domain of economics. No doubt you were not sure when I would entice you into the economist's lair. But doubtless you trusted me to do so somehow.

Let me then summarize the argument so far. You do not trust a person to do something merely because he says he will do it. You trust him

---

Yaari (1973). Analyses of such intertemporal games as these which are consistent with the backward-induction argument (see below) are provided in Dasgupta (1974), Hammond (1976), Yaari (1977), and Bernheim and Ray (1983).

because, knowing what you know of his disposition, his information, his ability, his available options and their consequences, you expect he will *choose* to do it. Commitment on his part merely alters the game that is to be played, and therefore alters your expectation of what he will choose to do and, what is subtly tied to this, simultaneously alters *his* expectation of what *you* will choose to do.

How is trust created? How is it perpetuated? Why is it not present when it is not? Why is it there when it is there, and why does it break down when it does? How can it be built up again when it breaks down? And finally what are we to make of the point made recently by Professor Albert Hirschman: that trust, like other moral resources, grows with use and decays with disuse?[5]

There are, it seems to me, two ways of approaching these questions, one of which is analytical and the other, for want of a better description, anthropological. The former pursues a general abstract route; the latter illuminates matters by compiling and analysing historical case studies. Several of the articles in this volume fall into the second category. What follows belongs rather to the first. But I make no pretence of *answering* these questions. The examples that follow are designed to indicate an avenue – a research strategy – for answering them. Along the way I hope the questions will be met in part.

SELF-FULFILLING EXPECTATIONS ABOUT HONEST AND DISHONEST BEHAVIOUR

Before presenting a detailed case (in the third and fourth sections) which, it seems to me, captures some of the crucial aspects of the formation of trust, I want to offer an intermediate example. This example at first blush seems promising for the problem at hand. In fact it captures something related, but something else. I want to discuss it because it is one of the first examples that comes to mind. It will also prove a useful prelude to my main example.

There is a large group of individuals in a society who meet pairwise at random in every period to transact. Each party at each encounter can do one of two things: X (transact honestly) and Y (cheat a little in the transaction). To have an interesting problem I must suppose that the parties choose their actions simultaneously. Each person would prefer to do X over Y if the person he encounters were also to choose X (it is nice to be honest when dealing with honesty), and he would prefer Y over X if

[5] 'These are resources whose supply may well increase rather than decrease through use; second, these resources do not remain intact if they stay unused; like the ability to speak a foreign language or to play the piano, these moral resources are likely to become depleted and to atrophy if *not* used' (Hirschman 1984: 93).

the person he meets were to choose Y (it is unpleasant to be a sucker). I now want to assume that each party prefers both to choose X rather than Y (it is preferable to have bilateral honesty than bilateral cheating).

In what follows I will suppose that while people appear to be the same there are in fact two types of persons in the population, one given to more honest urges (type 1) than the other (type 2). To make all this vivid I present in tables 4.1 and 4.2 the benefits (or pay-offs) to a person of each type when he transacts with someone. In table 4.1 the pay-offs to a person of type 1 are presented, and he is assumed to choose a *row* (the party he is transacting with is assumed to choose a column). In table 4.2 the pay-offs to a person of type 2 are presented, and he too is assumed to choose a *row* (the party he is transacting with is assumed to choose a column). For simplicity of exposition I have made the pay-off matrices the same except for the north-west box, and this is sufficient to indicate that a person of type 1 is more inclined towards honest dealing.

TABLE 4.1 *Pay-offs to a person of type 1, who chooses a row*

	X	Y
X	30	5
Y	5	10

TABLE 4.2 *Pay-offs to a person of type 2, who chooses a row*

	X	Y
X	20	5
Y	5	10

I want to suppose that the population is large, so that when two people meet at random to transact they cannot tell if they have met before. A person's past record of choices is thus not known by anyone (but see the fourth section). What then should an individual choose when he

randomly meets another for transaction? Clearly, a person's best policy
in this example depends on what he *thinks* the other will do. But what
thought should he rationally entertain?

Consider first a person of type 1. It is simple to confirm that his
optimal choice is X if he regards the chance that the other party will
choose X to be in excess of 1/6, and his optimal choice is Y if this chance
is less than 1/6.[6] Now consider a person of type 2. It is equally simple to
confirm that his optimal choice is X if he regards the chance that the
other party will choose X with a probability in excess of 1/4, and his
optimal choice is Y if this chance is less than 1/4.[7]

Let us now suppose, for the sake of vividness, that the proportion of
people of type 1 in the population is *P*, and suppose this is publicly and
commonly known. I want to concentrate attention on stationary (or
steady-state) behaviour patterns, and for simplicity I shall restrict myself
to equilibria where persons of the same type choose the same option.

Notice at once that if each person expects the others to choose X then
each will chose X, whereas if each expects the others to choose Y then
each will choose Y. Thus both X and Y are equilibrium behaviour. The
role of expectations is of course crucial: if everyone expects everyone to
be honest then everyone will be honest, and if everyone expects everyone
to cheat a little then everyone will cheat a little.[8] Note too that each is a
stable expectation, in that a slight departure from either equilibrium
expectation will bring the expectation back to equilibrium, provided
expectations at each period adjust in the direction of the past period's
average behaviour. We conclude, then, that if people are somewhat
cynical about one another (others will choose Y with a high probability),
everyone will emerge worse off than if people trust one another (others
will choose X with a high probability).

The population ratio *P* has not entered into the equation so far. It has
an interesting role to play if its value lies between 1/6 and 1/4. Consider
any value in this range. Then it is clear that in addition to the two
equilibria we have already identified there is another, where each person
of type 1 chooses X, and of type 2 chooses Y, on every occasion. At this
equilibrium it is common knowledge that type 1 people are always honest
and that type 2 people always cheat a little. But at no encounter does
either party know who he is dealing with. Behaviour according to type is
therefore what emerges at this equilibrium.

---

[6] To confirm this, suppose this chance is *p*. Then for the person of type 1 to be
indifferent between X and Y, *p* must satisfy the equation $30p + 5(1-p) = 5p + 10(1-p)$,
yielding $p = 1/6$.

[7] Because 1/6 is less than 1/4, a person of type 1 needs less 'persuasion' to choose X. It is
in this sense that type 1 people in the example lean more frequently towards honest dealing.

[8] Multiple self-fulfilling expectations have received careful attention in Schelling (1978).

The example on its own cannot, of course, tell us which stationary equilibrium will prevail in the long run, if indeed it is a stationary equilibrium towards which the society gravitates. For this we need more information about the dynamics of expectation formation. History clearly matters here, but it can matter in many ways and it is hard to tell how best to capture it.

Instructive though such an example might appear to be, it is not the right one for my purpose. For trust to be developed between individuals they must have repeated encounters, and they must have some memory of previous encounters. Moreover, for honesty to have potency as a concept there must be some *cost* involved in honest behaviour. And finally, trust is linked with reputation, and reputation has to be acquired. The example which follows attempts to take account of these issues.

AN EXAMPLE OF POSSIBLE COOPERATION

A salesman possesses a number of motor-cars. Their outward appearances are the same, but in fact some of them are reliable and the rest are 'lemons'.[9] The salesman knows each car intimately. In order to concentrate on what for us are the essential points, I shall assume that there is no haggling: the salesman has posted a fixed price in his showroom window. Any potential customer can, should he wish to, enter the showroom, pay the quoted price, and drive away in a car *the salesman picks out for him.* Alternatively, he can choose not to enter the showroom at all. I assume in this section that there is a single potential customer. Should this person not enter, the salesman sells no car, and in the event I assume (without loss of generality) that the *net benefit* (or *pay-off*) to each party is nil. However, should the person enter and pay the price, the salesman has two options: to hand over a reliable car (option A) or to saddle the customer with a lemon (option B). If a lemon is sold the net benefit (or pay-off) to the salesman is γ and that to the customer is $-\beta$, where $0 < \beta < 1$.[10] If a reliable car is sold the net benefit (or pay-off) to the salesman is α and that to the customer is $1 - \beta$.

---

[9] As mentioned earlier, a 'lemon' is a 'sour purchase', a commodity which is not worth the price paid for it. In a well-known article, Akerlof (1970) analysed a more complicated version of the example in this section.

[10] By hypothesis the customer realises subsequently that the car is a lemon, but by then there is nothing he can do. Since $-\beta$ is negative we are making the natural assumption that buying a lemon is worse than not buying a car at all. To be sure, salesmen usually offer warranties and the like, but they are a means of making the salesman's (or manufacturer's) claims about the reliability of the car credible. I am for the moment thinking of situations where such options are not available to the salesman, because I am discussing trust. Even when warranties are available, there is always the residual chance of being saddled with a lemon. Naturally, I want to consider such situations.

Thus the customer prefers buying a good car to not buying a car at all, and he prefers this in turn to buying a 'lemon'. (This is reflected in the hypothesis that $1 - \beta > 0 > -\beta$.) I now assume that these four pay-off values, $-\beta$, $1 - \beta$, γ, and α, are common knowledge.[11]

The tree describing this two-move game is depicted in figure 4.1. At the initial node of the tree (labelled 1) the customer chooses whether to enter and buy a car. (The customer thus has the first move.) Should he not enter, the game terminates. Should he enter, the game reaches the node labelled 2, the salesman chooses between A and B, and the game then terminates. Thus the customer has to choose between the two strategies 'enter' and 'not-enter'; and the salesman has to choose between the two strategies 'hand over a lemon' and 'hand over a reliable car'.

I begin by considering a 'dishonest' salesman, I formalize his disposition by the hypothesis that γ exceeds α. To have an interesting problem I assume further that α is positive, that is $\gamma > \alpha > 0$. In other words, the salesman would choose to sell the customer a lemon rather than a reliable car, but he would choose the latter option over not selling a car at all. Since the pay-offs are common knowledge it is, among other things, common knowledge that the salesman is dishonest; that he would

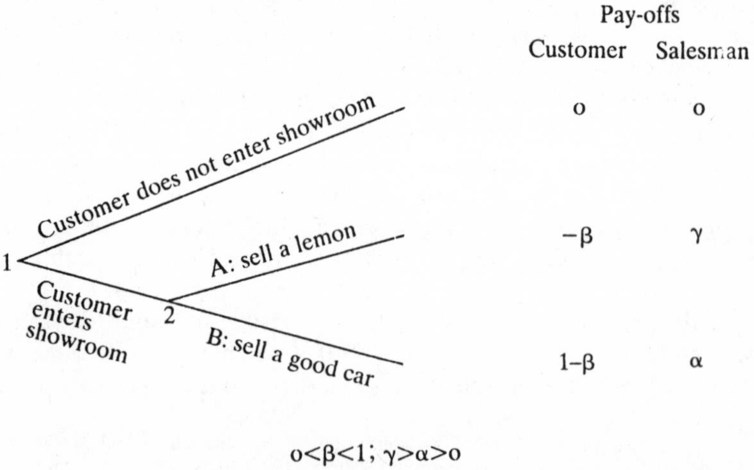

Pay-offs

	Customer	Salesman
	o	o
	$-\beta$	γ
	$1-\beta$	α

$o<\beta<1$; $\gamma>\alpha>o$

FIGURE 4.1 *Game tree: salesman dishonest*

[11] By this I mean that each knows them, that each knows that each knows them, that each knows that each knows that each knows them, and so on *ad infinitum*. For a non-technical account of the role that the common knowledge assumption plays in game theory, see Binmore and Dasgupta (1986). I should add that we do not require the full force of the common knowledge assumption in the simple two-move game I am considering now, but we will need it subsequently when we extend the game to discuss other matters.

choose A (selling a lemon) over B (selling a reliable car). So of course there will not be a transaction. The potential customer reasons *backwards*: 'If I enter the showroom and make a purchase the salesman wil sell me a lemon and my pay-off will be $-\beta$, which is less than zero – my pay-off in not buying a car at all. So of course I should not enter the showroom'. And he will not. We have thus a unique equilibrium of the game where no transaction occurs and where each party enjoys a pay-off of nil. This is worse for both than the (non-equilibrium) outcome where a reliable car is sold and where the customer and the salesman enjoy β and α respectively. A mutually beneficial transaction is thus unrealized.[12]

Notice that the salesman would love to persuade the customer of his 'good intentions', but mere words would not, in this example, be sufficient. If he could at little cost commit himself to choosing B – conditional upon the customer entering the showroom – he would do so. For example, if he could offer the potential customer a legally valid contract in which he would be liable to the customer for an amount something in excess of $\gamma - \alpha$ should the customer subsequently find that he has been sold a lemon, he would offer it. And if he were to offer it the customer's optimal strategy would be to accept it, and to buy a car, confident of the fact that the salesman would now be handing over a reliable car, it being now in his interest to do so. I shall suppose that the salesman cannot make such commitments, because I want to study the link between 'trust' and 'the reputation for being trustworthy'.[13] For this I must study a game in which people have incomplete information. I therefore make a minimal alteration to the game in figure 4.1: I suppose that the potential customer is unsure whether the salesman is dishonest, as in the game in figure 4.1, or honest and trustworthy. The relevant pay-offs for the dishonest salesman are as in figure 4.1; those for the honest type are as in the right-hand column in figure 4.2. Thus, to the honest salesman zero is the pay-off in not being able to sell a car, μ the pay-off in selling a lemon, and δ the pay-off in selling a reliable car. Naturally, I want to assume that δ is positive and that it exceeds μ. In other words, an honest salesman is one who would choose to sell a good car if he were given the option of selling a car and if he said it was a good car.[14]

[12] The idea of 'pay-offs' as represented by numbers such as β, α, and γ is one which I am appealing to only for expositional purposes. Behind it is the more general idea that each party can *rank* the outcomes (the eventualities) of the game and that choices conform to these rankings. These rankings can be based on as complex a set of considerations as we would like to include in our model of the choosers. The game tree I am discussing in the text is *not* based on an identification of choice with preference, or of preference with welfare.

[13] Warranties and the like reduce the need for personal knowledge on the part of the customer about the salesman's trustworthiness (i.e. his characteristics). But as noted earlier the need for trust cannot be eliminated entirely by such forms of commitment: the 'buck' is merely passed on to agencies that enforce contracts such as warranties. For this reason I assume that warranties do not exist in the game under consideration.

[14] We do not need to specify whether μ is positive or negative.

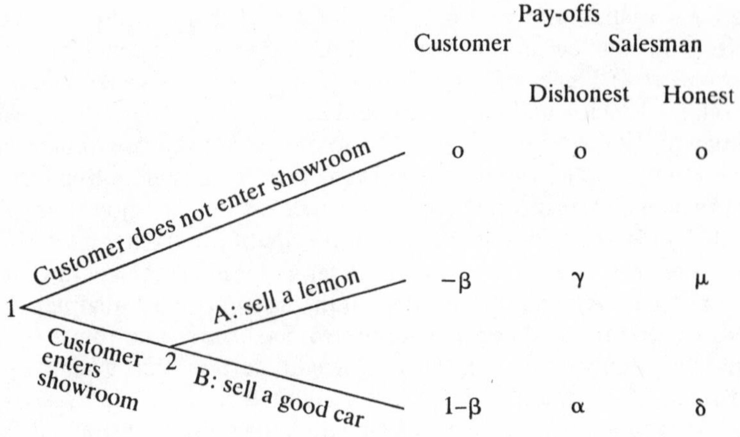

$\gamma > \alpha > o; \; o < \beta < 1; \; \delta > o; \; \delta > \mu$

FIGURE 4.2 *Game tree: salesman dishonest or honest*

I now suppose that the customer is unsure whether the salesman is trustworthy or untrustworthy, and that he imputes a (subjective) probability p to the salesman being honest. I want to think of p as being the 'reputation' the salesman has for honest dealing. This last move on my part needs elaboration, to which I now proceed.

Reputation is a capital asset. One can build it up by pursuing certain courses of action, or destroy it by pursuing certain others. Sometimes a reputation can be acquired by pure chance, as was the point of the short story *Luck* by Mark Twain. Sometimes it can be destroyed by misfortune, as in the case of Jean Valjean in *Les Misérables*. A reputation for honesty, or trustworthiness, is usually acquired gradually. This alone suggests that the language of probabilities is the right one in which to discuss reputation: a person's reputation is the 'public's' imputation of a probability distribution over the various types of person that the person in question can be in principle. Reputation is rarely of the all-or-nothing variety. And although a reputation for honesty may be acquired slowly, it can generally be destroyed very quickly. We will wish to see whether the framework we develop can accommodate this asymmetry.

At one level I am using the word 'reputation' somewhat loosely in the present customer–salesman example, for I am not explaining why p is what it is. The salesman in question may be a representative salesman of a population of salesmen, some of whom are known to be honest, some not. In this case p is not so much the salesman's as the *population's* reputation. For example, the Gurkhas have a worldwide reputation for bravery on the battlefield. No doubt individual Gurkhas vary in their bravery. But this group reputation has been won over the years by the bravery displayed by thousands of Gurkhas. A young Gurkha today enjoys a reputation painfully acquired by the efforts of others. We impute a high probability to his being brave, not necessarily because he has done anything – he may have gone untested so far – but because he is a Gurkha, he is one of *them*. In the next section I will discuss the much more difficult problem of reputation acquisition.

Now consider again the game tree in figure 4.2, where the potential customer does not know for sure whether the salesman in question is honest. As before, the left-hand column contains the pay-offs to the customer in the three possible eventualities of the game, the middle column the pay-offs to the salesman should he be untrustworthy, and the right-hand column the pay-offs to the salesman should he be trust-worthy. All the parameters of the game, α, β, γ, δ, μ, $1-\beta$, and p, are common knowledge. And I assume for the sake of simplicity that the potential customer chooses his action on the basis of his *expected net benefit*. This too is common knowledge.[15] Should he not enter the showroom, his net benefit is nil. Should he enter, his net benefit is clearly $p(1-\beta) - (1-p)\beta$, or in other words $p-\beta$. Whether he will choose to enter therefore depends upon whether p exceeds β.

I conclude that if the seller's reputation for honesty is high – specifically if p exceeds β – the potential buyer will engage in a transaction. If it is low – specifically if p is less than β – he will not enter and there will not be a sale. Each party will receive nothing in this case.

Simple as this example is, it nevertheless allows us to clarify two ideas at once. Firstly, if p is less than β to start with, an increase in p sufficient to tilt it over β is beneficial to all parties, in the sense that expected net benefits, in equilibrium, are thereby raised. The customer gains because the expected benefit from buying a car is now positive. But so does the salesman gain. If he is honest he gains δ, if dishonest then γ. Thus an honest salesman would be prepared to pay up to δ to find some way of increasing p from a figure below β to a figure above it. The dishonest salesman would, on the other hand, be prepared to pay up to γ. I conclude that 'reputation' is worth more to the honest salesman only if δ exceeds γ.

But we now have a mild paradox. If δ exceeds γ and if there is some mechanism in which by investing resources a salesman can tilt p from below β to a figure above it, the honest salesman can outbid his

---

[15] We do not need the expected net benefit hypothesis for this game. All we need to postulate is that the customer's preferences for entering the showroom are an increasing function of p.

counterpart, the dishonest one. To put it more accurately, if the salesman is willing to spend more than γ, and if he does so, he will reveal himself unambiguously as being honest (p will jump to the value of unity). But if γ exceeds δ there cannot be any such mechanism for raising p in this simple model. If the salesman is honest he will be willing to spend a maximum of δ. The dishonest salesman will be willing to spend more, but if he does he will reveal himself as being unambiguously dishonest! So of course he will not spend more. But if he does not, there is no way for the customer to distinguish the two possible types, and it is precisely because of this that the salesman (no matter which type he is) will not spend resources in improving his image.[16]

The second point this simple example brings to the surface is the underlying *externality* among persons that trust, or the lack of it, creates. Trust, as economists have noted before, is a public good, a social lubricant which makes possible production and exchange (see for example Akerlof 1970; Arrow 1974). To see this externality, suppose for example that δ exceeds γ. In this case the honest salesman would be willing to pay a maximum of δ to have his reputation increase from a figure below β to one above it. But the customer would also be willing to pay something towards this .increase – in fact to the extent of his own increase in expected net benefit. We may thus conclude that an honest salesman's willingness to pay for an increase in reputation falls short of society's willingness to pay. The point is that if *your* trust in me increases it certainly benefits me. But if there are good reasons for this increase in trust it benefits *you* as well. This latter benefit I do not take into account when I try to build up my own reputation. This is the source of 'market failure' and, in particular, why there might typically be an under-investment in trust formation.[17]

But what are the mechanisms through which one can buy and build one's reputation? Furthermore, how do we formalize Professor Hirschman's suggestion that trust grows with use? Although the questions are related the latter is easier to answer, at least in part. First of all, there is the fact that one feels a sense of obligation not to betray somone's trust if that someone has placed his trust in one. But this sense of obligation is not commonly overriding. If it were I would not be writing this essay now.

Secondly, there is the fact that society is not composed of culturally alienated beings. In dealing with someone you learn something not only

[16] This argument depends critically on there being a single play of the game and a single salesman. In the following section I will relax each of these assumptions. Readers who are familiar with the insurance literature will note that the argument in the text implies that equilibrium is *separating* when δ exceeds γ and that it is *pooling* when γ exceeds δ.

[17] Typically, but by no means necessarily. If there is competition among salesmen there may be excessive investment in reputation acquisition as each salesman tries to outdo his rivals – much as can happen in races for industrial patents. For a theoretical exploration of such races, see Dasgupta and Stiglitz (1980a; 1980b).

about him, but also about others in his society. You learn something about population statistics. Therefore, if you meet several honest persons and no dishonest ones you might want to revise your prior opinion of the society at large. It is unlikely that you would say you were especially fortunate to have met the few honest ones and so the chance that the remaining members are dishonest is now higher. You would display a good deal of ignorance of both social anthropology and statistical inference if you thought like that. By the same token, of course, if you were to meet several dishonest persons in your initial encounters you might also want to revise your prior opinion: the posterior distribution you would hold would reflect a lowered opinion in this case. Such initial runs of bad experience – leading to termination in relationships of production and exchange – can occur with positive chance. Thus suppose there are many salesmen, of whom some are honest (their pay-offs are given by the right-hand column in figure 4.2) and the remainder are dishonest (the middle column in figure 4.2), and suppose the proportion of honest salesmen is *p*. Suppose there is a single customer who encounters salesmen at random every week (i.e. a different salesman each week) and has to decide each week whether to make a single purchase of the commodity in question. (The commodity must, in this example, be non-durable and not a motor-car!) Now suppose the customer to begin with does not know the 'true' population average *p*, but entertains a subjective probability distribution of the population average. If his prior estimate of the population average is high, specifically in excess of *p*, he will purchase the commodity in his first encounter. If the commodity is of good quality he will revise his initial estimate upward. If, on the other hand, the commodity is bad, he will revise it downward. The point is, however, that even if the *true* population average *p* exceeds β, he will, with a *positive* probability, have a run of bad encounters leading to so low a revised estimate of the population average that he will, as a rational agent, no longer wish to make a purchase. Once he ceases purchasing he will cease forever, because a non-purchase yields no information about the population at large. Thus, if *p* exceeds β there are two possible outcomes: one where after a finite number of purchases transactions cease, and another where the initial run turns out on average to have been favourable, so that purchases continue indefinitely and the customer's posterior estimate of the population average converges in the long run to the actual figure of *p*. (If *p* is less than β then of course the only long-run equilibrium is a cessation of purchase.)[18]

[18] Formally, this model is akin to the model of a 'two-armed bandit' – two adjacent fruit machines – in statistical decision theory, where the gambler knows the true odds offered by one of the arms and not those of the other. For an excellent presentation of the two-armed

The third point which explains Professor Hirschman's observation is the fact that bonds develop among people who encounter one another repeatedly. A sharp dealer will not sell a defective piece of merchandise to a previous customer, and this is not necessarily because otherwise the customer would not come again. The point is psychologically deeper.

THE ACQUISITION OF A REPUTATION FOR HONESTY

While all this is true, none of it throws light on the idea of a person acquiring a reputation for honesty by his act. For this we need to discuss repeated plays of our basic game and to assume that the salesman's behaviour (whether he has sold a reliable car or a lemon) is recorded after each transaction, so that future customers know the seller's history.[19]

Suppose that the game in figure 4.2 is repeated over time, and suppose – although this is not essential, since the salesman's past behaviour is, by assumption, common knowledge – that a different potential customer appears in each period. But assume that the salesman remains the same since it is his reputation we are trying to model.

Consider first the extreme, but well-known, case of $p = 0$; customers (subjectively) know for sure that the seller's pay-offs are as in figure 4.1. If the game is repeated a finite number of times, say T, where T is known in advance, no customer will ever enter the showroom. This follows from the familiar backward-induction argument.[20] Thus a move from a single-encounter game to a finitely repeated game does not alter the conclusion if $p = 0$. In other words, our refusal to deal with a fly-by-night operator, if we *know* he is untrustworthy, will remain the correct strategy even if he were to cease being a fly-by-night operator and announce that he was

---

bandit problem, see Rothschild (1974). The model in the text can be extended, with only a little difficulty, to include many (identical) buyers and, as in the example in the second section, to have customers and sellers meet each week at random. The natural assumption to make here is that customers never encounter the same salesman twice (or what is the same thing, have no memory of who the past salesmen were) and that each customer can see how many other customers are continuing to purchase the good. (This latter assumption allows each customer to glean something about others' experiences in the market.) If p exceeds β there is a unique long-run equilibrium, with each customer purchasing each week. If p is less than β the unique long-run equilibrium is a complete cessation of trade.

[19] In actual markets, word of mouth is the most common mode in which such records are kept.

[20] See for example Luce and Raiffa (1957) for this argument applied to finite repetitions of the Prisoner's Dilemma game. See also Axelrod (1984). The argument 'proceeds' as follows. There is no way a cooperative outcome can be realized within the structure of the game. The point is that no matter what promises the salesman makes he will, given that his pay-offs are as in figure 4.1, sell a lemon at the last date T should a customer come. This is common knowledge. So in effect $T-1$ is the last date, when again he will sell a lemon should a customer arrive at his showroom. And so on.

offering business for the next 50 years. We should still not deal with him.[21]

Now continue to assume that $p = 0$ but that the encounters are to go on forever. That is, set T equal to infinity.[22] If the salesman is known to discount his future benefits at a low enough rate then it is the case that the outcome, where at each period the customer enjoys $1 - \beta$ and the salesman α – that is, where at each date the customer enters the showroom and the salesman hands over a reliable car – is an equilibrium outcome even if there is no possibility of binding commitment of any sort. The point here is that customers and salesman have available to them what can be shown to be a set of credible strategies whereby future customers refuse to enter the showroom should the salesman ever sell a lemon. Since the salesman discounts future benefits at a low enough rate it is in his interest to sell reliable cars only: by reneging on his promise he enjoys a one-period gain of $\gamma - \alpha$ but loses an infinite flow of benefits, α at each period, for customers never again enter his showroom. The above, of course, does not constitute an argument, merely a strong indication that there may *be* an argument establishing the claim that there are credible strategies – that is, strategies which jointly satisfy the backward-induction argument – supporting the 'cooperative' outcome.[23]

But while this example fits in part the notion of trust as I have defined it, it captures only one aspect of the idea of trust, namely that customers can trust the salesman to hand over a reliable car. It cannot convey the idea of the salesman trying to acquire a reputation for honesty – trying, through his behaviour, to alter people's perception of what kind of person 'he really is'. For notice that in the foregoing infinitely repeated game customers do not revise their opinion of him. They *know* he is dishonest (in the sense of having the pay-off structure of figure 4.1) and behaves honestly only because of the punishment (loss of customers) that will be meted out to him should he never renege. To represent the idea of reputation formation we will, if we are followers of the good Reverend Thomas Bayes, have to assume that customers are initially uncertain as

[21] This seemingly paradoxical result really tells us that the model is a bad one, not that we have a deep philosophical problem on our hands, because the result hangs on a number of highly unrealistic assumptions pertaining to human motivation and knowledge. Radner (1980) has shown how cooperative outcomes can be sustained even in finitely repeated games if individuals are not fine-tuned optimizers. In the text below I shall explore cooperation by introducing ignorance on the part of potential customers about the characteristics of the salesman in question, that is, by supposing that the initial reputation p is positive.

[22] Actually, we need only assume that there is a chance that encounters will not terminate at any finite date.

[23] Readers unfamiliar with infinitely repeated games will find an excellent account in Axelrod (1984). The most complete account to date of repeated games is Fudenberg and Maskin (1986); see also Friedman (1971).

to whether the salesman is honest. They all assign a positive probability p that he *is* honest; that is, a probability p that his pay-off structure is the right-hand column of figure 4.2. We assume that this is common knowledge. (This initial assignment is provided historically, as it were, by the past behaviour of other salesmen. For example, imagine that we are all queueing outside a store in a Cairo bazaar.)

To focus on the idea of reputation acquisition, I assume that p is less than β. We noted in the third section (figure 4.2) that if the salesman is in business for only one period the customer will not enter the showroom. So I suppose that the salesman is in the market for T periods, where T is some large positive integer.[24] Assume finally for simplicity of exposition that the salesman does not discount future benefits to himself.

Notice that given the data available to all potential customers, if the salesman were ever to sell a lemon (i.e. choose option A in figure 4.2) he would reveal himself as having the pay-off structure in the middle column of figure 4.2. The game would end then and there, because his reputation would plummet from whatever positive probability assessment customers had assigned him to a solid zero.[25] Once he was found out, no customer would ever come to him. (This is a finitely repeated game, so the backward-induction argument sketched in footnote 20 would now be valid.) Trust would be totally destroyed. Of course, a dishonest seller can reason the consequences of reneging. So can each potential customer. Equally, if the seller is in fact honest he will *always* sell a reliable car (i.e. choose option B in figure 4.2) when called upon. Each participant can reason thus, just as we have done. But what if the seller is *actually* untrustworthy? He will certainly sell a lemon in the final period should a customer come to him. He no longer cares for his reputation. In the final period he is truly a fly-by-night operator.

What of previous years though? Might it not be in a dishonest seller's interest to sell a reliable car in the initial period, simply to keep open in the public mind the possibility that he is honest and thus encourage future customers to enter his showroom? Furthermore, since customers can mimic this reasoning, may they not arrive in the early periods,

[24] I do not suppose that T is infinity (that is, an infinitely repeated game), because we would not then know from our analysis which part of our answer is based on the reputation effect.

[25] I have not allowed in the model for the salesman to make a genuine mistake. In the world as we know it a salesman's reputation *usually* does not collapse on the basis of his selling, say, one lemon. This is because we like to think that even the salesman may not know the true characteristics of his own merchandise. The possibility of genuine mistakes or, more generally, bad luck on the part of the salesman can be incorporated into the present model by invoking the important recent investigation by Radner (1981). The effect of such considerations is as one might expect. In equilibrium customers will keep track of the time series of the ratio of lemons sold to the total number of cars sold. If this ratio ever exceeds some critical value – a value determined by among other things the chance at each stage that the salesman has made a genuine mistake – customers dump the salesman.

anticipating correctly that even if the seller is dishonest his behaviour will be honest; that is, he will choose B so as not to destroy his original reputation p of being honest? For the point to note is that, to an untrustworthy seller, playing B in any period yields a loss amounting to $\gamma - \alpha$ in that period. Set against this one-period loss is the gain of α at each period in the future that he would enjoy if, by choosing B, he could keep the customers' trust in him. Using techniques developed in the important work of Kreps and Wilson (1982) on games of incomplete information, we can show that such reasoning on the part of participants is mutually consistent if T is large. I shall not go into technicalities. But it can be shown that if T is large there is a set of *credible* strategies, one per participant, where for a large number of initial periods customers come to the showroom, one by one, and where the salesman sells a reliable car (i.e. chooses B) *irrespective of his true disposition*, thus maintaining his reputation at the initial estimate p. (The reason the estimate does not change is that behaviour in these periods is independent of the salesman's disposition, that is, independent of whether he is honest or dishonest. This being so, the fact that he sells reliable cars provides no information about his true disposition. Hence his reputation does not change.) The remaining periods are a bit harder to describe, since this involves the salesman, *if he is dishonest*, bluffing by choosing between A and B in random manner (if he is honest he always chooses B).[26] As long as during this set of periods customers see the salesman selling reliable cars, they update their assessment. His reputation as an honest salesman rises, and if the run of Bs continues it rises to a value in excess of β. (The reason the salesman's reputation increases along an uninterrupted run of Bs in those periods when the dishonest salesman is *known* to choose B randomly follows from Bayes's rule. The honest salesman will in any case choose B, and the dishonest salesman is known to choose B with a positive probability *less than one*. So if in fact B obtains, the possibility that the salesman in question is genuinely honest is enhanced.) If the salesman is truly honest, all is well: customers continue to come until the very end (but see footnote 26) and only reliable cars will be sold. But if the salesman is dishonest one of two things will happen. Firstly, in some period while the salesman is randomizing over A and B, A will be chosen by the 'luck of the draw'; customers will realize the salesman is dishonest, and no further exchange will occur. Alternatively, the random draws will continue to produce B in each period until, towards the end, it is the dishonest salesman's equilibrium strategy to choose A with probability one. In either event a trusting customer will at *some* date be saddled with a lemon and from then onwards transactions will cease.

---

[26] It may also involve potential customers randomizing over whether to enter. But for expositional ease I shall ignore this.

I think this is the right sort of framework to capture the idea that people *invest* resources for the purpose of building a reputation for honesty. The gains from honest behaviour are built directly into the model. The fact that the dishonest salesman builds his reputation by going against his short-term interests is an important feature to highlight. This is *his* investment.

The first, and to my mind most serious, weakness of this model is that there is nothing which enables the honest salesman to distinguish himself from the dishonest one. Everything the former can do the latter can do as well. The dishonest type is the cancerous cell which 'acts' like the healthy one. It is here that the role of commitments can assume importance. If the stake is high enough the honest salesman will search for ways of persuading customers that he really is honest; he will be willing to spend resources to distinguish himself from his possible counterpart. This is not included in the foregoing model of reputation acquisition.

The second weakness is that the strategies I sketch for the various participants are not the only credible ones. It follows that the outcome I describe is not the only viable one. There are other, equally credible, sets of strategies that result in outcomes which do not have this form of reputation acquisition, where transactions are not undertaken for a great many periods. In short, such repeated games possess more than one equilibrium outcome (see Fudenberg and Maskin 1986). There is therefore no guarantee that the one I have outlined will prevail. It is here that historical accidents may matter. I have assumed a single salesman in the model. But there are usually many sellers in the world, some of whom are honest, some dishonest. And of course there are many customers. Chance events may set off transactions among some protagonists, the associated sellers embarking on the acquisition of reputation, while others – some of whom are truly honest – are left by the wayside for want of customers. It seems plausible to suppose that if a record is kept of salesmen's past behaviour (say through word of mouth) customers will gravitate towards salesmen with a good track record. But I do not know how to prove it. Adding competition among salesmen enlarges the initial game, enlarges the class of strategies from which participants can choose, and makes the problem very difficult to analyse.

One way to simplify the problem is to assume that participants have a very limited number of strategies at their disposal. An extreme case, explored by socio-biologists, is that where each participant has only one strategy available to him; that is, no one has any choice. In socio-biological models such as those of Maynard Smith (1982) and Axelrod (1984), a participant in a game *is* a strategy. Such models are a great deal easier to analyse because the long-run outcomes can be readily traced to the initial distribution of strategies in the population. The question socio-biologists have asked is not: 'What outcomes are viable when participants are rational calculators?' They have asked instead: 'What strategies have survival value?' Mercifully, people in the world we know are not as restricted in their choices as participants in socio-biological models. But the moral must surely be that repeated games need some form of 'friction' to generate predictable outcomes.[27] Moral codes are a form of friction. There are certain things, while feasible, that are 'not done'. This may well be a route to pursue in exploring the emergence of trust in analytical models.

REFERENCES

Akerlof, G. 1970: The market for 'lemons': qualitative uncertainty and the market mechanism. *Quarterly Journal of Economics* 84, 488–500.

Arrow, K. J. 1963: Uncertainty and the economics of medical care. *American Economic Review* 53, 941–73.

Arrow, K. J. 1974: *The Limits of Organization*. New York: Norton.

Aumann, R. and Shapley, L. 1976: Long term competition: a game theoretic analysis. Hebrew University, Jerusalem: unpublished paper.

Axelrod, R. 1984: *The Evolution of Cooperation*. New York: Basic Books.

Bellman, R. 1957: *Dynamic Programming*. Princeton: Princeton University Press.

Bernheim, D. and Ray, D. 1983: Altruistic growth economies. IMSSS technical report no. 419, Stanford University.

Binmore, K. and Dasgupta, P. 1986: Game theory: a survey. In K. Binmore and P. Dasgupta (eds), *Economic Organizations as Games*, Oxford: Basil Blackwell.

Blackorby, C., Nissen, D., Primont, D., and Russell, R. R. 1973: Consistent intertemporal decision making. *Review of Economic Studies* 40, 239–48.

Dasgupta, P. 1974: On some alternative criteria for justice between generations. *Journal of Public Economics* 3, 405–24.

Dasgupta, P. and Stiglitz, J. E. 1980a: Industrial structure and the nature of innovative activity. *Economic Journal* 90, 266–93.

Dasgupta, P. and Stiglitz, J. E. 1980b: Uncertainty, industrial structure and the speed of R&D. *Bell Journal of Economics* 11, 1–28.

Elster, J. 1979: *Ulysses and the Sirens: studies in rationality and irrationality*. Cambridge: Cambridge University Press.

Friedman, J. 1971: A non-cooperative equilibrium for supergames. *Review of Economic Studies* 38, 1–12.

Fudenberg, D. and Maskin, E. 1986: A folk-theorem in repeated games with discounting and with incomplete information. *Econometrica* 54, 533–54.

Hammond, P. J. 1976: Changing tastes and coherent dynamic choice. *Review of Economic Studies* 43, 159–73.

---

[27] By 'predictable' I mean narrowing down the set of viable (or equilibrium) outcomes.

Hirschman, A. O. 1984: Against parsimony: three easy ways of complicating some categories of economic discourse. *American Economic Review* Proceedings, 74, 88–96.

Kreps, D. and Wilson, R. 1982: Reputation and imperfect information. *Journal of Economic Theory* 27, 253–79.

Laffont, J.-J. and Maskin, E. 1981: The theory of incentives: an overview. University of Cambridge: unpublished paper.

Luce, R. D. and Raiffa, H. 1957: *Games and Decisions*. New York: Wiley.

Maynard Smith, J. 1982: *Evolution and the Theory of Games*, Cambridge: Cambridge University Press.

Peleg, B. and Yaari, M. 1973: On the existence of a consistence course of action when tastes are changing. *Review of Economic Studies* 40, 391–401.

Phelps, E. S. and Pollak, R. A. 1968: On second-best national savings and game equilibrium growth. *Review of Economic Studies* 35, 185–99.

Radner, R. 1980: Collusive behaviour in non-cooperative epsilon equilibria of oligopolies with long but finite lives. *Journal of Economic Theory* 22, 136–54.

Radner, R. 1981: Monitoring cooperative agreements in a repeated principal-agent relationship. *Econometrica* 49, 1127–48.

Rothschild, M. 1974: A two-armed bandit theory of market pricing. *Journal of Economic Theory* 9, 185–202.

Rubinstein, A. 1979: Equilibrium in supergames with the overtaking criterion. *Journal of Economic Theory* 21, 1–9.

Schelling, T. 1960: *The Strategy of Conflict*. New York: Oxford University Press.

Schelling, T. 1978: *Micromotives and Macrobehaviour*. New York: Norton.

Selten, R. 1965: Spieltheoretische Behandlund eines Oligopolmodels mit Nachfragetragheit. *Zeitschrift fur die Gesampte Staatswissenschaft* 121, 401–24 and 667–89.

Selten, R. 1975: Re-examination of the perfectness concept for equilibrium points in extensive games. *International Journal of Game Theory* 4, 25–55.

Singer, P. 1981: *The Expanding Circle: ethics and sociobiology*. Oxford: Oxford University Press.

Strotz, R. H. 1955–56: Myopia and inconsistency in dynamic utility maximization. *Review of Economic Studies* 23, 165–80.

Trivers, R. I. 1971: The evolution of reciprocal altruism. *Quarterly Review of Biology* 46, 35–57.

Yaari, M. 1977: Consistence utilization of an exhaustible resource – or how to eat an appetite arousing cake. Research memorandum no. 23, Hebrew University.

5

Trust and Political Agency

John Dunn

Trust is both a human passion and a modality of human action: a more or less consciously chosen policy for handling the freedom of other human agents or agencies.[1] As a passion, a sentiment, it can be evanescent or durable. But as a modality of action it is essentially concerned with coping with uncertainty over time (Luhmann 1979: 30; Luhmann, this volume). A human passion, let us agree with David Hume, is an original existence (Hume [1739] 1911: II, 127). Human beings can certainly affect their own feelings through time, by more or less ingenious strategic dispositions (Schelling 1984: chapter 9). But they cannot at a particular time simply choose these feelings. In contrast – and on any defensible theory of the causation of human actions – they can and do often and decisively choose their own policies and modalities of action. On a holist view, to be sure, these choices may in the last instance be made for them by structural features of the economic, political, or social setting of their lives (James 1984). But the most intrepid holist view denies merely the analytic or explanatory significance of individual choice. It does not (and, to be coherent, it *must* not) deny either the pheomenological reality or the causal efficacy of individual decisions as such. (To lengthen a causal chain is not to remove its later links.)

The claim that trust is central to the understanding of political action needs to be stated with some care. Defenders of absolutism throughout the ages, from Bodin, Richelieu, and Louis XIV to Stalin and Mao Tse-tung, have sought to present their own putatively legitimate political authority as founded in fact upon the profound and pervasive trust of its faithful and law-abiding subjects, contested only by the wilfully and inexcusably

[1] I am extremely grateful for the challenges levelled at the first version of this paper at the King's College seminar on trust, especially by Frank Hahn and Bernard Williams, for the editorial suggestions of Diego Gambetta, for the stimulus of two papers by Allan Silver and, once again, for the extensive assistance of Quentin Skinner.

contumacious. But one may doubt in fact whether the passion of trust can ever have been a very prominent characteristic of intricate and massively inegalitarian political relations – perhaps indeed of any political relations of substantial demographic or geographic scope.[2] Certainly it is scarcely a prominent feature or a natural consequence of either of the leading forms of contemporary state: the huckstering interest brokerage of advanced capitalist democracies or the petulant accents of monopolistic party authority in existing socialist states. Nor, it may be as well to add, would there be any great cognitive appropriateness in the passion itself being at present markedly more widespread in political relations. The absolutist case for the benefits of subject docility continues to have plenty of utilitarian force: lowered expenditures on surveillance and repression, and the smoother concertation of productive energies for projects of which many of the benefits are likely to extend far beyond ruling circles. But for a belief to be consequentially advantageous is very far from its being true.

Trust as a human passion may rest on close familiarity or massive social distance. Many have trusted their Queen (or Stalin) as implicitly as ever they have trusted their spouse or favourite sibling. The essence of trust as a passion is the confident expectation of benign intentions in another free agent. Compare Hobbes's sharp behaviourist account:

> *Trust* is a Passion proceeding from the *Belief of him* from whom we *expect* or *hope* for Good, so *free* from *Doubt* that upon the same we pursue no other Way to attain the same Good: as *Distrust* or Diffidence is *Doubt* that maketh him endeavour to provide himself by other Means. And that this is the Meaning of the Words Trust and Distrust, is manifest from this, that a Man never provideth himself by a second Way, but when he mistrusteth that the first will not hold,' (Hobbes [1640] 1750: 19)

Since at the moment of experience it is necessarily unchosen, trust as a passion cannot be in any way strategic, though of course like any other psychic state it can in practice prove to have either good or bad consequences (Good, this volume). As a modality of action, however, trust is ineluctably strategic, however blearily its adopter may conceive the circumstances in which he or she comes to adopt it, and however inadvertently they may carry through the adoption itself. When it proves to have been strategically well conceived, trust as a modality of action may well generate its passive concomitant, convert a policy of trust into a

[2] Honesty and loyalty may have been the watchwords of the European *ancient régime*. But they were the canoniccal values of an intensively imposed system of social discipline, not the spontaneous overflow of grateful hearts (Clark 1986: especially 86). Contrast William Paley's *Reasons for Contentment Addressed to the Labouring Part of the British Public* (1793).

condition of confidence. But when less happily placed, naturally, it is more apt to generate acute anxiety, or even paranoia. To see trust as a modality of action as central to the understanding of politics is certainly not to commend a strategically inept credulity or a sentimental misconstruction of the intelligence, ability, or benignity of the great. How, then, should we see the claim that an assessment of the presence or absence of trust and of the cognitive justification or folly of trust must be amongst the central elements of any adequate understanding of politics?

I

It may help initially to contrast this claim with a range of other understandings of the character of politics with which it is clearly incompatible. One such understanding is given by a common version of anarchism. We may take this to assert: firstly, that centralized coercive power can never be justified; secondly, that it is never a precondition for organized social life; thirdly, that it never (or at least seldom) on balance has consequences more desirable than those which would follow from its absence; fourthly, that human beings who belong to a single community potentially have both the will and the capacity to cooperate with each other to whatever degree such cooperation will be necessary to serve their several (real?) interests; and fifthly, that individual communities in their turn have both the potential will and the potential capacity to cooperate with each other to the same degree. The serious case in favour of anarchism is, as Michael Taylor has well argued, a case in favour of the efficacy of community (Taylor 1982).

On this view centralized coercive power, whenever and wherever it is present, can only be a ground for acute rational distrust and resentment; and whatever grounds for interpersonal and intercommunal distrust may emerge and persist at different times and in different places can be sufficiently and best dealt with by interpersonal and intercommunal cooperative responses which do not rely on the concentration and alienation of coercive power. The core conviction of anarchism is the conviction that such coercive capacity must never be permitted to congeal, to settle down into a distinct institutional complex under the control of a distinct set of persons. Anarchism depends upon (or can be expressed as) two key presumptions: firstly, concentrated coercive power cannot be made trustworthy (or less utopianly, it cannot be made *sufficiently* trustworthy for its existence to be endorsed); secondly, dispersed coercive power (what Locke called 'the executive power of the law of nature'; Locke 1967: II, paragraphs 7–9) just is trustworthy, or at any rate it can readily be made and kept trustworthy (or less utopianly, it can readily be made and kept *sufficiently* trustworthy).

The anarchist thesis is that there is nothing wrong with the state of nature; or, that there is nothing wrong with it which is not even more dramatically wrong with organized and concentrated coercive power. Of these two beliefs the second, especially since the invention of nuclear weapons, is very substantially more plausible than the first (indeed, in a wide variety of settings at different times – from Buenos Aires to Phnom-Penh – it has been proved very evidently valid). It is helpful to present the deficiencies of anarchism as a theory not by stressing its exceedingly skimpy and implausible conception of the causal determinants of collective social life and its vicissitudes (a charge which can scarcely be denied), but rather by underlining its blatantly capricious views about the incidence of trust in human social relations.

The anarchist judgement that organized coercive power cannot be made entirely trustworthy, while despondent, has much persuasive force and is in fact shared with a number of thinkers who are certainly not anarchists (Locke 1967: II, paragraphs 159–68, 199–243). What really marks anarchism out as a political theory is the judgement that dispersed coercive power either is in itself, or would be if instantiated, or could readily be caused to become, quite sufficiently trustworthy for the living of acceptable human lives. At its most optimistic anarchism simply consists in the universalization of trust towards all humans who are not themselves bearers of concentrated coercive power. Its sociological realism therefore varies very greatly with historical setting, from the Nuer ('deeply democratic, and easily roused to violence': Evans-Pritchard 1940: 294) to the *classes dangereuses* of a great Third World metropolis like Cairo (or Beirut) or a centre of advanced capitalist civilization like Manhattan. As Locke pointed out (1967: II, chapter 5), and as most subsequent social and political thinking has amply confirmed, this sociological realism diminishes markedly with a deepening division of labour, enhancement of productive power, and widening of economic inequalities. To restore to anarchism a measure of sociological plausibility, it would be necessary to extricate an anarchic community from the modern world economy and to reconcile its members to decidedly more modest standards of living than those which prevail in, for example, Sweden or Spain or the Soviet Union. It would also be necessary to reconcile the existing holders of territorial sovereignty (and perhaps their neighbours) to this withdrawal. The problems of anarchism so conceived are certainly problems of its potential stability within a world of comparative economic dynamism. But they are also, and at least as acutely, problems of its mere accessibility within that world.[3] As a policy,

---

[3] I take this way of expressing the distinction from an essay of Frank Hahn's (in Dunn 1988a). For the crucial political importance of accessibility see Dunn 1984.

accordingly, anarchism prescribes the universalization of trust in conditions which it gives no good reason for supposing will prove available. As a strategy for conditions which are at all likely to obtain, it has, therefore, very little to recommend it. In anarchism trust as passion swamps trust as potentially well-considered policy.

A second understanding of politics which regards trust as potentially unproblematic, because dependably available under particular circumstances, is Marxism. In contrast with anarchism, Marxism certainly has an explanation of why rational trust is unavailable in principle in many (perhaps, thus far, most) historical circumstances, and of why in contrast it is (or will be) available in others. It does, in that sense, have some explanation of the asymmetry for which anarchism provides no explanation whatever. And it certainly offers a sociologically fuller and more realistic representation of the practical settings within which rational trust cannot hope to be reproduced. (It is decidedly weaker on the settings in which it *can* reasonably hope to be reproduced.)

Like anarchism, unfortunately (and partly because one key element in its political theory simply *is* a form of anarchism), Marxism's grounds for rejecting the dependable availability of rational trust where it sees this as absent are decisively more cogent than its grounds for affirming this availability where it presumes it to be potentially, readily, or even necessarily present. The core Marxist view is that rational trust is precluded in principle by exploitation. It is unavailable, plainly, in a slave or feudal mode of production, and equally unavailable under capitalism. The theory of surplus value may be of little or no use for economic analysis; but it does offer a vivid idiom for disputing the justice of capitalist property relations. Justice may or may not be precluded in principle by capitalist relations of production (compare Rawls 1972); but it is scarcely routinely encountered in practice under such relations. There is plainly a strong case for claiming, as both Marxists and modern liberals like Rawls and Dworkin do, that rational trust is precluded by a structurally unjust social order. Contrast, however, the flimsiness and aberration of the judgement that rational trust will readily be generated (let alone guaranteed) by the presence of a structurally just social order: a society in which all productive property has been subjected to collective ownership or its modern liberal surrogates.

There are many difficulties with this ingenuous expectation:

1   Can a structurally just social order even be coherently conceived in principle? Is it possible to furnish a non-contradictory and reasonably full description of such an order? (Modern liberals here can at least not be accused of failing to try.)

2   Could a structurally just social order be causally viable in principle? Is rational economic planning a real causal possibility? Does not the democratic organization of an economy necessarily demand: one person, one economic plan? Could there be cooperative ownership and control of productive property and reasonable economic efficiency without in due course engendering just those arbitrary and unjust disparities of property rights which are characteristic of capitalist economies? How can such a social order be reconciled with the ineluctable existence of a political division of labour? How, within such a social order, are we to understand the cultural self-formation of society?

3   Is a structurally just social order (could it ever realistically be) causally accessible in practice (Dunn 1984)?

There certainly are very grave doubts as to Marxism's capacity to resolve either the second or the third of these sets of difficulties, a central problem about both being the recalcitrant presence of a highly obtrusive division of political labour: a set of institutional structures for political action, reproducing through time. Marxists at present scarcely have much claim to rational trust over the purely economic effectiveness of a productive system founded upon communal or cooperative property (Nove 1983; but compare Elster and Moene 1988). But even if they did possess such a claim, they would remain drastically inadequate in their conception of politics. The political creation and reproduction of a structurally just social order is presented within Marxism as an occasion for rational and unproblematic trust on the part of all those who are not structurally opposed to its inauguration in the first place. But even if it were in fact historically possible to create and reproduce such an order, the choice of strategies for attaining it, and the assessment of commitment to doing so, would always remain savagely demanding exercises in appraising the rationality of trust.

A third understanding of politics which regards trust as politically unproblematic does so from a dramatically contrasting point of view. It insists that we have no option but to take the concentration of power in human societies as given, and that we must take the less edifying motives and the less impressive levels of cognitive insight of most human beings as equally given (that is what human society and human beings are like: that *is* the existential reality of human society). Classical natural law or natural right theories it sees as confused, sentimental, and in bad faith. The world and human beings are to be taken the way they are and are going to remain. Coercive power may sometimes be humanly ugly; but it is here to stay and is, moreover, certainly no uglier than the more socially extended impotence that it confronts, reproduces and, to a large degree, protects from a still worse fate.

This putatively realist perspective can be expressed in notably unapologetic terms – as it is, for example, by Thrasymachus in Plato's *Republic*, to some degree by Machiavelli in *The Prince*, and subsequently by Nietzsche. Thus presented, it is a perspective on power from the viewpoint of the powerholder (or of claques of intellectuals who more or less grovellingly identify themselves with the powerholder). But it is commoner for it to appear in a decidedly more apologetic vein, explicating not the pleasure of exerting coercive power but the practical services which this can and does furnish to those over whom it is exercised.

An instructive thinker to consider in this respect is Joseph de Maistre, who combined a strong feeling for the absurdity of rationalist politics and for the massive role of the heteronomy of ends within political experience with a powerful utilitarian critique of the actual consequences of rationalist politics in revolutionary France and a gleeful providentialist celebration of the extent to which the victims of revolutionary violence on all sides had it coming to them (Maistre 1964). De Maistre, to be sure, is scarcely a promising starting point for constructing a modern political theory. But the way in which he conceived politics is sufficiently unlike our own to bring out some aspects of the latter with some sharpness. In particular he makes it clear that it is possible to reject the view that the problematic availability of trust is of any great significance for the understanding of politics on grounds other (and intellectually more bracing) than misplaced credulity over the merits of particular political agencies. A necessitarian theodicy which sees political society as something for which human beings are not genuinely causally responsible – and for which they are in principle incapable of making themselves fully causally responsible – is less than enticing for most inhabitants of the modern West. But it is important to note how little it differs in its practical implications from the alienated and egoist individualism characteristic of the most sophisticated contemporary thought (Dunn 1980: chapter 10). There is, therefore, considerable admonitory force to de Maistre's point of view; and there are certainly today still a fair number of human settings to which it directly applies. Who has the least idea how South Africa, or Cambodia, or the Lebanon, or even Afghanistan could be turned into humanly acceptable habitats once again?

II

Over considerable areas of the world, however, it is now reasonable to believe that establishing or sustaining a social frame that facilitates human flourishing does depend upon establishing and sustaining structures of government and responsibility which in some measure merit and earn trust (Dunn 1986). Where such institutions already exist and happen to be operating successfully it is reasonable for individuals to feel a stolid indifference towards the exertions which have brought them into being and to see them merely as occasions for current confidence. But where they have yet to be established the need for direct and exigent forms of trust is altogether more importunate. Whether or not such structures will be established depends upon two sorts of factors. It depends obviously, and passively, on the way things already are, on the historical inheritance of the society in question. But it also depends, *pace* de Maistre, on human agency; and this in its turn depends upon human intelligence and practical skill.

This last is a delicate claim, but it is of fundamental importance. Much of human life, plainly, is shaped by forces which no human beings at all at the time of happening genuinely understand; and even if a few select human beings did happen to comprehend those forces, they could scarcely significantly affect them. There are important cognitive perspectives on human life (for humans themselves, often perspectives of a retrospective kind) which are views from well above or beyond politics. A political perspective upon human life, if it is to be coherent, must necessarily be more modest. It is a view focused upon, and restricted by, human capacities: by the possible consequences of possible intended actions. It is within this (world historically, somewhat mole's-eye) view of human circumstance that the incidence of well-founded or ill-founded trust occupies such a key position. It does so because within this perspective what happens to a human society *does* depend both on the intelligence and practical skill of at least some of its members and on the use they elect to make of their freedom of action. Fundamentally, trust is a device for coping with the freedom of other persons (Luhmann 1979; and this volume). It is because of the phenomenological plausibility of this conception of trust that it plays such a prominent role in shaping collective life.

Most of what is true and worth saying about the role of trust in making possible human flourishing is severely particular. To develop a clearer sense of the bearing of trust on political agency in general it may be more helpful to consider a pair of seventeenth-century generalities. We may take these, conveniently, from the political theory of Locke (Dunn 1985: chapter 2), though the viewpoint they represent was characteristic of a wide range of European political thinkers of the period of the sixteenth- and seventeenth-century wars of religion (Skinner 1978: II). The first of them is the claim which Locke shared with many natural law thinkers before and after him: that the fundamental bond of human society – what makes it possible for human beings to associate with each other as human beings at all – is *fides*, the duty to observe mutual undertakings and the virtue of consistently discharging this duty. Truth and the keeping of faith, as he put it elsewhere, belong to 'Men, as Men, and not as Members of Society' (Locke 1967: II, paragraph 14). As human beings actually exhibit it (or fail to do so), it is a socially acquired attribute. But for Locke it both helps to explain what makes benign social existence possible at all and sets a standard for judging how far social existence is indeed benign. Locke himself believed that such mutual dependability could only be rationally and stably coherent when backed by the sanctions of an avenging deity: 'the Hand of the Almighty visibly held up, and prepared to take Vengeance' (Locke 1975: 74, and see also 69; and for the judgement compare Williams, this volume). But he was far from insensitive to the psychic impact of human socialization (Wood 1983: chapters 5–7; Locke 1975: 353–7). His eighteenth-century critics were far more sanguine about the efficacy of socialization (Dunn 1985: chapter 3), anticipating the verdicts of Talcott Parsons and, with a rather different emphasis, Michel Foucault. No modern political thinker has mustered a very impressive treatment of this issue.

Most seventeeth-century natural law thinkers laid particular emphasis upon the promise as a type of social performance on which human cooperation depends and on the role of language in defining the scope and limits of human commitments to one another; and Locke was emphatically amongst them. But his root conception of what makes social existence possible does not really depend on the role of words in expressing such commitments. Rather, it depends (and in ways which perhaps extend with comparative ease to some other species) on the presence or absence of relatively well-founded expectations about the conduct of others – expectations which can serve, until too harshly violated, as premises for partially cooperative conduct of one's own. What the root conception consists in is a picture of the conditional meshing of mutual interaction.

One great political merit of this root conception is that it discourages excessively credulous and optimistic expectations, recognizing that such forms of interaction arise and persist because all human beings need and rely upon a large measure of cooperation from others, but also recognizing that all may at any time discover that such cooperation is in fact unavailable. In some measure it certainly is true, as Locke put it, that men 'live upon trust' (Locke 1976: 122). But the twin of trust is betrayal. However indispensable trust may be as a device for coping with the freedom of others, it is a device with a permanent and built-in possibility of failure (compare Gellner, this volume). The central, if equivocal, role of mutual commitment and understanding in rendering social cooperation possible is one important seventeenth-century generality which needs to bulk a great deal larger in late-twentieth-century political theory. In so far as a political life is conceived exclusively in terms of manipulation and ideological befuddlement, the issue of trust need not feature prominently within it. But even in this vision those whose role it is to manipulate and befuddle will in practice face the constant problem of how to concert in carrying out their venture. In so far as politics is conceived at all in terms of agency, the cooperative and strategic interaction of individuals and groups, the issue of the rationality of trust is ineliminable from it.

A second seventeenth-century generality with an equally strong claim to a place of honour in modern understandings of politics is the vision of the nature of legitimate political authority as a structure of well-founded trust set out in the political theory of Locke, and particularly in his *Two Treatises of Government*. This theory is expounded as a theory of duties and rights; but it survives in modern ideological practice, particularly in the United States of America, as a theory of rights which have sloughed off their concomitant (and markedly demanding) duties – and lost along with them the theoretical basis which gave the right claims whatever intellectual force they initially possessed (Dunn 1988b). But in Locke's own thinking the right claims are principally important for establishing one categorical distinction: between the political units within which governmental power is essentially legitimate, and those in which it is essentially illegitimate. Locke's account of this distinction is a bit rough and ready (Dunn 1980: chapter 3), though it is a marvel of intellectual intricacy and elegance in comparison with any realistic twentieth-century reflections on the same issue.

Anarchists, of course, deny that there can ever be legitimate governmental power, while providentialist thinkers like de Maistre, in well-merited revenge, deny that there can ever be illegitimate governmental power. But on less flighty views it is perhaps evident enough that there can be, though all too often is not, at least imperfectly or partially legitimate governmental power. The view that a number of existing governments are blatantly illegitimate arises naturally out of listening to the morning news or reading the front pages of a reasonably honest newspaper (in any country that permits reasonably honest newspapers). The view that a number of existing governments are at least partially legitimate is perhaps harder to defend, at least to an audience of trained social scientists. But there can be little doubt that if most of the past population of the world were to be transported into many countries in the present, they would (once they had recovered from the shock of arrival) be extremely clear that the governments of these countries had gained markedly in legitimacy over their historical predecessors. Modern political theory is obsessively interested in the question of what could make a modern government truly legitimate; but it has not succeeded in developing at all a convincing way of handling this question (contrast Hare 1972; 1976). Locke, on the other hand, distinguished sharply between true civil societies in which governmental power derives in more or less determinate ways from the consent of their citizens, and political units which possess at least equivalent concentrations of coercive power but in which there is neither the recognition nor the reality of any dependence of governmental authority upon popular consent. For him, legitimate political authority was itself a product of human will and action, a verdict in one version or another essentially common to all major seventeenth- or eighteenth-century contractarian thinkers (Riley 1982). Within illegitimate governments, in Locke's view, the psychological relation of trust between ruled and ruler was likely for the most part to be absent, though it was also apt to be affirmed by those in authority with particular unctuousness. The more complex and the more economically differentiated the society in question, the more likely it was to be absent (Locke 1967: II, chapter 5). It was within the former – true civil societies with governments of at least partial legitimacy that the category of trust played a second important role in Locke's understanding of the nature of politics.

What legitimate governmental authority is, Locke insists, is a range of freedom to act on behalf of what the governors take to be the rights and interests of the members of a society. To possess this freedom of action the governors must be in some ways released from the control of those over whom they govern. But in a legitimate political society they are accorded the discretion and the coercive power which they need, solely in order to serve their subjects; they claim it solely for this purpose; and they use it, to the best of their abilities, solely for this purpose (Dunn 1969: especially chapter 11). In legitimate political societies, accordingly, governmental power is in fact conceived both by rulers and ruled as a trust and (with whatever modifications are due for the moral and cognitive limitations of both rulers and subjects) the psychic relation between rulers and ruled can also consequently aspire to be one of trust: confidence, the giving and receiving of clear, veridical, and carefully observed mutual understandings, a relation of trust deservedly received and trust rationally and freely accorded. Seen in this way, politics at its best is an intricate field of cooperative agency, linking a multiplicity of free agents, none of whom can know each other's future actions but all of whom must in some measure rely upon each other's future actions.

The most striking feature of Locke's conception, to a modern eye, is its readiness to conflate two issues which most (though not all: see Silver 1985a; 1985b) modern traditions of political understanding regard as so drastically discrepant as to be essentially irrelevant to one another: the psychic and practical relations between individual citizens across the space of private life, and the structural relations between bureaucratic governments and the subjects over whom they rule. Locke (who had some experience of the seventeenth-century version of bureaucratic government) sees these relations as connected in meaning rather than identical in practical character. But his political theory as a whole represents a determined resistance to the depersonalization and demoralization of political authority which already in his day constituted the main thrust of modern political thinking (Skinner 1978: II; 1988). This resistance was strongly linked to his uniquely individualist analysis of the basis of political legitimacy and to the sometimes exceedingly radical political implications he drew from this analysis (Tully 1986).

The point of his emphasis upon the personal and moral character of political relations was not to embrace the political routines of a decaying feudal order (Silver 1985b), founded very explicitly upon *fides* as a concrete social relation of an eminently instrumental character (Benveniste 1969: I, 103–21, especially 118–19). He had, in fact, little more enthusiasm for factious grandees or a Frondeur nobility than Cardinal Richelieu himself (Dunn 1969, especially 236 n.; Church 1972). Nor was it to herald or applaud the emergence of a social and economic order in which all human relations aspire to the condition of overt and definite contracts (Dunn 1969: chapters 15–19; compare Macpherson 1962). Nor, indeed, was it in any way to slight the merits of, or discourage the search for, risk-reducing and trust-economizing institutions over time. The very purpose of political society itself is precisely to stand in – by clear and predictable legal and judicial arrangements, backed by effective powers of enforcement – for the erratic and dangerous conditions generated by the collision of institutionally unrestrained human partiality. The best condition open to human beings, in his eyes, was the enjoyment of an environment in which men were fortunate enough to be able to have well-founded confidence (Locke 1979: 148; Dunn 1980: 243). But the thread which ran through all his political judgements and which set him so tenaciously against the modern penchant for purely institutional solutions was the vision of the most benign of human environments as in the end a habitat created and sustained by free human agency (Locke 1967: II, 6, line 9). Since any state as its subjects actually encounter it at any time behaves as it does merely because a particular set of human beings chooses one course of action rather than another, the most important single point about a state's claims to authority always remains that they are claims of particular human beings to be obeyed (Dunn 1969: 148 n.l). (It was not a trivial matter to elect Ronald Reagan President of the United States.) In political agency what there is in the end for human beings to reckon with is only their judgement of how other human beings can be expected to act. No one can *know* how another human being will act in the future. Trust is a policy apt for conditions where knowledge is unavailable, as in the case of the free acts of another person (in Locke's view) it will always remain. Trust does not have to be any more credulous or sentimental than the judgement of those who decide how to allocate it, though it will in practice, naturally, not be any less so either.

There is, to be sure, an alternative to trust: a consistent and strategically energetic distrust. But even in a small *latrocinium* (Augustine 1884: book IV, chapter iv, in volume I, 139) this is apt rapidly to paralyse all capacity for cooperative agency. Across the space of national, let alone global, politics this perspective, if held with any pertinacity and clarity of mind, will crush political energy and creativity in a sense of overwhelming futility. For most human beings, to envisage politics as a relentless quest for the maximization of personal advantage is to consign its practice to a sorry blend of immediate impotence and protracted disappointment. Indeed for most human beings most of the time, from the narrow viewpoint of instrumental advantage, there is almost everything to be said for pushpin over politics as a field for the expenditure of their energies. Those who live off politics, of course, can narrow their evaluative sights without condemning themselves to miscalculation or absurdity. But only an ampler array of values and a less parsimonious conception of what is worth doing can rescue politics for most as a relatively sane and coherent preoccupation. Locke in effect foresaw this quite early in his life when he acknowledged the radical contradictions between human terrestrial interests (Locke 1954: 204–14). The busily opportunistic optic of game theory has done much to confirm his assessment. (It has also, of course, identified a bewildering array of impediments to rational cooperation that are quite independent of assumptions about individual motivation or interest.) A purposeful determination to avoid being a sucker, we now know, if generalized to the human race, would subvert human sociality more or less in its entirety (Williams, this volume).

In the extraordinarily complicated division of labour on which modern social life necessarily depends no one could rationally dispute (Luhmann, this volume; Silver 1985b; Elster and Moene 1988) that human beings need, as far as they can, to economize on trust in persons and confide instead in well-designed political, social, and economic institutions. One of the main battle lines in modern political theory has been the dispute as to how far such economy of trust can go. On the one side are ranged thinkers from James Mill (Lively and Rees 1978: chapter 2; Thomas 1979: chapter 3) and Bentham (Hume 1981; Rosen 1983) to Anthony Downs (1957) and the younger Robert Dahl (1956), who insist on the possibility (or in some cases on the actuality) of institutions which produce a predictable 'common good' from the consequences of the rational pursuit of interest by individual role-players. On the other are thinkers from Locke and Macaulay (Lively and Rees 1978: chapter 3) to Mancur Olson (1965) and the older Robert Dahl (1985), who insist on the antinomies of individual egoism or stress the key role of improvisatory leadership in facilitating the production of collective goods.

In this setting Locke's insistence upon the centrality of trust was already in some respects archaic by his own day. Even in the feudal monarchies of medieval Europe the impress of Roman public law had prompted a strong theory of the priority of claims of public utility over those of private right, in determining the content of the *rationes status*, and thus in guiding the ruler in the discharge of his or her responsibilities (Post 1964: 241–309, 316–18). It was a priority which might on occasion fully license a breach of *fides* between ruler and individual subject or an emergency encroachment for public purposes upon private property throughout the realm. (The latter claim, notoriously, was one which Locke in contrast with Richelieu (Church 1972: 34–5, 303–15) was especially anxious to repudiate.) In the trenchant pages of Machiavelli's *The Prince* (Machiavelli 1961: chapter 18) the idea that a ruler would be well advised to (or even that he could possibly afford to) confine himself to telling the truth and keeping faith with his subjects was held up to vivid scorn. More recently, and more pertinently, Cardinal Richelieu and his busy apologists pondered long and hard on the question of how far public utility, the *raison d'état*, could justify the breach of a ruler's solemn undertakings to individual subjects or to foreign or domestic heretics (Church 1972: 190–6, 205, 244–7, 278–81, 424–6, 433, 501–2).

There is an important parallel in these construals[4] between the clash of feudal defenders of private right and personal faith with modernizing monarchs and intellectuals pressing the claims of state interest, and more recent encounters between utilitarians and exponents of the primacy of justice. True, the crucial thought experiments considered have changed a trifle over the centuries. Utilitarians today clash with rights theorists over the issue of whether it is ever legitimate to torture an individual to save the city (Gewirth 1984), a question over which it might be hard to muster a single medieval critic of the utilitarian viewpoint (compare, later, McManners 1985: 375–9, 550–3). Medieval conceptions of a truly hard case centre more on the regulation of sexuality than on the infliction of pain. Could it be legitimate, for example (a lesser evil), to commit adultery with the wife of an intending tyrant in order to save the city from destruction (Post 1964: 305 n.)? Would the Pope's *plenitudo potestatis* entitle him to dispense from her vows of chastity a fetching young nun, if marrying her to a tyrannical Saracen emperor would deter

---

[4] I am indebted to Quentin Skinner for underlining the importance of this point to me.

the latter from destroying the Christian faith and all the faithful along with it (Post 1964: 266–7)? (Philosophical examples have gained little in unreality over the last seven centuries.) Even in the early Middle Ages, however, it is plain that contemporaries had a clear sense of the claims of utility in the discharge of public office. When Pope Zachariah deposed the last of the Merovingians from the crown of France and absolved his subjects from their oaths of loyalty, he did so quite explicitly because the latter was *inutilis* for the exercise of his *potestas* (Post 1964: 376).

In the context of this clash, however, Locke's espousal of trust assumes a rather less archaic character. For him the political primacy of *fides* is certainly not a matter of the priority of private rights over public utility. What divided him on this score from Richelieu and other exponents of the claims of state authority (Skinner 1988) was not any lack of sensitivity to the *rationes status* (Dunn 1969: chapter 11 and 12). Rather, it was a more disabused and less alienated conception of the state itself. For him the state was only an organizational system through which some human beings are enabled to act on behalf of (or against) others. Above all, it was an eminently fallible human contrivance, not a divine provision. Men and women need in their rulers a power of agency which they can themselves only very marginally control. The subjects of every state are committed permanently by their political subjection to acts the character of which they cannot know and the consequences of which may embellish or devastate their lives. In so far as these actions are genuinely undertaken on behalf of the public good and in so far as their consequences in fact subserve this, human beings can ask no more of politics, even if the means deployed are sometimes ones which under other circumstances would have been open to moral censure.

In political life after a certain stage of economic development the only policies which are open to human beings carry massive risks. In particular they expose men and women to appalling harm through the treachery or fecklessness of those in a position to exert concentrated coercive power. Trust in the relation between ruled and ruler is not a supine psychic compulsion on the part of the former. Rather, it is an eminently realistic assessment of the irreversibility of a political division of labour and a sharp reminder, from the former to the latter, of the sole conditions that can make that division humanly benign.

There is no doubt that Locke's conception of political legitimacy is a remarkably optimistic picture. But its optimism is conditional and in no sense absurd. For, unlike the anarchist view or the Marxist vision of the socialist or communist community, it is a picture of a continuing and inordinately demanding collective human project. It is *not* a picture of a state of affairs that is effortlessly and routinely available at any stage of history, still less of one which depends on something other than myriads of intended and free actions. It is a goal at which to aim, not a destination at which it is reasonable to expect ever fully to arrive, let alone to remain forever. Locke did not expect well-founded trust to be actualized at all frequently even in an essentially legitimate political society. But he thought that in political communities which were fortunate enough to be essentially legitimate the problems of political agency for all socially and politically active groups were always problems of how best to construct, reproduce, or repair structures of well-founded mutual trust. Even in political units which were far from being legitimate he supposed that all socially and politically active groups whose aims were not intrinsically malign had reason to do their best to establish structures of well-founded trust – at least at reasonable risk to themselves and in so far as they stood any reasonable chance of success.

III

How do these two Lockean conceptions bear upon the understanding of modern democratic politics? There are two distinct and not readily compatible conceptions of a democratic political order current in the modern world. One of these, harking back to the institutional forms if not the social or economic realities of the ancient *polis*, denies the need for and the legitimacy of any clear division of political labour. This view is fully current as ideology in contemporary political conflict (to say nothing of contemporary Western higher education). But in a world of economies of immense intricacy, all of which are founded upon an elaborate social and economic division of labour and none of which, plainly, could maintain their productive efficiency on the basis of any less elaborate organization, it is a view in very evident bad faith – where it is not simply hopelessly confused (it is not infrequently both). As a view it neither has had nor could ever have any very firm and lasting purchase on the real political history of societies, being based upon the systematic rejection of the attempt to consider, let alone control, political causality. But none of this implies that it is a view devoid of political consequences: on the contrary.

It certainly is not true, as Moses Finley made exceedingly clear (1983), that the participatory democracy of the ancient *polis* dispensed with an elaborate division of political labour. All modern states likewise display and depend upon such division. Indeed what a modern state actually *is*, in large measure is a strongly institutionalized division of political labour, though not one which in any sense occludes the exercise of coercive force. The interesting question in modern political theory is not whether there is going to be a political division of labour (there is). It is the question of what forms that division is going to take and what are going to be the consequences of its taking those and not other forms. More acutely still it is the question of what, if anything, could make such a political division of labour at least partially legitimate.

There is no extant model of the most minimal plausibility which suggests that such legitimacy could be sustained other than momentarily and in extreme crisis without at least freedom of political speech and association and the right to organize and choose political representatives on the basis of the opinions which citizens actually hold. There are not many places in the world today where these conditions are plainly satisfied. We know, too, rather close to home, how painful it may be to satisfy them in, for example, Armagh or Belfast or Haringey or Brighton. But even within a political order which *was* legitimate by these criteria, the issue of how to conceive an acceptable division of political labour or an acceptable structure of representation remains an extremely demanding one (see, for example, Przeworski 1985). The favoured political agency for modern representation has been the political party, a vaguely conceived and in practice a notably unreassuring mode of human agency. Faced with the choice between a state with a variety of competing political parties and a state evasively related to a single monopolist political party which determines its own membership, it is not hard to see the merits of the former model. But in the less auspicious periods of modern capitalist democratic experience (themselves related to the less promising periods of modern capitalism's economic experience) it is discouraging how far their sole convincing ideological merit has become their not instantiating the latter model. A state founded upon political parties may well be a necessary condition for modern political legitimacy of any real durability. But it is distressingly far from being a sufficient condition.

What might serve to flesh it out a little, and render it more of an aid in practical political thinking, would be a more strenuous attempt to think through the character of a modern political party in terms of the project of constructing, reproducing, or repairing structures of well-founded mutual trust. Any such attempt would have fully to acknowledge the reality of the distinction between leaders and led; and it would have to give a much clearer account of the attributes that leaders need to display if trust in them is to stand any chance of proving well founded. It would need to construe the party as agency of representation more as a medium of social identification and less as a structure for the manipulative pursuit of interests (Pizzorno 1981; 1983; but compare Przeworski 1985). But by the same token it would also need to distinguish more sharply than is customary in modern political ideologies between trust in the good intentions of more or less professional politicians and trust in their practical capacities. Trust in either might often be an agreeable start. But if it is necessary to choose between the two, it is wiser in most circumstances (the more so, the more democratic or legitimate the polity in question) to opt for trust in practical capacity. Politics is not on the whole good for the character; and it is unlikely that there really are sound reasons for viewing the intentions of most of those who have devoted decades to it with unreserved trust. But this provides no reason for welcoming the chance of being ruled by the well intentioned but hopelessly ineffectual. Modern political theory, both liberal and socialist (because it is so vacuously and evasively moralistic), gives inadequate weight to the human importance of practical skill in politics. Here, especially, we can see how misguided it would be to hope to replace trust as policy (the properly sceptical choice of human political expedients) with trust as passion (in its characteristic modern form, an unreflective confidence in the efficacy and decency of existing institutions: state, party, government, union, or firm).

With this caveat in mind we may take as a final plain illustration of the soundness of Locke's insight into what politics is really about – and as a quite novel problem of practical trust – the question of human coexistence after the point at which human beings have learnt how to exterminate themselves.

Anyone who is minimally informed is aware that the invention and deployment of nuclear weapons has created a condition of considerable danger (Bracken 1983). There is dispute – and probably rationally unresolvable dispute – about the scale of the disaster that is now possible and about the intensity of the risk that any particular assessment of this scale will in fact be actualized over any particular span of time. There are also a miscellany of proposals as to what different political actors would be well advised to do about these risks: few, if any, of them intellectually at all compelling. One point which is clear, however, is how centrally the nature of the problem of what to do is captured by conceiving it in terms of the construction, reproduction, and repair of structures of well-founded mutual trust. There are two simple reasons why this is so, perhaps individually necessary and certainly jointly sufficient to ensure that it is so. The first is that the knowledge of how to make these instruments of destruction is ineliminable in principle except by their large-scale use. This knowledge and the possibilities which it embodies are with us for as long as anything we could sensibly think of as our way of life, or civilization itself, is going to continue. The problem is not how to rid ourselves of this knowledge. We cannot unlearn it. The problem is to stop it getting rid of us. The second reason is that the level of threat, and its erratic but rapid intensification, are themselves a product of obtrusive structures of well-founded mutual mistrust.

These structures are not going to vanish into thin air in the face of moral disapprobation, more particularly of moral disapprobation on the part of those who are essentially bystanders. Building the structures of mutual trust that would be required to diminish the urgency of the risk cannot be done by burying one's head in the sand, still less by encouraging others to do so. It can only be done by focusing more clearly on the scale of the risk itself and establishing a clear mutual understanding of the priority of the need to reduce it over the need to diminish other – often in their own terms equally realistic and indisputably grave – anxieties.

Once such structures were built they might in due course relapse into occasions for confidence. But until they have been built the project of erecting them will remain as perilous and as urgent an exercise in the pragmatics of trust and betrayal as any staged in the mountains of the High Atlas (Gellner, this volume).

REFERENCES

Augustine, St 1884: *The City of God*, trans. Marcus Dods, 2 vols. Edinburgh: T. and T. Clark.

Benveniste, E. 1969: *Le Vocabulaire des institutions indo-européennes*. Paris: Editions de Minuit.

Bracken, P. 1983: *The Command and Control of Nuclear Forces*. New Haven: Yale University Press.

Church, W. F. 1972: *Richelieu and Reason of State*. Princeton: Princeton University Press.

Clark, J. C. D. 1986: *English Society 1688–1832*. Cambridge: Cambridge University Press.

Dahl, R. 1956: *A Preface to Democratic Theory*. Chicago: University of Chicago Press.

Dahl, R. 1985: *A Preface to Economic Democracy*. Berkeley: University of California Press.

Downs, A. 1957: *An Economic Theory of Democracy*. New York: Harper and Row.

Dunn, J. 1969: *The Political Thought of John Locke*. Cambridge: Cambridge University Press.

Dunn, J. 1980: *Political Obligation in its Historical Context*. Cambridge: Cambridge University Press.

Dunn, J. 1984: *The Politics of Socialism*. Cambridge: Cambridge University Press.

Dunn, J. 1985: *Rethinking Modern Political Theory*. Cambridge: Cambridge University Press.

Dunn, J. 1986: The politics of representation and good government in post-colonial Africa. In Patrick Chabal (ed.), *Political Domination in Africa*, Cambridge: Cambridge University Press.

Dunn, J. (ed.) 1988a: *The Economic Limits to Modern Politics*, forthcoming.

Dunn, J. 1988b: Rights and political conflict. In Larry Gostin (ed.), *Civil Liberties in Conflict*, London: Tavistock Publications, forthcoming.

Dworkin, R. 1978: Liberalism. In Stuart Hampshire (ed.), *Public and Private Morality*. Cambridge: Cambridge University Press.

Elster, J. and Moene, K. (eds) 1988: *Alternatives to Capitalism*. Cambridge: Cambridge University Press.

Evans-Pritchard, E. E. 1940: The Nuer of the Southern Sudan. In M. Fortes and E. E. Evans-Pritchard (eds), *African Political Systems*, London: Oxford University Press.

Finley, M. I. 1983: *Politics in the Ancient World*. Cambridge: Cambridge University Press.

Geuss, R. 1981: *The Idea of a Critical Theory*. Cambridge: Cambridge University Press.

Gewirth, A. 1984: Are there any absolute rights? In Jeremy Waldron (ed.), *Theories of Rights*, Oxford: Oxford University Press.

Hare, R. M. 1972. The lawful government. In Peter Laslett and W. G. Runciman (eds), *Philosophy, Politics and Society*, third series, Oxford: Basil Blackwell.

Hare, R. M. 1976: Political obligation. In Ted Honderich (ed.), *Social Ends and Political Means*, London: Routledge and Kegan Paul.

Hobbes, T. [1640] 1750: Human nature. In *The Moral and Political Works of Thomas Hobbes of Malmesbury*, London.

Hume, D. [1739] 1911: *A Treatise of Human Nature*. London: J. M. Dent and Co.

Hume, L. J. 1981: *Bentham and Bureaucracy*. Cambridge: Cambridge University Press.

James, S. 1984: *The Content of Social Explanation*. Cambridge: Cambridge University Press.

Lively, J. and Rees, J. 1978: *Utilitarian Logic and Politics*. Oxford: Clarendon Press.

Locke, J. 1954: *Essays on the Law of Nature*, ed. W. von Leyden. Oxford: Clarendon Press.

Locke, J. 1967: *Two Treatises of Government*, ed. P. Laslett. Cambridge: Cambridge University Press.

Locke, J. 1975: *An Essay Concerning Human Understanding*, ed. P. H. Nidditch. Oxford: Clarendon Press.

Locke, J. 1976: *The Correspondence of John Locke*, ed. E. S. de Beer. Vol. 1. Oxford: Clarendon Press.

Locke, J. 1979: *The Correspondence of John Locke*, ed. E. S. de Beer. Vol. 4. Oxford: Clarendon Press.

Luhmann, N. 1979: *Trust and Power*, ed. T. Burns and G. Poggi. New York: Wiley.

Machiavelli, N. 1961: *The Prince*, trans. G. Bull. Harmondsworth: Penguin Books.

McManners, J. 1985: *Death and the Enlightenment*. Oxford: Oxford University Press.

MacPherson, C. B. 1962: *The Political Theory of Possessive Individualism*. Oxford: Clarendon Press.

Maistre, J. de, 1964: *The Works of Joseph de Maistre*, ed. and trans. J. Lively, New York: Macmillan.

Nove, A. 1983: *The Economics of Feasible Socialism*. London: George Allen and Unwin.

Olson, M. 1965: *The Logic of Collective Action*. Cambridge, Mass.: Harvard University Press.

Olson, M. 1982: *The Rise and Decline of Nations*. New Haven: Yale University Press.

Pizzorno, A. 1981: Interests and parties in pluralism. In Suzanne D. Berger (ed.), *Organizing Interests in Western Europe*, Cambridge: Cambridge University Press.

Pizzorno, A. 1983: Sulla razionalità della scelta democratica. *Stato e Mercato* 7, 1–46.

Post, G. 1964: *Studies in Medieval Legal Thought: public law and the state 1100–1322*. Princeton: Princeton University Press.

Przeworski, A. 1985: *Capitalism and Social Democracy*. Cambridge: Cambridge University Press.

Rawls, J. 1972: *A Theory of Justice*. London: Oxford University Press.

Riley, P. 1982: *Will and Political Legitimacy*. Cambridge, Mass.: Harvard University Press.

Rosen, F. 1983: *Jeremy Bentham and Representative Democracy*. Oxford: Clarendon Press.

Schelling, T. C. 1984: *Choice and Consequence*. Cambridge, Mass.: Harvard University Press.

Schumpeter, J. 1959: *Capitalism Socialism and Democracy*. London: George Allen and Unwin.

Silver, A. 1985a: 'Trust' in social and political theory. In G. D. Suttles and M. N. Zald (eds), *The Challenge of Social Control*, Norwood, NJ: Ablex Publishing Company.

Silver, A. 1985b: Friendship and trust as moral ideals: a historical approach. Unpublished paper, American Sociological Association meeting, Washington DC, 26–30 August.

Skinner, Q. 1978: *The Foundations of Modern Political Thought*, 2 vols. Cambridge: Cambridge University Press.

Skinner, Q. 1988: The state. In T. Ball, J. Farr, and R. Hanson (eds), *Political Innovation and Conceptual Change*, Cambridge: Cambridge University Press.

Taylor, M. 1982: *Community, Anarchy and Liberty*. Cambridge: Cambridge University Press.

Thomas, W. 1979: *The Philosophic Radicals*. Oxford: Clarendon Press.

Tully, J. 1986: Political individualism. Unpublished paper, Canadian Political Science Association Meeting, Winnipeg, June 1986.

Wood, N. 1983: *The Politics of Locke's Philosophy*. Berkeley: University of California Press.

6

Familiarity, Confidence, Trust: Problems and Alternatives

Niklas Luhmann

I

Trust has never been a topic of mainstream sociology. Neither classical authors nor modern sociologists use the term in a theoretical context. For this reason the elaboration of theoretical frameworks, one of the main sources of conceptual clarification, has been relatively neglected. Furthermore, empirical research – for example, research about trust and distrust in politics – has relied on rather general and unspecified ideas, confusing problems of trust with positive or negative attitudes toward political leadership or political institutions, with alienation (itself a multidimensional concept), with hopes and worries, or with confidence. In their monograph on patrons, clients, and friends, Shmuel Eisenstadt and Luis Roniger (1984) use the concept of trust as roughly equivalent to solidarity, meaning, and participation. This makes it possible to show that unconditional trust is generated in families and small-scale societies and cannot be automatically transferred to complex societies based on the division of labour. Trust, then, needs for its reconstruction special social institutions; friendship networks and patron–client relations are examples for this adaptation. But this is merely to reiterate well-known statements about the division of labour and the need to reconstruct solidarity, about *Gesellschaft* and *Gemeinschaft*. It does not give any new insight into the particularities of trusting relations. To gain such insights we need further conceptual clarification.

Bernard Barber at least perceives this need. In his recent monograph *The Logic and Limits of Trust* (1983; see also Barber 1985) he tries for the first time to provide some kind of ordering. He proposes to distinguish between three different dimensions in which trusting expectations may fail: the continuity of the natural and the moral order, the technical competence of actors in roles, and the fiduciary obligations of actors, that is, their duty and their motives to place the interests of others before their own. This distinction refers to the content of expectations and, indirectly, to causes of disappointment. It leaves unspecified, however, the social mechanisms which generate trust in spite of possible disappointment. It is this question, and in a more general sense the problem of the *function of trust*, which is my primary interest (Luhmann 1979), and which leads to a different approach to conceptual problems.

To begin with, we have to avoid confusion between *familiarity* and *trust*. Familiarity is an unavoidable fact of life; trust is a solution for specific problems of risk. But trust has to be achieved within a familiar world, and changes may occur in the familiar features of the world which will have an impact on the possibility of developing trust in human relations. Hence we cannot neglect the conditions of familiarity and its limits when we set out to explore the conditions of trust.

Soon after we are born we begin making distinctions. An observer might think we were applying the beautiful logic of George Spencer Brown (1971). We arrive (and find ourselves included) in an unmarked space. We execute the first command: draw a distinction! In doing this we are forced to indicate which side of the distinction we mean. Indicating what we mean (maybe our own body), we elaborate on the distinction. We tend to repeat that indication. This will condense the form. Through condensation the indicated side will assume not simply the logical quality of sameness but, in addition, the metalogical quality of familiarity. The distinction develops, ripening into a distinction between familiar and unfamiliar. It remains possible to cross the distinction; otherwise it would not be a distinction. We can use the opposite side (which remains the opposite side, the *un*familiar) to return to the preferred side, the familiar side. As soon as one side grows thick with condensations the distinction reinforces its own asymmetric structure, and we begin to live in a familiar world with familiar dangers within boundaries which mark off the unfamiliar. And we – or at least our ancestors – have invented myths in order to reintroduce the distinction into the distinguished, into the marked space. This again follows Spencer Brown: the distinction 're-enters' its own space.

If this is the operative version, phenomenology describes its results. In fact, I have begun to reformulate the famous concept of the 'life-world' (Luhmann 1986). We can live within a familiar world because we can, using symbols, reintroduce the unfamiliar into the familiar. We never have to leave the familiar world. It remains our life-world. We never cross the boundary. It remains a horizon that moves as we move. But we know in a familiar way about the unfamiliar. Familiarity breeds unfamiliarity.

We develop forms to account for the other, the hidden side of things, the secrets of nature, the unexpected surprise, the inaccessible, or (in modern terms) the complexity. We can operate only in familiar terms, but when we observe and describe our operations we proceed paradoxically. We use the familiar distinction between the familiar and the unfamiliar.

I cannot continue to elaborate on an operational theory of familiarity. However, one further point is essential for the following discussion of confidence and trust. I shall use the concept *symbol* in a particular way, returning in fact to its original meaning: *sýmbolon* as distinct from *diábolon* (Müri 1931). Symbols are not signs, pointing to something else. They presuppose the difference between familiar and unfamiliar and they operate in such a way as to enable the re-entry of this difference into the familiar. In other words, symbols represent the distinction between familiar and unfamiliar within the familiar world. They are forms of self-reference using the self-reference of form. In fact, symbols have developed as the successors of myth, replacing it first by symbolic interpretation and later by pure symbolism.[1]

Traditionally, the symbolic function of using familiar terms to cope with the unfamiliar has been the province of religion (Luhmann 1984a and 1985). Only in early modern times did a new term (*riesgo, rischio*, risk) appear to indicate that unexpected results may be a consequence of our decisions, and not simply an aspect of cosmology, an expression of the hidden meanings of nature or the hidden intentions of God. This discovery of 'risk' as a general feature of life – roughly replacing what had previously been known as *fortuna* – does not facilitate the task of religion, but it adds another dimension to human experience. It becomes ever more typical and understandable that decisions cannot avoid risk. Such awareness of risk – the risks of technological development or of investment, of marriage or of prolonged education – is now a very familiar aspect of everyday life, but it does not necessarily convey a cosmological or religious meaning. Secrecy, and therefore dissimulation and distrust, are no longer the essence of life and of prudence,[2] but trust is bestowed at your own risk (Short 1984).

This transformation of historical semantics, this shift from cosmology to technology, in highly simplified terms, must be presupposed when we try to understand the function of symbols in general and the differentiation between confidence and trust in particular. Trust and confidence are placed in a familiar world by symbolic representation, and therefore

[1] Assmann (1984) is particularly aware of this non-symbolic or pre-symbolic original meaning of myths.

[2] 'El secreto es vida de las determinaciones saludables' (Ramírez [1617] 1958: 25) was a common opinion at the time. See also Bacon (1895); Accetto ([1641] 1930).

remain sensitive to symbolic events which may suddenly destroy the basis for their existence. Observing events which contradict previous trusting relationships – becoming aware, for instance, that scientific data have been falsified with the intention of publishing spectacular results – may lead to a sudden collapse of confidence or trust. Thus a symbolic basis for confidence or trust emerges, only to vanish again and leave unmarked a position which briefly provided, as you may retrospectively realize, for the unity of the familiar and the unfamiliar within the familiar life-world.

II

All this has been a prelude to my main topic. I want to propose a distinction between confidence and trust. Both concepts refer to expectations which may lapse into disappointments. The normal case is that of confidence. You are confident that your expectations will not be disappointed: that politicans will try to avoid war, that cars will not break down or suddenly leave the street and hit you on your Sunday afternoon walk. You cannot live without forming expectations with respect to contingent events and you have to neglect, more or less, the possibility of disappointment. You neglect this because it is a very rare possibility, but also because you do not know what else to do. The alternative is to live in a state of permanent uncertainty and to withdraw expectations without having anything with which to replace them.

Trust, on the other hand, requires a previous engagement on your part. It presupposes a situation of risk.[3] You may or may not buy a used car which turns out to be a 'lemon'. You may or may not hire a baby-sitter for the evening and leave him or her unsupervised in your apartment; he or she may also be a 'lemon'. You can avoid taking the risk, but only if you are willing to waive the associated advantages. You do not depend on trusting relations in the same way you depend on confidence, but trust too can be a matter of routine and normal behaviour.

The distinction between confidence and trust thus depends on perception and attribution. If you do not consider alternatives (every morning you leave the house without a weapon!), you are in a situation of confidence. If you choose one action in preference to others in spite of the possibility of being disappointed by the action of others, you define the situation as one of trust. In the case of confidence you will react to disappointment by external attribution. In the case of trust you will have

---

[3] This is a point made in psychological research. For a recent report see Petermann (1985).

to consider an internal attribution and eventually regret your trusting choice.

Moreover, trust is only possible in a situation where the possible damage may be greater than the advantage you seek (Deutsch 1958; 1962: 302ff.). Otherwise, it would simply be a question of rational calculation and you would choose your action anyway, because the risks remain within acceptable limits. Trust is only required if a bad outcome would make you regret your action.

The distinction between confidence and trust depends on our ability to distinguish between dangers and risks, whether remote or a matter of immediate concern. The distinction does not refer to questions of probability or improbability. The point is whether or not the possibility of disappointment depends on your own previous behaviour. Since 'risk' is a relatively new word, spreading from whatever sources into European languages via Italy and Spain only after the invention of the printing press, we may suppose that the possibility of making this distinction is likewise a result of social and cultural development. The degree to which our own behaviour, in spite of social dependencies, is thought to have an impact on our future state, has varied considerably in the course of history. Whereas in the Bible, for instance, the Last Judgement comes as a surprise, the late Middle Ages began – under the influence of the confessional – to represent it as the predicted outcome of risky behaviour. In committing sins you risk the salvation of your soul, which thereby becomes a matter not of church practice but of individual life-style and effort.[4]

If this is true, the relation between confidence and trust becomes a highly complex research issue. The question is not simply to assign expectations to types and to sort them according to whether they are based respectively on confidence or on trust. A relation of confidence may turn into one of trust if it becomes possible (or is seen to be possible) to avoid that relation. Thus elections may to some extent convert political confidence into political trust, at least if your party wins. Conversely, trust can revert to mere confidence when the opinion spreads that you cannot really influence political behaviour through the ballot. As a participant in the economy you necessarily must have confidence in money. Otherwise you would not accept it as part of everyday life without deciding whether or not to accept it. In this sense money has always been said to be based on 'social contract' (for a recent example see Lagerspetz 1984). But you also need trust to keep and not spend your money, or to invest it in one way and not in others.

---

[4] A kind of empirical proof may be that this change is in no way the result of the Protestant movement but can be observed in Catholic circles as well (Hahn 1982; 1984). It is the result of an increasing awareness of risk, traditionally defined in religious terms.

Seen from this point of view, political and economic liberalism attempts to shift expectations from confidence to trust. Insisting on freedom of choice, liberalism focuses on the individual responsibility for deciding between trust and distrust with respect to politicians, parties, goods, firms, employees, credit, etc. And it neglects the problems of attribution and the large amount of confidence required for participation in the system. Mobilizing trust means mobilizing engagements and activities, extending the range and degree of participation. But what does this mean, if people do not perceive a condition of trust or distrust but a condition of unavoidable confidence? They will not save and invest if they lack trust; they will feel alienated if they lack confidence.

Moreover, we have to acknowledge that the relation between confidence and trust is not a simple zero-sum game in which the more confidence is given the less trust is required and vice versa. Such a theory would neglect the structural complexity of social systems as an intervening variable. But a social evolution which achieves increasingly complex societies may in fact generate systems which require more confidence as a prerequisite of participation and more trust as a condition of the best utilization of chances and opportunities. Confidence in the system and trust in partners are different attitudes with respect to alternatives, but they may influence each other; and in particular, a decline in confidence or an increasing difficulty in finding situations and partners which warrant trust may unleash deteriorating effects which diminish the range of activities available to the system.

III

Familiarity, confidence, and trust are different modes of asserting expectations – different types, as it were, of self-assurance. However, they use self-reference in different ways.

Familiarity and confidence presuppose asymmetric relations between system and environment (Luhmann 1984b: 35ff., 242ff.). Familiarity draws the (asymmetric) distinction between familiar and unfamiliar fields and puts up with the familiar. The unfamiliar remains opaque. There is no need for conscious self-reflection: one is familiar, not unfamiliar, with oneself. Confidence, on the other hand, emerges in situations characterized by contingency and danger, which makes it meaningful to reflect on pre-adaptive and protective measures. The source of disappointment may be social action. Anticipation therefore differentiates between social actors. Whereas the difference between the familiar and the unfamiliar is controlled by religion, the difference between social actors as sources and victims of disappointing behaviour is controlled by politics and law.[5] The degree to which religion on the one side and politics and law on the other are differentiated in ancient societies can be taken as an indicator that contingency increases (Gunnell 1968) and that distinct control techniques are required for coping with problems of familiarity and problems of confidence. With respect to the distinction between familiar and unfamiliar, religious techniques of symbolization suffice. The political distinction between enemies and friends, between potentially dangerous and reliable people, amounts largely to a question of maintaining peace within territorial boundaries. In both cases a self-assertive individualism develops. It is sufficient to maintain one's position in the face of an opaque, fateful destiny and visible sources of danger: the hero is the appropriate symbol for this demand.

The case of trust is very different and requires quite another type of self-reference. It depends not on inherent danger but on risk. Risks, however, emerge only as a component of decision and action. They do not exist by themselves. If you refrain from action you run no risk. It is a purely *internal* calculation of *external* conditions which creates risk. Although it may be obvious that it is worth while, or even unavoidable, to embark on a risky course – seeing a doctor, for instance, instead of suffering alone – it nevertheless remains one's own choice, or so it seems if a situation is defined as a situation of trust. In other words, trust is based on a circular relation between risk and action, both being complementary requirements. Action defines itself in relation to a particular risk as external (future) possibility, although risk at the same time is inherent in action and exists only if the actor chooses to incur the chance of unfortunate consequences and to trust. Risk is at once in and out of action: it is a way action refers to itself, a paradoxical way of conceiving action, and it may be appropriate to say that just as symbols represent a re-entry of the difference between familiar and unfamiliar into the familiar, so too risk represents a re-entry of the difference between controllable and uncontrollable into the controllable.

Whether or not one places trust in future events, the perception and evaluation of risk is a highly subjective matter (Kogan and Wallach 1967; Fischhoff et al. 1981). It differentiates people and promotes a different type of risk-seeking or risk-avoiding, trusting or distrusting, individuality. Among the many sources of modern individualism this may have had considerable importance. The individualism of risk-calculating merchants, learning from experience, attentive to news, making decisions on the basis of a well-judged mix of trust and distrust, replaces the individualism of the hero holding out against all kinds of danger and fit for all manner of unhappy surprises. Combining both types, Robinson Crusoe fascinated the period of transition.

[5] However, an early sociological pamphlet about the new crimes of abusing confidence and trust uses the term 'sin' in its title (Ross 1907).

Of course, the relative emphasis on familiarity, confidence, or trust is not simply prescribed by social structures or cultural imperatives. To a large extent this remains a matter of definition, and particularly with respect to confidence and trust one can choose to see the relation – the decision to see the doctor – as either unavoidable confidence in the medical system or a matter of risky choice. Belonging to the same family of self-assurances, familiarity, confidence, and trust seem to depend on each other and are, at the same time, capable of replacing each other to a certain extent. It is not possible, of course, to completely replace with yourself something on which you also depend. Hence, we have to assume a complicated relation between dependence and replacement that depends itself on further conditions. These conditions are not given *a priori* but change in the course of social evolution, and this affects the extent to which familiarity, confidence, and trust become variously important in social life.

IV

The conditions of familiarity have been dramatically changed over the ages by the invention of writing, by literacy, and in particular by the printing press.[6] Now a huge amount of knowledge can be stored with which one may be and forever remain unfamiliar, although others may know and use it. In the first instance these developments must have led to increasing social tension. Already the sophisticated art of rhetoric, with its emphasis on remembering the places, inventing (and that meant: finding) ideas, and amplifying effects, was a reaction to this new situation. It challenges the speaker because the audience is no longer debarred from secret knowledge: it may know the texts and may even know more texts, and others, and better ones. The printing press made rhetoric obsolete by enlarging the problem.[7] The world itself could be compared to a book, written by God in partly illegible letters; and immediately Protestants, philosophers, and scientists began to read it in different ways. The unfamiliar no longer screens off possible dissensus, tension, and conflict. The social world is reconstructed in terms of 'interests' (Raab 1965: 157ff., 246ff.; Gunn 1969; Hirschman 1977). Now, you may try to calculate and to outwit interests; you may see ways to use the interests of others which are reliable precisely *because* they are interests (Gunn 1968).

6 See also, from a different point of view, Horton (1967: 64ff.).

7 It took, as we well know, several centuries to realize this effect. Latin rhetoric was institutionalized and taught in schools and, in spite of the emphasis in the sixteenth century on 'self-improvement' through reading, it certainly was not possible to stop teaching (Ong 1967; 1971; 1977).

These considerations lead to the hypothesis that the printing press has completely changed our modes of coping with the unfamiliar. The distinction of familiar and unfamiliar becomes blurred; the religious technique of reintroducing the unfamiliar into the familiar through symbolization loses its former potence. There is no longer any need to distinguish *símbolon* and *diábolon*, good and bad forces, at a cosmological level. These schemes are replaced by the question of whether knowledge and power are used in a positive or a negative way, given particular interests. Thus confidence and eventually trust are the decisive issues, and familiarity survives as a purely private milieu[8] without function for society as a whole. Differences in familiar milieux may now explain cultural and national differentiation, or the diverging results of socialization; they no longer describe the human condition.

A second major change comes about when the predominant type of social differentiation shifts from stratification to functional differentiation. People[9] are no longer placed in a fixed social setting but must have access to all functional subsystems of the society on which they simultaneously depend. Structures become contingent; the law can be changed, if not by statute then by judicial practice (Horwitz 1977). The fluctuations of the economy are no longer thought to be limited by the boundaries of 'just prices'. Science surprises the public with new discoveries and new theories as a matter of routine.[10] Essential structures and territorially bounded cultural entities are largely displaced by time-limited entities such as fashion and style.[11] These new conditions,[12] of access and temporal pressure, of opportunity and dependence, of openness and lack of integration, change the relation between confidence and trust. Trust remains vital in interpersonal relations, but participation in functional systems like the economy or politics is no longer a matter of personal relations. It requires confidence, but not trust.

The inclusion of persons in important social systems is thus neither a matter of nature, nor a matter of trusting, risk-taking, or rational decision. The forms of exclusion likewise have changed. They no longer consist in having no place to live or being in a state of mortal sin (having

---

[8] In fact, during the eighteenth century the term 'milieu' changes its meaning accordingly. It no longer denoted a mediating position, a middle between extremes, but concrete surroundings, something for which the nineteenth century would invent the term 'environment'.

[9] Even the word 'people' changes its meaning, losing in the eighteenth century its customary connotation of property owners.

[10] Tenbruck (1975) speaks of the 'trivialization of science', and by this means that there will never again be a Newton.

[11] The semantic career of fashion begins with the terminological bifurcation of *le mode* and *la mode* at the end of sixteenth century. The concept of 'style' assumes a temporal meaning only in the second half of the eighteenth century.

[12] 'Condition' too (from the Latin *condicio*, not *conditio*) changes its meaning, no longer being given by birth.

lost the *habitus* of faith); nor are they the result of rational distrust. At the level of social inclusion there is no choice of opting in or opting out; nor is it a question of being well born or of being 'elected'.[13] Both these bases of forming social trust have disappeared. Modern life depends on contingent structures and changeable conditions. One cannot avoid participation because 'such is life', but there is no rational basis for accepting what is unavoidable. There is neither the need nor even the occasion to decide about confidence in the system. One can only feel unhappy and complain about it.

Given these conditions the relation between confidence and trust is once again important. The large functional systems depend not only on confidence but also on trust. If there is a lack of confidence there will also be a diffuse sentiment of dissatisfaction and alienation or even anomie. This may have no immediate impact on the system. If trust is lacking, however, this changes the way people decide about important issues. Trust, as may be recalled, is an attitude which allows for risk-taking decisions. The development of trust and distrust depends on local milieu and personal experience. These conditions may be extended by television culture, for instance in the case of political leaders. The testing and control of trust and the continuing perception of those symbolic events that eventually destroy it require a relatively concrete setting. They depend on a previous structural reduction of complexity. Moreover, they require a visible relation to one's own decisions about accepting a risk. Under modern conditions they depend, in addition, on confidence. A lack of confidence may mean, without further reflection, a lack of trust, and lack of trust means that behaviour which presupposes trust will be ruled out. So wealthy Brazilians invest in superfluous apartment buildings for wealthy Brazilians, but not in industry. Whole categories of behaviour may effectively be precluded, and this further reinforces a situation in which one cannot have confidence in the system.

Thus lack of confidence and the need for trust may form a vicious circle. A system – economic, legal, or political – requires trust as an input condition. Without trust it cannot stimulate supportive activities in situations of uncertainty or risk. At the same time, the structural and operational properties of such a system may erode confidence and thereby undermine one of the essential conditions of trust.

This does not lead to the conclusion that the distinction between confidence and trust is obsolete. On the contrary, if complex societies do indeed show a lack of confidence and trust the distinction becomes more important, because denial and retreat in each case have different consequences. The *lack of confidence* will lead to feelings of alienation,

---

[13] Except, it seems, in South Africa (Loubser 1968). Note also the correlation of this type of inclusion/exclusion with an almost exclusive socialization in families.

and eventually to retreat into smaller worlds of purely local importance, to new forms of 'ethnogenesis', to a fashionable longing for an independent if modest living, to fundamentalist attitudes or other forms of retotalizing milieux and 'life-worlds'. This may have indirect repercussions on the political system and the economy, depending very much on the actual state of these systems, on the unpredictable coincidence with other factors within what Michel de Certeau (1980: 337f.) has called *le temps accidenté*. The *lack of trust*, on the other hand, simply withdraws activities. It reduces the range of possibilities for rational action. It prevents, for example, early medication. It prevents, above all, capital investment under conditions of uncertainty and risk. It may lead to a bad life in moral terms, because one no longer expects to be rewarded after death. It may reduce public interest in innovative art which is not yet recognized and confirmed by the establishment of experts.[14] Through lack of trust a system may lose size; it may even shrink below a critical threshold necessary for its own reproduction at a certain level of development. However, the distinction between confidence and trust throws light on the fact that the withdrawal of trust is not an immediate and necessary result of lack of confidence.

A conceptual distinction, of course, is not yet an empirical theory. We need, in addition, to construct hypotheses about, and conduct research into, those special conditions in particular systems which may interrupt such a vicious circle of losing trust by losing confidence by losing trust by losing confidence. The economy, for example, may enjoy periods in which it is possible to have reasonable trust in investment, and stable political conditions may assist in this. Results may then strengthen confidence in monetary stability – that is, in the system. The law may protect civil rights, freedom, and property even in the face of political opportunity. Thereby, it may create a confidence in the legal system and in positions of security which then makes it easier to place trust in other relations.[15] Moreover, we know from many empirical studies that a negative stereotype of the system, the bureaucracy, 'capitalistic' enterprises, and international corporations is not incompatible with positive experiences in individual cases. *Your* bank gives you good service; *your* doctor, although state employed, has proven to be very careful and considerate. Hence it may be possible to build up trust on the micro-level and protect systems against loss of confidence on the macrolevel.

Seen from this point of view, the distinction between confidence and trust gives an additional flavour to the notorious micro/macro distinction

[14] See the study of fine distinctions, which of course have to be 'safe' distinctions, by Bourdieu (1979).
[15] Barber (1983) also makes this point about the cooperation of law and trust building.

that is so difficult to handle in empirical research. We know perfectly well how to come down from the macro-level to the micro-level, considering the impact of societal structures and changes on individual attitudes. It is much more difficult to ascend again and to speculate about the effects of an aggregation of individual attitudes on macrophenomena. Did Weber really prove his point, when he stated that new types of ascetic and thrifty motivation brought about the transition from traditional to capitalistic society? We could reconsider this issue by asking whether there were special conditions available for creating confidence through providing occasions for trusting commitment. Above all there is the vanishing importance of the distinction between familiar and unfamiliar fields of activity and the transition from adventurous capitalism to risk-calculating capitalism;[16] but there is also the increased reliability of the law, the protection of individual property against political expropriation, and the increased visibility of interdependence within the market economy. Disturbing events could be identified, and specifiable possibilities of attribution could make it possible to think of the next case as different.

We should, of course, avoid overstating a single explanatory device. The concept of trust cannot replace the concept of *Gemeinschaft* or of solidarity. Trust or distrust: this is certainly not the distinction we should use to characterize modern society. In describing modern society it may be more important to accept two interdependent structural changes: firstly, the increasing diversification and particularization of familiarities and unfamiliarities; and secondly, the increasing replacement of danger by risk, that is by the possibility of future damages which we will have to consider a consequence of our own action or omission. If this is true our rationalities will, as a matter of course, require risk-taking; and risk-taking will as far as others are involved, require trust. And again, if this is true, we are likely to enter sooner or later into the vicious circle of not risking trust, losing possibilities of rational action, losing confidence in the system, and so on being that much less prepared to risk trust at all. We may then continue to live with a new type of anxiety about the future outcome of present decisions, and with a general suspicion of dishonest dealings.

I do not claim that conceptual clarification and theory building provide us with an effective instrument to avoid such a fate. But they may help us to see clearly what happens.

---

[16] This was partly an effect of recent discoveries of unknown territories and, finally, of the 'globalization' of the earth, but also of improved news services.

REFERENCES

Accetto, F. [1641] 1930: Della dissimulazione onesta. In B. Croce and S. Caramella (eds), *Politici e moralisti del seicento*. Bari: Laterza.

Assmann, J. 1984: *Ägypten: Theologie und Frömmigkeit einer frühen Hochkultur*. Stuttgart: Kohlhammer.

Bacon, F. 1895: Of simulation and dissimulation. In F. G. Selby (ed.), *Bacon's Essays*, London: Macmillan.

Barber, B. 1983: *The Logic and Limits of Trust*. New Brunswick: Rutgers University Press.

Barber, B. 1985: Trust in science: a paper in honor to Professor Ben-David. Unpublished paper.

Bourdieu, P. 1979: *La Distinction: critique social du jugement*. Paris: Editions de minuit.

Certeau, M. de 1980: *L'Invention du quotidien*. Paris: Union générale d'éditions.

Deutsch, M. 1958: Trust and suspicion. *The Journal of Conflict Resolution* 2, 265–79.

Deutsch, M. 1962: Cooperation and trust: some theoretical notes. Nebraska symposium on motivation, 275–319.

Eisenstadt, S. N. and Roniger, L. 1984: *Patrons, Clients and Friends: interpersonal relations and the structure of trust in society*. Cambridge: Cambridge University Press.

Fischhoff, B. et al. 1981: *Acceptable Risk*. Cambridge: Cambridge University Press.

Gunn, J. A. W. 1968: Interest will not lie: a seventeenth-century political maxim. *Journal of the History of Ideas* 19, 551–64.

Gunn, J. A. W. 1969: *Politics and the Public Interest in the Seventeenth Century*. London: Routledge and Kegan Paul.

Gunnel, J. G. 1968: *Political Philosophy and Time*. Middletown, Conn.: Wesleyan University Press.

Hahn, A. 1982: Zur Soziologie der Beichte und anderer Formen institutionalisierter Bekenntnisse: Selbstthematisierung und Zivilisationsprozess. *Kölner Zeitschrift für Soziologie und Sozialpsychologie* 34, 408–34.

Hahn, A. 1984: Religiöse Wurzeln des Zivilisationsprozesses. In H. Braun and A. Hahn (eds), *Kultur im Zeitalter der Sozialwissenschaften: Friedrich H. Tenbruck zum 65. Geburtstag*, Berlin: Reimer.

Hirschman, A. O. 1977: *The Passions and the Interests: political arguments for capitalism before its triumph*. Princeton: Princeton University Press.

Horton, R. 1967: African traditional thought and Western science. *Africa* 31, 50–71, 155–87.

Horwitz, M. J. 1977: *The Transformation of American Law 1780–1860*. Cambridge, Mass.: Harvard University Press.

Kogan, N. and Wallach, M. A. 1967: Risk taking as a function of the situation, the person, and the group. In *New Directions in Psychology*, III. New York.

Lagerspetz, E. 1984: Money as social contract. *Theory and Decision* 17, 1–9.

Loubser, J. J. 1968: Calvinism, equality, and inclusion: the case of Africaner

Calvinism. In S. N. Eisenstadt (ed.), *The Protestant Ethic and Modernization: a comparative view,* New York: Basic Books.

Luhmann, N. 1979: *Trust and Power.* Chichester: Wiley.

Luhmann, N. 1984a: *Religious Dogmatics and the Evolution of Societies.* New York: Edwin Mellen.

Luhmann, N. 1984b: *Soziale Systeme: Grundriss einer allgemeinen Theorie.* Frankfurt: Suhrkamp.

Luhmann, N. 1985: Society, meaning, religion – based on self-reference. *Sociological Analysis* 46, 5–20.

Luhmann, N. 1986: Die Lebenswelt – nach Rücksprache mit Phänomenologen. *Archiv für Rechts- und Sozialphilosophie* 72, 176–94.

Müri, W. 1931: *Symbolon: Wort- und sachgeschichtliche Studie.* Bern: Beilage zum Jahresbericht über das städtische Gymnasium Bern.

Ong, W. J. 1967: *The Presence of the Word: some prolegomena for cultural and religious history.* New Haven: Yale University Press.

Ong, W. J. 1971: *Rhetoric, Romance, and Technology: studies in the interaction of expression and culture.* Ithaca: Cornell University Press.

Ong. W. J. 1977: *Interfaces of the Word: studies in the evolution of consciousness and culture.* Ithaca: Cornell University Press.

Petermann, F. 1985: *Psychologie des Vertrauens.* Salzburg: Müller.

Raab, F. 1965: *The English Face of Machiavelli: a changing interpretation 1500–1700.* London: Routledge and Kegan Paul.

Ramírez de Prado, L. ([1617] 1958:) *Consejo y consejero de príncipes.* Madrid: Instituto de Estudios Políticos.

Ross, E. A. 1907: *Sin and Society: an analysis of latter-day iniquity.* Boston: Houghton and Mifflin.

Short, J. F. 1984: The social fabric of risk. *American Sociological Review* 49, 711–25.

Spencer Brown, G. 1971: *Laws of Form.* London: George Allen and Unwin.

Tenbruck, F. H. 1975: Wissenschaft als Trivialisierungsprozess. In N. Stehr and R. König (eds), *Wissenschaftssoziologie: Studien und Materialien.* Special issue 18 of *Kölner Zeitschrift für Soziologie und Sozialpsychologie.* Opladen: Westdeutscher Verlag, 19–47.

Part II

Trust Observed

7

Three Ironies in Trust

Geoffrey Hawthorn

I

I want to explore what could be thought to be three ironic and even disquieting truths about trust.[1] I want first to argue that a socially extensive trust, that is to say, something more than trust between friends, cannot be created except in and by what I call 'aristocracies'; second, that having been so created, there is good reason to believe that the aristocrats will undermine it; and therefore, and third, that if trust is to be maintained, this will have to depend on conditions which are external to the social arrangements in question or which, if internal to them, might at first sight seem to be conditions that pre-empt anything one would want to call 'trust' at all.

II

There are at least three reasons to believe that a socially extensive and enduring trust is not an easy thing to create. The first of these is clear in Bernard Williams's contribution to this volume. Williams distinguishes a class of what he calls 'micro' motives which are 'non-egoistic'. These are the motives of individuals, rather than of any larger entity, and are motives to something other than those individuals' strictly individual, or selfish, interests. It is not unreasonable, except to those who uninterestingly wish to translate every motive into selfishness, to suppose that such motives might exist. Most of us have at least some of them towards at least some others for at least some of the time. An extreme instance

[1] I am grateful to Diego Gambetta for very helpful comments on the first version of this paper.

would be many of the motives that a parent has towards his or her child. A more ordinary instance would be the motives we have for others whom we just like. But as Williams explains, such motives cannot either analytically or practically do the work for a more extensive and properly social or political trust that we might wish them to do. This is because the four 'reality' conditions that have to be met – that people know what each other's motives actually are, that they know that they know, that this knowledge is not too expensive to obtain and maintain, and that the outcomes of any course of action are not too difficult and themselves too expensive to determine – are separately and together conditions that reality can never meet. If this is correct then the common and, on the face of it, uncontentiously common-sensical claim that the less information we have, the more interpersonal trust we need, is at once sensible and insufficient. It is sensible in that we do, in that circumstance, need more trust; but it is insufficient in its implication that in that circumstance, we can easily obtain it.

The second reason to believe that an extensive and enduring trust is not easy to create follows from the first. Williams again makes it clear. He asks which combinations of motive make sense in which circumstances, and suggests that a necessary condition of any combination making sense in any defined set of circumstances is that the four reality conditions should not be too difficult to meet, and also that the strains of commitment – the strains, in any real set of circumstances, of and on what will be our various and perhaps not consistent commitments – should not be too great. If this also is right, and I believe that it is, then there would seem to be only one kind of interpersonal relation, only one kind of relation between persons as persons, which can satisfy the condition: and that is friendship.

The romantic and, if they are distinct, the fortunate too, might say that love is also a candidate. But too often 'love's best habit', as Shakespeare said in sonnet 138, 'is in seeming trust'. Trying to know her motives, and to know that one knows – quite apart from the 'costs', so to speak, of trying to find out what they are, and the strain that all this imposes both on her commitment and on one's own – would seem often to force Shakespeare's own conclusion:

> Therefore I lie with her, and she with me,
> And in our faults by lies we flattered be.

In friendship, by contrast, sufficient knowledge is easy to come by, it is possible to imagine that there can *be* sufficient knowledge, and the strains of commitment are few. Were this not the case, friendship would not be friendship: transparency and ease are its point. Indeed one might put it more strongly and agree with Aristotle and Montaigne that although my friend is another self, I do not have motives *for* him and act for him at all, but for and as myself; my relation to him is a relation which is at once one of complete self-love and perfect altruism (Shklar 1985: 158–9).[2] It is, in the American legal phrase, the one wholly no-fault relation there is, and if like Shakespeare's lovers the friends in it lie, they simply cease to be friends.

But it is clear that if friendship is the model of interpersonal trust, it is also clear that interpersonal trust itself cannot, as it stands, be a model for enduringly cooperative and trusting relations between strangers. If a society of friends is imaginable at all, then it will be like the Society of Friends itself – a society held together, as Locke argued, not only by the fact that 'human beings can and do take pleasure in each other's company' and 'the emotional impact of moral socialisation within a particular family and community', but also and inescapably by something like 'the revelation to them of God's requirements for his creatures, weakly enforced by prudential sanctions within this life but backed by overwhelming sanctions in the next' (Dunn 1985: 46–7).[3] In a Godless order, however, it would seem at first sight impossible to hold up either friendship or Friendship as a model for enduringly cooperative and trusting relations between strangers. But this is not so. Some of what is met in true friendship can in fact be met in wider social settings. Motives which in all their complexity are transparent as the motives they are between friends can be made transparent between strangers. And the relations between strangers can remain relations between persons and, thus, sites for an interpersonal and wholly general – that is to say, not

2 Shklar refers to Aristole, *Nicomachean Ethics* (VIII, 1161b) and Montaigne (n. d.: 189–91). Her discussion of 'the ambiguities of betrayal' (138–91) suggests a sharper distinction than I do between friendship and *honra* (see notes 3 and 4 in this chapter); but it is the best recent published account that I know of the complexities of the beliefs and sentiments in trust.

3 There are John Dunn's paraphrases. As he goes on to explain, Locke also set a fourth condition, 'the public law of particular political communities, backed by the coercive sanctions at the disposal of their rulers'. But Dunn claims that 'the central premiss of the *Two Treatises* is that men belong to their divine Creator and that their rights and duties in this earthly life derive from his ownership of them and from the purposes for which he fashioned them' (Dunn 1985: 49). If this is an indispensable condition of trust, Locke's conclusions do indeed seem bleak as conclusions for us. (One should also remember that what Locke had in mind was a Protestant community, in which the believers' communication with their God was direct. In a community, for instance of Catholics, in which that communication is mediated by a hierarchy, an 'aristrocracy' may still be necessary.) As Dunn explains in his contribution to this volume, as Luhmann asks, and as I too go on to discuss here, the question for us is whether some more interest-based functional interdependence can do God's work in a larger society. In a smaller one, which is my point here, 'friendship' may be sufficient. In contrast to Shklar, Dunn (1985: 195 n. 57) chooses to distinguish between relations of kinship and relations of friendship, to describe all relations between equals as the latter, and rightly adds that relations between patrons and clients 'tend to be moralised in terms of a vocabulary of friendship'; as he there says, the use of these terms in the anthropological and sociological literature, not least in virtue of their use in life, is loose and unsteady.

functionally specific – trust. All this is possible if, but perhaps only if, the relations are simplified, stylized, symbolized and given ritual expression: if, that is, they are coded in convention. Such motives and conventions do not have the transparency and innocence of friendship. Opacity and hence, a doubt about innocence are their *raisons d'être*. But once they are in place, they can achieve something of what friendship does.

Such codes present themselves as self-justifying, but they are not. The virtues of virtue, unlike the motives of friends, may be self-evident, but they are by no means self-evidently secure. Hence the point that I take to be implicit in Dunn's discussion of Locke, the third of the three reasons for believing that a socially extensive and enduring trust is not an easy thing to create: that 'motive' cannot do all the work, in theoretical reason or in practical reason, that we would like it to do. It has to be buttressed by 'belief', by some more explicit and elaborated and perhaps also more *im*personally grounded set of reasons to act.

If we put these three reasons together – if we accept that the less information we have, the more trust we need, if we accept that if we are even to approximate interpersonal trust in wider social settings, and reliably reproduce it, we have to concede the codification of virtue in convention, and if we accept that we have to have explicit and elaborated reasons to adopt it and act on it – then I think that we are driven to the conclusion that the only possible society is an aristocracy. I do not by this mean, or do not only mean, a society bound together by a militaristic code of honour and propped up by a toiling mass in bondage and felt boots. I mean more generally a society which turns on a code, in which the quality of persons is measured by the extent to which they observe this code, in which there can, that is, be said to be 'persons of quality' – a society, in the familiar phrase, of 'virtue and honour'. Its members may be officers or gentlemen, 'very parfit gentil knights'; they may be Max Weber's Calvinists; they may be instances of 'the new socialist man', or woman; they may take one, although – because such conventions are absolute and exclusive – I think always only one, of several forms.[4]

---

[4] As Anthony Pagden explains in this volume, the early modern European understanding of honour was complicated and can be confusing; and this was not only so in Naples or other places in which men had to deal with Spain (see e.g. Shklar 1985: 158 on Montesquieu). Here, I am talking about the honour that is supposed to inhere in a virtuous public life, the Spaniards' *honra* as Pagden distinguishes it, and not that which is private and does not require public witness, *honor*, and which has to do with the chastity of women and other such matters. Nevertheless, Pagden's point that *honor* in part derives from self-love – a wife's carelessness reflects on her husband – shows that no sharp line can be drawn between what I have been calling friendship and virtue; and accordingly serves further to make the point that it does at first sight make sense to consider virtue to embody some of the same features as friendship.

Yet as Williams says in the course of his discussion of what he calls 'non-egoistic macro-motives', the motives which such persons socially embody, this is not a causally adequate state of affairs. I trust my friends, but just as there can be treachery in a kiss, so too there can be betrayal in an honourable mien. It has repeatedly proved too much to ask of persons of quality that they always remain so in those societies, which are all the societies there are, in which people will be presented with conflicting claims. It may indeed be the case that betrayal is something that we have always to expect and accept where there is any honour and virtue at all; that it is, in Judith Shklar's phrase, an 'ordinary vice' (1985: 138–91). I can trust my friends in so far as I trust myself. I can even be brought in principle to see the virtue in virtue. But I see no reason to believe that the reason to believe in it will, just *as* that reason, hold. As Elizabeth said to Parliament in 1586, we all, if less dramatically than she, 'in trust have found treason'. I see no reason to trust trust just as trust. And so, I see no reason to trust its markers. Given the syntactical and sartorial corollaries of aristocracies, I see no reason to trust someone who speaks and dresses too well; and given the sartorial corollaries of the new socialist person, I see no reason to trust one who dresses with too ostentatious a drabness either.

III

Hence the interest in the other side of Williams's typology (this volume), the interest in 'egoism'. This is the interest in the reply that Brzezinski, Carter's National Security Adviser, is reported to have given when he was asked before the start of the arms talks in Geneva at the end of 1985 whether one could trust the Russians: 'The point', he said, 'is not to trust them; it's to find an agreement that is self-reinforcing.' It is the interest, if one's concern is with establishing and maintaining a mutually profit-able economic life, in reinventing Adam Smith.

The Adam Smith I have in mind is the one illuminatingly reconstructed by Istvan Hont and Michael Ignatieff (Hont and Ignatieff 1983: 1–44). This is the Smith who argued that if one were to go over to an economy of high wages and a high division of labour, one would not only generate more wealth; one would also insure the poor against the capricious charity of the rich; one would replace an unpredictable provision by persons of quality with a predictable if minimal quantity; one would replace trust, which was not self-reinforcing, with a mutual interest in the results of the pursuit of self-interest, which would be.

Opinions differ on the extent to which Adam Smith's expectations, against say Rousseau's, have been borne out. But if one is contemplating the persistent stagnation of the Italian Mezzogiorno and many other such areas still in the world, there is a prior question: how does one go over to such an economy in the first place?

Albert Hirschman asked this question in Colombia in the early 1950s. And he offered an original answer to it. Bogotá in the 1950s was not Glasgow in the 1770s, and none of the recipes that had been proposed in the years in between for achieving Adam Smith's ends by other means – by taking control, for example, of the commanding heights, or by planning, or by trying to reproduce the Reformation – was practicable for the Colombian economy. What might be practicable, Hirschman thought – because it could in principle and in practice be a recipe for anywhere, regardless of social, political, and cultural conditions – was to introduce technically complex systems (Hirschman 1971: 41–62).[5] To precipitate people into such a system was to precipitate them into an unavoidable and unavoidably self-perpetuating interdependence. 'The lag of understanding behind motivation', as Hirschman puts it, 'is likely to make for a high incidence of mistakes and failures in problem-solving activities and hence for a far more forthcoming path to development than the one in which understanding [or a mere belief in the importance of trust] runs ahead of motivation.' Against the conventional wisdom that development had to start at the foundations and link forwards through time, Hirschman suggested that it could start in the middle, or even at the top, and link backwards.

One of his examples, very much against the conventional wisdom of the time, a wisdom which scorned the pretension, was an airline and all that is required to maintain it. It was not, as it happens, the most fortunate example. It may have been the case, as he said it was, that in the early 1950s the air services in Colombia were 'excellent'. But I have heard that in a classification some years later by the International Airline Pilots' Association of the degree of hazard presented by the world's airports, more 'black star' fields, more of the most hazardous of all, are in Colombia than in any other single country. Nevertheless an airline is a good example, because it unfortunately shows how limited can be Hirschman's argument, characteristically ingenious though it is.

An aircraft's cockpit, like an operating theatre in a hospital, or the water regulation point at a dam, or the mixing point in a chemical plant, is indeed a system in which rules have to be rigid, cooperation and coordination infallible, and the outcome certain. If they are not, catastrophes can happen and people can die. There are, however, relatively

---

[5] This essay of Hirschman's was his first on general questions of economic development. It was written in 1954, immediately after a period of two years as an adviser in Bogotá. Many of the ideas in it were subsequently elaborated in Hirschman (1958). Hirschman (1984) is an interesting retrospect on the larger train of thought of which it was an early part.

few systems, even in the high-technology industries and services, which are as tightly self-reinforcing as they have to be to overcome any prior disinclination to cooperate. And a large number of those there are, especially in still 'developing' societies, are in the armed services, which in a perverse vindication of Hirschman's point does something to explain the distribution of power in some Third World countries. Moreover, although these self-reinforcing systems do depend on other systems to support them – that was Hirschman's point – they do not in fact guarantee that those ancillary systems will work. They will work, of course, if pecuniary incentives are already in place. But it is part of the point of the argument that such incentives may not exist. All Third World airlines are fine in the air, but as many of us have experienced, and as I once understood from a reflective executive who had been seconded from the United States to establish one in South-West Asia, they can often be obstinately awful on the ground. No one who has travelled in some of the poorer parts of West Africa forgets the sorry sight of rusting jets on every perimeter, languishing for lack of parts and service. And if systems such as airlines requiring ground services are carelessly introduced, they can actually set the intended progress back. One solution, of course, is more deliberately to introduce more efficient ancillary systems. But that requires either pecuniary incentives, which may not exist; or the imposition of a foreign corporation; or planning; or some other device or set of devices which undermines the original hope of a self-generating linkage. And most severely of all, even if the backward linkages do link, either in the way that Hirschman envisaged, or in some other way, they can do so in such a way as actually to strengthen those social and political relations – the hierarchical relations of patronage and so of 'corruption' that Hirschman, like Adam Smith, so disliked – which it is their purpose to override. The examples are numerous: the construction of dams and the extension of irrigation in India, the introduction of breweries (not to mention the national airline) in Zaire, the consequences in the 1960s of putting a new Alfa-Romeo plant in Naples and not in Milan or Turin, and many more (Wade 1981–82; Gould 1980; Schatzberg 1980; Allum 1973).[6]

Nevertheless, although the sociology of vicious circles is not a cheering subject, it is not an irredeemably dismal one either. Such circles do get broken, as Adam Smith hoped and Hirschman saw. To see further why this is so, and thus to see how some more enduring cooperation can

---

[6] One of the most vivid instances of this remains Scarlett Epstein's study (1962) of two villages in Karnataka, south India, in the 1950s. In one, irrigation was extended, more crops could be taken, and the pre-existing forms of organizing labour and the attendant subordinations of caste were actually strengthened; in the other, persistent aridity had caused these relations to atrophy and by default to be replaced by what would elsewhere be seen to be healthy self-interest.

emerge – some 'trust', although trust of a more partial and prudential kind than that which I have so far been discussing – one has to look again at viciousness. One has to look at the obstructive viciousness of aristocracies and their equivalents: at the viciousness, as it were, that is inherent in virtue.

I V

I said earlier that although one could see the sorts of social phenomena that aristocracies are as extensions in code of interpersonal trust, there was no good reason to believe that they could be trusted. I cannot conceive of any mechanism by which such an extended interpersonal trust could, by itself, reinforce itself, however elaborate a belief in it might be, however well justified this belief might be, or however well justified we might succeed in making it. And there is certainly little encouragement in the evidence. 'The beautiful, the excellent and the brave' themselves, for instance – this is the connotation of the Arabic word from which 'mafia' may derive – are only one of the more extreme examples of a set of such persons who find it necessary repeatedly to remind each other and outsiders of their excellence by other means. And this is the far from uncommon exception that proves the rule that rules alone do not do.

One can characterize the means that such 'aristocracies' use to enforce their virtue according to the motives which they elicit and exploit; or according to the institutions in which these motives are pursued.

The motivational strategy is essentially very simple. It is to play, positively and negatively, on fear. Positively, fear is induced with the ceremonial paraphernalia of kingship and lordship and rhetoric and ritual and their latter-day equivalents: Mao suits and flags and speeches and parades, or silk shirts and Mercedes and retinues of flunkeys (one thinks, for instance, of Jonathan Miller's entirely plausible transposition of the action of *Rigoletto* in his 1982 production of the opera from the court in early modern Mantua to Manhattan's Little Italy). But this inducement of fear is not altogether reliable. Jon Elster has several times reminded us of the force of the point of Veyne's account of civic giving, 'evergetism', in antiquity (Elster 1983: 67–8). The tyrants who set out to impress the *plebs* with overwhelming amounts of bread and circus failed, Veyne claims, to do so. Only those who concentrated on celebrating their own supposed divinity succeeded, and therefore did so unintentionally. If, however, one lacks the charisma to do this, there can be a temptation to play more directly and negatively on fear: to place the People's Liberation Army behind the Mao suit, to darken the Mercedes' windows and the flunkeys' glasses, or more decisively, and as Anthony Pagden (in this volume) describes the Spanish having done in Naples, to exacerbate the uncertainties in the environment; to cut off the well or irrigation water, for instance, to make housing or employment or some other such good dependent upon loyalty, or at the limit simply to present a physical threat.

Institutional strategies likewise vary from the positive to the negative and include the same mixture of display, inducement, and threat. They too range from the almost invisibly subtle to the utterly overwhelming. Positively and most subtly and to most of us, even now, most familiar, there is the almost imperceptible nod of acceptance, the other side of which was so effectively if ambiguously lampooned in England in the 1930s and 1940s in Bateman's cartoons of 'the man who . . .' Positively and rather less subtly, there are all the more public sorts of performance I have just described. In early modern Europe, and certainly in the post-colonial Third World, these tend generally to parade one or another sort of patrimonialism, entailing more or less elaborate and confining relations of patronage, and often depending upon the symbolism, if not the reality, of kinship: godfatherhoods, brotherhoods, fictive 'families' of all kinds. Negatively, and where display and shame are insufficient, as they often are, particularly in societies which are changing, the institutional forms range from warlordism – feudal Europe, China in the 1920s and 1930s, the Lebanon in the 1970s, the mafia, the small protection rackets on the streets of every modern city – to the more coordinated, comprehensive, and assertive apparatus (in which opaque dark glasses play an important part) of what has come to be called the 'bureaucratic authoritarian state'.

V

How are these vicious circles, these consequences of the motivational strategies which persons of quality tend to deploy, undermined or overriden? The answers are, in a general way, in the question itself. If the devices are not – the second of my three ironies – undermined by the aristocrats themselves, they can be undermined by a more predictable environment. And they can be overriden by a power – even an alternative aristocracy – which is independent of the interests which maintain them. So much is obvious. The interest is in the examples, and in what the examples more exactly show about how the changes can occur.

An interesting example of the first case is that of changing relations in agricultural areas in the western Gangetic plain. It is interesting because it is an instance of a move away from what I have been calling 'aristocratic' arrangements to arrangements which are not only socially rather different but also economically more advantageous to everyone involved except, perhaps, the already very poor. The example is also interesting because the means by which the status quo has been undermined are far from simple. They are not the important but readily comprehensible and, from colonial history, familiar means, for example, of flood control, or the opening up of communications, or the external imposition of peace. They are means which have been introduced by a democratic state that is actually dependent on 'aristocratic' arrangements which, in spite of its political interests, it has undermined.

In 1973, in a widely cited paper on what he called 'agricultural backwardness under semi-feudalism', Bhaduri assumed that Indian landlords wished to retain total local power. He accordingly explained the persistence of share tenancy, in which the tenant is a sharecropper, by the landlords' interest in retaining a monopoly of credit and employment, each of which would bind tenants to them. And he used this in turn to explain why the landlords had an interest in resisting technical change and the improvements in productivity that such change might bring. Meanwhile, others had repeatedly pointed to the political advantage to the Congress Party in supporting these landlords. In return for such support, the landlords would in elections duly deliver from what had come to be widely known as their captive 'vote banks'.

But in 1974, Bliss and Stern (1982) began a close study of Palanpur, a village in western Uttar Pradesh, which showed that Bhaduri and those who argued like him were no longer correct. The study also showed, although this was not its purpose, why the vote banks had lately begun to collapse. On the face of it, Bhaduri's description appeared still to hold. Tenancy persisted. Bliss and Stern discovered that because a public source of reliable and relatively cheap credit had emerged, and the landowners' private lending correspondingly had declined, and because it had become possible to market whatever was produced at a reasonable and relatively reliable price outside the village; also because the risks of cultivation remained high for ecological reasons, because the landlords preferred to lease land out to tenants rather than cultivate it themselves, and because active cultivators preferred to be tenants rather than labourers; so it had indeed come to be in the interests of both landlords and tenants to continue tenancy. But the reasons were not Bhaduri's. Production was maximized and risk minimized; there was interdependence, not dependence, and accordingly no monopoly of power. The status quo had been undermined, although its external institutional shape had been retained, by the partial intrusion of a market for credit and for produce which had made continuing the previous sharecropping arrangements unacceptably expensive and comparatively risky.

And thus the Congress Party itself has been gradually undermined. The tenants, realizing that the landlords depend on them just as much as they depend on the landlords, have come to resist a party which has always been doubly offensive to them, a party whose practice is patrimonial and yet whose rhetoric, at least by the end of the 1960s and the first half of the 1970s, was becoming increasingly socialist. They therefore formed a political party of their own, and at least until the mid 1980s and the perhaps merely temporary political interval caused by Mrs Gandhi's assassination, it commanded growing support (Brass 1984). The greater variety of acceptable credit, and the development of a more reliable market for agricultural produce, which together caused the change in the status quo, are the result of moderate innovations introduced by a state whose governing party, Congress, has had as strong a reason for withholding them as for not.[7]

A state or a governing party, however, which unlike those in India since 1947 is not committed to universal suffrage and owes nothing to any particular interest, can if it so wishes simply override vicious circles. Students of politics have in recent years been paying increasing attention to such states. This is partly because they have become more common, and partly because they have been so successful in promoting not only the economic growth but also, in some cases, the social equity too that 'development' is held to consist in.[8] Trimberger, who has looked at four of them – the Meijis' Japan, Ataturk's Turkey, Nasser's Egypt and Velasco's Peru, experiments ranging from 1868 to 1968 – has explained that where they have been successful, this has been due to four things. The rulers of such states have not been recruited from a dominant landed, commercial, or industrial class; they do not form close ties with any one such class after they come to power; they do not create or themselves become such a class; and they establish an efficient administration (Trimberger 1978: 4). They usually rule over states in whose

---

[7] The irony is not lost on those who advise Congress: the political reason for keeping the rate of agricultural taxation so low, at effectively only about 1 per cent of income, is to serve as a disincentive to improved production. The argument for mutual benefit extends only to the tenants; agricultural labourers in these parts of India, as I mentioned, are now more exposed than before, and overt and covert violence against them has increased. The protection that patrons offer can have its advantages. One can see Marx to be arguing this: to be mounting what is in fact a conservative reply to Adam Smith, to the effect that if the market and the capitalism on which it depends in fact make things worse, some way has to be found of combining the care that was characteristic of aristocratic patronage at its best with the productive efficiency of competitive capitalism and equality. Indeed, Marx's insistence on the importance of a collective ethic, rather than individual interest, further aligns him as closely with literally conservative (that is to say aristocratic) thinking as it does with the radicalism with which he is more conventionally associated. And notoriously, his aristocracy of labour – in this sense and not that of the labour historians – has proved to be as riddled with deception and distrust as any of the older sorts.

[8] There is a concise review of the literature and the issues in Skocpol (1985).

inception and even direction the military has played a part. The Republic of Korea is a case in point.

The Korean peninsula was occupied by the Japanese between 1910 and 1945. In this occupation, 'a highly articulated, disciplined, penetrating colonial bureaucracy', as Cumings has described it (1984: 6), 'substituted both for the traditional regime and for indigenous groups and classes that under "normal" conditions would have accomplished development themselves.' In Korea these 'indigenous groups' included, as they did not in Taiwan, which the Japanese also occupied, and which is often now compared with it, a large and established landed class. For this reason, as Cumings reports the colonial administrators saying at the time, what could be achieved with incentives in Taiwan required coercion in Korea. Moreover, the Japanese promoted industrialization in Korea in exactly the way in which they had earlier begun to promote it in Japan itself. They connected their directive colonial administration to a few large conglomerates, *zaibatsu*, and several big banks. This served further to centralize the society and consolidate their power. And to reinforce it, the Japanese 'foisted upon Koreans . . . an ideology of incorporation emphasizing a structural family principle and an ethical filiality' (Cumings 1984: 13–14).

The policy nevertheless had a price. The changes in the society, the moving of peasants from the land, the emergence of an industrial working class and the consequent and rapid urbanization generated tensions which came to the surface in a series of outbursts between 1945 and the start of the war on the peninsula in 1950. The nature of the Japanese administration also produced a pervasive distrust. No one knew who had been colluding and collaborating with whom. Yet since 1953 and the end of the war, the governments in both north and south, the Democratic People's Republic and the Republic, have attempted to contain the lasting consequences of these disruptions in exactly the same way. The DPRK has had what might be described as its 'corporate familism' with a self-described 'great leader' in the Confucian manner; the ROK, directed in the 1960s and 1970s by a man who had been an officer in the Japanese army, has had its 'New Spirit' movement. In the one, there has been a direction and nominally socialist corporatism; in the other, a directive and nominally capitalist one. And the similarities between them are much greater than conventional distinctions between the two sorts of system would suggest. Economically, the DPRK is wholly socialist, but there is also in the ROK what Amsden, talking about Taiwan, has called 'a total interpenetration of public and private interests' (1979: 362).[9] Politically, with the exception of a brief and

---

[9] The difference in this respect between the ROK and Taiwan lies only in the fact that whereas South Korean enterprises are often large *chaebol* (conglomerates) on the model of the Japanese *zaibatsu*, those in Taiwan tend to be much smaller.

entirely unsuccessful experiment in the ROK in 1960, neither society has approached an even moderately open democracy.

The ROK has been an extraordinary economic success. Its rate of growth in the 1980s has slowed, but at 7 or 8 per cent per year is still high; and although its international debt is now in the order of $45 billion, it is still regarded as creditworthy by the International Monetary Fund and thus by private banks. In its high rate of growth since the 1960s it has, unlike some other fast-growing countries, provided high rates of employment and considerable security of employment too, and if it has spent less on health than some other 'developing' countries, including the DPRK, it has effectively abolished illiteracy. It is, in short, a demonstration case of the economic benefits of directive rule.

Yet Tocqueville believed that centralization, as he put it, 'excels at preventing, not doing'. The putatively omnipotent, he thought, are practically impotent, because 'the sovereign can punish immediately any faults he discovers, but he cannot flatter himself into supposing that he sees all the faults he should punish' (quoted by Elster 1983: 88). Elster suggests that:

> The most fundamental reason [why despotic rulers are unable to achieve their goals] is found in the lack of reliable information. . . . The flaw of the system is that all acts tend to have an immediate political significance, which means that information degenerates into informing and so becomes worthless for planning purposes. Or else the information is offered that the informant believes his superiors want to hear, even if they insist on information that reflects the world as it is rather than the world as they would like it to be.

Reality conditions, in Williams's phrase (this volume), cannot be met. Elster's own example is the USSR, and at first sight he would seem to be right. One would similarly suppose that the despotism of the governments in Seoul since 1961, and the pervasive distrust between Koreans that came down from the Japanese occupation and the disarray of the period between 1945 and 1953, would have made it impossible for them to have avoided this too.

It has not, and this fact has not only impressed scholars. Some years before the ROK's economic success had become apparent to many in the West, Suharto, as soon as he had assumed power in Indonesia in 1967, sent his closest political associate, Modani, to Seoul to discover how this success had been achieved.[10] The answer was indicated in Modani's appointment in 1974 as director of Suharto's internal intelligence agency. He had discovered that the South Korean government had

[10] I owe this fact to Robert Taylor.

built up an extremely effective agency of its own, the Korean Central Intelligence Agency. Exploiting the persistent fear of imminent invasion from the DPRK, a fear encouraged by the Americans, and assiduously gathering information on a large number of putative subversives in a wide variety of places in society, the KCIA had in turn exploited the pre-existing distrust in the society to the government's advantage. Indeed, the KCIA's power may have exceeded that of any comparable agency in any country in the world, even, *pace* Elster, the KGB. The present president and prime minister are both former directors of it. Its reputation is understandably unsavoury; so much so that the president, Chun Doo-hwan – who is changing tack in an attempt to liberalize the society – has recently renamed it the Agency for National Security Planning.

Nevertheless, even if it is conceded that the government of the ROK has in this way overcome what might otherwise have been an economically debilitating vicious circle, it cannot be said that it has created trust. On the contrary. And it is indeed perfectly possible that if and when the present pattern of rule changes in the country, as Chun Doo-hwan intends it to do in 1988, existing cooperations and the successful economic organization which depends on them could dissolve or even collapse. The despotism could turn out not to have broken the circle after all, or simply to have instituted another. It could turn out not, as it certainly seems at present to have done, to have created that 'restless activity, superabundant force, and energy that' in Tocqueville's view (quoted by Elster 1983: 95) is 'never found elsewhere' than in democracies and 'which, however little favoured by circumstances, can do wonders'.

But it may also be the case that the ROK qualifies or even overturns Tocqueville's expectation. Even if it is said that there is no reason in the recent political history of Korea to believe that the pattern of rule will change, and certainly no reason to believe that any such change will be in a democratic direction,[11] there *is* reason to believe that it has already surmounted what Tocqueville and Elster suggest no such regime can surmount, which is insufficiency of information. Yet there is at the same time no good reason not to think that its economic organization is – like Japan's, which has recovered in several fundamental respects the character it had assumed in the 1930s – one which has already generated a sufficient interest in its continuation.

---

[11] There are arguments for this both from the internal character of the country and from its external conditions (Hawthorn 1986); and if there is a successful move to a more democratic rule after 1988, this rule may well assume the form it has in Japan rather than in, say, the United States or even France.

VI

I have argued that a socially extensive trust cannot be created except in and by what I have called 'aristocracies'; that having been so created, there is good reason to believe that the aristocrats will undermine it; and that if trust is to be maintained, this will have to depend either on conditions which are external to the social arrangements in question or on strategies which are internal and which, although perhaps directed by what could be called an 'aristocracy', might at first sight seem to pre-empt anything one would want to describe as 'trust' at all. If these arguments are right, they suggest two qualifications to existing discussions, including this one, of trust and its conditions.

The first is that even if one accepts with Luhmann (1979) that there are two sorts of trust, one founded on belief, characteristic of the 'pre-modern', and one founded on mutual self-interest and functional inter-dependence, characteristic of the 'modern', it is not clear that these are causally independent of each other. In their different ways, the failures of backward linkage even in high-technology systems, the changes in agricultural practice and political affiliation in northern India, and the developmental successes of South Korea, each suggest that whatever may eventually result, a self-reinforcing and functional trust may not be able to generate itself, but may require something analogous to an 'aristo-cracy' to impose the initial conditions of its generation. The second qualification, most evident from the example of Korea, is that it may be possible deliberately if deviously to create trust, which cannot always therefore be seen as a 'by-product', as Elster claims; and that at least one way of doing so is the way that Elster, after Tocqueville, does not believe is possible. If this in turn is right, it would seem to follow that in some conditions some 'aristocracies' – a political party, for instance, or an army – can create trust after all, and can do so by creating *dis*trust.

REFERENCES

Allum, P. A. 1973: *Politics and Society in Post-War Naples*. Cambridge: Cambridge University Press.

Amsden, A. M. 1979: Taiwan's economic history: a case of *étatisme* and a challenge to dependency theory. *Modern China* 5, 341–80.

Bhaduri, A. 1973: Agricultural backwardness under semi-feudalism. *Economic Journal* 83, 120–37.

Bliss, C. J. and Stern, N. J. 1982: *Palanpur: the economy of an Indian village*. Oxford: Clarendon.

Brass, P. R. 1984: National power and local politics in India: a twenty-year perspective. *Modern Asian Studies* 18, 89–118.

Cumings, B. 1984: The origins and development of the northeast Asian political economy: industrial sectors, product cycles and political consequences. *International Organisation* 38, 1–40.

Dunn, J. 1985: 'Trust' in the politics of John Locke. In J. Dunn, *Rethinking Modern Political Theory*, Cambridge: Cambridge University Press.

Elster, J. 1983: *Sour Grapes: studies in the subversion of rationality*. Cambridge: Cambridge University Press.

Epstein, T. S. 1962: *Economic Development and Cultural Change in South India*. London: Oxford University Press.

Gould, D. J. 1980: *Bureaucratic Corruption and Underdevelopment in the Third World: the case of Zaire*. New York and London: Pergamon.

Hawthorn G. P. 1986: The political economy of the arms race in northeast Asia: the case of the Republic of Korea. Paper given to Korean Association of International Relations conference on the arms race and arms control in North-East Asia, Seoul, 28 August.

Hirschman, A. O. 1958: *The Strategy of Economic Development*. New Haven and London: Yale University Press.

Hirschman, A. O. 1971: Economics and investment planning: reflections based on experience in Colombia. In A. O. Hirschman, *A Bias for Hope: essays on development and Latin America*, New Haven and London: Yale University Press.

Hirschman, A. O. 1984: A dissenter's confession. In G. M. Meier and D. Seers (eds), *Pioneers of Development*, New York: Oxford University Press for the World Bank.

Hont, I. and Ignatieff, M. 1983: Needs and justice in the *Wealth of Nations*: an introductory essay. In I. Hont and M. Ignatieff (eds), *Wealth and Virtue: the shaping of political economy in the Scottish Enlightenment*, Cambridge: Cambridge University Press.

Luhmann, N. 1979: *Trust and Power*. Chichester: Wiley.

Montaigne, n. d.: Of friendship. In *The Essays of Montaigne*, trans. E. J. Trechman, Oxford University Press.

Schatzberg, M. G. 1980: *Politics and Class in Zaire: bureaucracy, business and beer in Lisala*. New York: Holmes and Meier.

Shklar, J. N. 1985: *Ordinary Vices*. Cambridge, Mass.: Harvard University Press.

Skocpol, T. 1985: Bringing the state back in: current research. In P. B. Evans, D. Rueschemeyer, and T. Skocpol (eds), *Bringing the State Back In*, Cambridge Cambridge University Press.

Trimberger, E. M. 1978: *Revolution from Above: military bureaucrats and development in Japan, Turkey, Egypt and Peru*. New Brunswick: Transaction.

Wade, R. 1981–82: The system of administrative and political corruption: canal irrigation in south India. *Journal of Development Studies* 18, 287–328.

8

The Destruction of Trust and its Economic Consequences in the Case of Eighteenth-century Naples

Anthony Pagden

I

In this essay I wish to consider an example not of how trust might be created or sustained within a society but of how it might be destroyed.[1] For although it may well be the case that no central agency is capable of intentionally creating trust where none previously or independently existed, it clearly does lie within the power of most effectively constituted agencies to destroy it, or, in Thomas Schelling's words, to 'spoil communication, to create distrust and suspicion, to make agreements unenforceable, to undermine transition, to reduce solidarity, to discredit leadership' (1984: 211).

What I shall attempt to explain in this essay is how a group of eighteenth-century Neapolitan political economists interpreted what they saw as an attempt by their Spanish rulers to achieve just such objectives in order to increase their social and political control over the kingdom. I have chosen Naples because it provides, I think, a paradigmatic example of the way trust was thought to operate in pre-industrial Europe, and because an understanding of this, as I shall suggest at the end of this essay, might offer some answers to larger questions about the necessary conditions for economic growth and social development in the early modern world.

Under its Angevin and Aragonese rulers in the Middle Ages the Kingdom of Naples – which included the whole of the peninsula south from the border of the Papal States, that is south from the modern

[1] I would like to thank John Dunn, Geoffrey Hawthorn, and Diego Gambetta for their comments on an earlier version of this essay.

province of Lazio – had enjoyed a large measure of political autonomy. It had for long been the seat of the Aragonese kings, and like most parts of the Aragonese empire possessed extensive liberties expressed in a legendary, and probably apocryphal, oath of allegiance to the king which ended with the telling phrase 'and if not, not'. When the kingdom passed to the Habsburgs it became increasingly marginalized and the older representative assemblies, the *Eletti* and the *Università*, became little more than the instruments of a feudal aristocracy which was entirely beholden to the crown. As the Spanish empire steadily declined during the late sixteenth and early seventeenth centuries, the Spanish kings demanded more and more in taxes from their subjects. In Naples and Sicily they purchased these by granting the baronry ever increasing power. In 1647 the people of Naples, by now reduced to living off melons, rose in what was to become the most spectacular and widely discussed revolt of the period. For a few months the *populo minuto*, the 'common people', and what was called the *populo civile* (see Galasso 1982: I, xv–xvi) – comprised, for the most part, of merchants and lawyers – managed to establish an independent republic with the Duc de Guise as its sometimes reluctant doge. The Spaniards returned by force in 1648, but the revolt had shaken the crown's confidence in the barons and compelled it to recognize that its policies were in no one's long-term interests. These policies, as we shall see, consisted largely in the destruction of trust and the cultural networks which sustained it. In 1707, after the War of the Spanish Succession, Naples passed to the Austrians and in 1724 became an independent kingdom under Bourbon rule.

It is with the political economists of this last period, from the early 1720s until the 1790s, that I shall be concerned. The first of this group, Paolo Mattia Doria, was, paradoxically for such a fierce opponent of the Spanish monarchy, a member of the Genoese family which had provided Philip II with a navy in the Mediterranean and an army in the Netherlands. He was born in the year of the revolution, became a member of the Academia del Medinaceli, whose prime concern was to reform the political and economic structure of the kingdom in the aftermath of the revolt, and lived long enough to discuss the reasons for the collapse of the Spanish empire with Montesquieu. The last are Antonio Genovesi (1713–79), the first man to hold a chair of commerce at the university of Naples, or indeed at any university anywhere (see Bellamy 1987), and Gaetano Filangieri (1753–88), the author of an immensely influential treatise on the science of legislation.[2] All of these men, the leading figures in their

2 Galasso (1982: I, xi) rightly notes that 'nel periodo fra il Doria e il Genovesi fossero posti i temi principali della discussione su Napoli, che sarebbe proseguita, in termini solo parzialmente mutati, anche dopo che nel 1860 la città aveva cessato di essere la capitale di uno Stato independente.' If we allow for certain changes in vocabulary, and a far greater emphasis on the means of production, the debate continues to this day.

different ways of the Neapolitan Enlightenment, were engaged – as were the perhaps better-known figures of Giambattista Vico and Pietro Giannone – in the project or reviving and reinterpreting their humanistic past, a project which was to be taken up again by the liberals of the nineteenth century and which has had a marked influence on more recent Italian social thought.

II

For Doria and Genovesi, the notion of trust as a dimension of social behaviour involved a crucial element of the incalculable, of the non-rational. Trust clearly depends, as several of the essays in this book stress, on the availability of information about the object of one's trust. I will trust my friends, or even my trading partners, because I believe that I can predict how they will behave. But although it may be perfectly rational for me to hold such a belief, I cannot in fact ever be in possession of sufficient information to *know* that they will not act in entirely unforeseen ways. I *trust* them not to do so. What I have will always be a *belief*. Like Pascal's view of faith, trust relies in the end upon a wager; and in Italian as in Latin (and most Romance languages), the term most commonly used for trust, *fede*, is the term English translates as 'faith'. John Dunn refers in this volume to Locke's understanding of the Latin *fides* as 'the duty to observe mutual undertakings and the virtue of consistently discharging this duty'. So defined, it stands, as he has said elsewhere, not only as an antithesis to understanding (*cognitio*), but also in direct contrast to 'untrustworthiness' (Dunn 1985: 41). For Genovesi and for Doria, trusting someone involved the belief that the object of trust would perform just such a duty.

Trust – *fides* – was also, for anyone reared (as all eighteenth-century Italian theorists were) on Machiavelli, the necessary condition of all political association. Trust, wrote Doria in his *Della vita civile* of 1710, 'is the sole sustenance of states and leads to their stable maintenance' (1852: 352).[3] *Fede* here is a purely social and a visibly public virtue. It is, in Genovesi's telling phrase, *fede pubblica*. It is this, he says, and this alone, which not only sustains the state but also constitutes its credibility with respect to other states. But *fede pubblica* has to be distinguished from what he calls *fede privata*, which is a purely familial association, where private rather than public interests are involved since the family, the kin group, is merely an extension of the individual. Genovesi is clear,

[3] For an account of the theoretical underpinning of Doria's work, which in the psychology and metaphysics it employs is markedly different from that of Genovesi and Filangieri, see Nuzzo (1984).

however, that *fede privata* is a necessary condition of *fede pubblica*, since trust like charity begins at home. When, as happened in the republics of Rome and Athens, 'first private trust [grows] weak and then the public' (Genovesi 1803: 94), societies degenerate into one or another form of tyranny.[4] But he is equally certain that a society where *only* private trust was available would – since it would consist solely of small self-interested groups united by kin – be no society, no *societas*, at all. This distinction between public and private, between conditions within the kin group and without, was, as we shall see later, central to the accounts provided by Doria, Genovesi, and Filangieri of the necessary conditions for social stability and economic growth.

Trust – *fede pubblica* – depends, of course, upon security of expectation. But a trusting society must also be one in which men are prepared to surrender their instinctive habits of distrust, where they are prepared to 'have faith' in their neighbour's word. And such a society must itself be capable of generating high levels of expectation in its citizens (Genovesi 1803: 80).[5] Cooperation, as Genovesi conceived it, works through conscience and cultural – or in some cases divine – sanction. Deviation from what is regarded as an acceptable mode of conduct is met with expulsion from the community. A merchant whom no one trusts will not be able to remain in business for very long. Economic transactions are clearly more heavily dependent on the agencies of trust than any other, and in every European language they share a common vocabulary: 'commerce', 'credit', 'honour', and 'trust' itself are all terms which have specific economic applications. Confidence, as Filangieri pointed out, 'is the soul of commerce', and the credit it alone can generate must be regarded as a 'second species of money'. Any individual who betrays his trust by, for instance, issuing false bonds is likely to find himself excommunicate. Fraud, forgery, and bankruptcy, claimed Filangieri, constituted the severest threats to the social and economic order (1804: 290–1).

For both Genovesi and Doria it was axiomatic that the only kind of society capable of generating and maintaining the high levels of expectation which would render its people prosperous and happy was the virtuous republic, the Ciceronian *bene ordinate respublica* where all laws were directed towards the public good and the sovereign ruled in the interest of his people (Genovesi 1803: 69–71; Doria 1852: 353–4). Citizenship, as Weber observed of the ancient Greek *polis* and the medieval city, cancelled out the power of the kinship group (1925: I, 201–4). Brutus's *virtù*, claimed Genovesi, lay not in self-sacrifice but in

---

4 This also of course distinguishes this use of *fede* from simple faith.

5 Education, Genovesi claimed, was the only effective way to enhance the citizens' awareness of, and corresponding willingness to invest in, the community.

preferring the interests of the community to those of even his most immediate family.

As long as *fede pubblica* always dominated *fede privata* the polity itself might take the form of either a monarchy or a republic. Genovesi, like Rousseau, however, believed that true republics were more likely to succeed, for in a republic public instruction is 'more severe'; there is less luxury – there are fewer purely private goods – and as a result it is more 'creditable' ('si puo avere piu credito in una repubblica che in una monarchia') and 'trust [*fede pubblica*] is more rigorously upheld' (1803: 57-8). Doria, on the other hand, shared the view of the Milanese merchant who, offering sage northern advice to disordered southerners, wrote to a Neapolitan friend in November 1647 that Naples had been too long used to monarchical rule to be able to make a republican government work. What the Neapolitans required was not what the Dutch and the Swiss had achieved, for such peoples are 'hard, slow, cold and long-suffering'; but the elective monarchy which the Catalans briefly, and the Portuguese more lastingly, had acquired.[6] For Doria, too, the enlightened and elective monarchy provided the best guarantee of the well-ordered state. Such a virtuous and well-ordered society had existed in Naples, or so it was popularly believed, under the Aragonese kings, but this happy state of affairs had been systematically undermined by the Habsburgs. The point was to understand how.

III

Shortly after the establishment of the Austrian government, Doria composed a treatise entitled *Massime del governo spagnolo a Napoli* in which he attempted to explain just how the Spanish Habsburgs had governed Naples and reduced a once flourishing state to economic ruin. What his treatise provides is, in fact, a carefully considered list of the necessary macro- and micro-conditions for dissolving trust within a society while still preserving its condition *as* a society. He begins with the commonplace observation that all princes who live far from their states have to employ 'some malicious art' if they are to preserve them (Doria 1973: 21-2). As the Spaniards had discovered to their cost in the Netherlands, simple coercion is not enough, if only because at such distances the resources of the state are not up to providing the policing required. The Spanish strategy in Naples was founded on two classical maxims: *divide et impera* and *depauperandum esse regionem*. The Spanish kings had preferred weak dependencies to strong ones, which is

---

6 'Lettera di un Milanese a un Napolitano amico suo' (Milan, 29 November 1647), in Conti (1984: 45-8).

why, Doria explained, they had deprived their subjects of 'virtue and wealth and introduced instead ignorance, villainy, disunion and unhappiness' (1953: 175). For the Castilian crown, concerned only with securing from its subjects sufficient revenue to fight its foreign wars, there existed a trade-off between *relative* poverty and political compliance. As long as sufficient numbers of the nobility were able, with Castilian assistance, to maintain a properly 'noble' life-style, they could be relied upon to provide – or to compel their subjects to provide – the fiscal support the crown demanded. Excessive wealth, particularly when concentrated in the hands of the *populo civile*, might, as it had done on occasion in Milan, lead to the creation of a powerful political group eager to rise out of the tax-paying class. But, of course, as at least one viceroy recognized, the custom of beggaring the better part of the economy in such relatively short-term interests produced a downward spiral from which ultimately it might prove impossible to recover. For as Guilio Genoino (a man who was to play a major role in the revolt of 1647) pointed out in 1620, since the nobles could not escape the general decline of the economy they became increasingly unable 'to maintain themselves with the necessary decorum, but feeling compelled to do so they [were] obliged to oppress their vassals, which greatly [damaged] the public good'.[7]

Trust, in Doria's view, was a necessary condition of both wealth and virtue. In the interest, then, of reducing the wealth of the citizens of Naples to a politically and fiscally acceptable minimum, and their political virtue to zero, the crown had set out to destroy the pre-existent bonds of trust within the society. At one level this had been achieved by means which the French kings too had found useful in coping with their nobility. They had created large numbers of new nobles whose loyalty flowed, not between the members of the community, but directly from the individual to the king, and in whom the king could have complete 'trust'. The French monarch, or his prime minister, trusted the service nobility he had created, and they him. Similarly, the Castilian crown had created in Naples an inordinately large number of 'new nobles' whose presence, and whose pretensions, helped to generate hostility and unrest among the older aristocracy (Doria 1973: 30–2). The crown had then set out to replace the society's normative values (*ordini e costumi*) – precisely, of course, those values on which *la fede pubblica* depended – by new Hispanic ones. The policy of 'hispanization' which the Spaniards adopted in all their dependencies, spearheaded by such institutions as the Inquisition – which had nearly resulted in the Spaniards being driven out of the kingdom in 1585 – consisted largely in this, for as Doria pointed out, once a 'mutation of customs' had been successfully effected the laws

---

[7] *Relatione del stato di Napoli*, quoted in Villari (1980: 166).

which guaranteed the continuation of the *respublica* would collapse of their own accord (1973: 22). Just how Doria thought this had been done I shall come to shortly.

What in effect this translation of cultural values achieved was the replacement of a virtuous society based upon the mutual trust of all its members by an aristocratic tyranny based on suspicion and self-regard, 'arrogance and self-love'. In other terms, it replaced a society based on trust by one based on another, equally slippery concept: honour.

Historically there are two distinct senses in which the term 'honour' may be understood. In the sense Doria used it when describing what he, and indeed most European contemporaries, regarded as the single defining characteristic of Spanish culture, it implied the existence of a self-love vested in, and consequently at risk through, the persons and objects –and most particularly the persons viewed *as* objects, that is, the women –by which a man (for a woman's honour is merely a repository for the man's) is surrounded. If, as I was once told, a gentleman is he who uses a butter-knife when dining alone, a true man of honour is one who, like so many of the protagonists – they cannot be called heroes – of the Spanish theatre of the seventeenth century, is content to have the wife who has dishonoured him murdered in private by a hired assassin. His dishonour is a private affair, a family matter, and as such cannot find redress in law. As Charles Duclos observed in 1750, the man of honour 'seems to be his own legislator' (1820: I, 56).[8] But there is also that other kind of honour which derives from Aristotle's account in the *Nichomachean Ethics* of τιμή (book 1, chapter V, 5). This is public, in that it requires a witness, and thus implies a relationship between two or more parties and with persons outside the kin group. This understanding of honour –the sense in which the term is used in such phrases as 'honouring one's bond' – is, of course, a crucial component of trust. As Genovesi said, *onore e virtù* (honour and virtue), in the absence of any effective coercive mechanism, can be the only guarantors of a debtor's reliability. But, as we shall see, no virtue is possible in a society of honour understood in the first sense. Spanish, which has the richest lexicon of terms for relations of honour of any European language, uses the term *honra* to describe honour in the first sense, *honor* to describe it in the second.

The virtuous republic is, of course, a society grounded on a set of shared and stable values. These values – trust in and concern for one's fellow citizens, the triumph of public over private good – depend crucially upon the amount of information each party has. In order, then, to destroy the trusting society, the Spaniards had systematically reduced

---

[8] Duclos also notes that 'today' the term has come to mean nothing more than self-respect (pp. 61–3), a piece of wishful thinking. See Julian Pitt-Rivers (1977: 9), who has some interesting reflections on the relationship between honour and legality.

the amount of information available to the citizenry, which is why Genovesi insisted that the new enlightened administrations should hold a census after the Roman model and make its findings public (1803: 109) The viceregal administration, 'in keeping with the best rules of reason of state' (something obnoxious to the virtuous republic, which can have no reason independent of the good of its members), made a secret out of the business of government so that it should be 'reserved to them alone'. It obliged the University to go on teaching Aristotelian logic 'because it never explained anything'. And in religion it decreed 'that everyone should follow the priest in the ritual without examining it' (Doria 1973: 33–4).

This last observation brings us back to the definition of *fede pubblica*. For Doria and for Genovesi, who had read Rousseau on the subject, religion should be, as far as was possible without falling into heresy, a civil affair – what Genovesi, so as to avoid the Machiavellian and atheistical implications of the phrase 'civil religion', called a 'rational religion' (1803: 80); since it is religion, *fides* as 'faith', which provides the ultimate sanction against preferring private interests over public ones. On this point both Doria who was, as far as I know, a good Catholic and Genovesi, who had once hoped to hold a chair in theology, would have been in broad agreement with Locke's claim that once you remove God from the picture, 'neither faith [*fides*], nor agreement, nor oaths, the bonds [*vincula*] of human society, can be stable and sacred' (quoted in Dunn 1985: 43). But although faith in the certainty of divine sanction may indeed constitute the ultimate guarantee for trust, in Genovesi's account of the 'rational religion' there is more than a mere suggestion that faith may be subsumed under trust and, and within the sphere of interpersonal relations, the public good come to replace a private God. What is clear is that whatever religion the society embraces – even if it consists simply in believing in the virtues of that society – it must be comprehensible to all those who participate in it; and it must be available for participation. Lack of information destroys trust. So too, of course, does mystification.

The elaborate religious ceremonies, the obsessive veneration for San Gennaro and the Virgin of the Carmine, which played such a prominent, and in Doria's view lamentable, role in the revolt of 1647 were hardly 'rational' and certainly had not made religion civil. Instead they made civil society religious and, as a consequence, provided the Spaniards with yet another set of devices for distracting the people from the correct understanding of their civic responsibilities.

The Spaniards also sought to undermine the harmonious relationship which had previously existed between the various orders in the kingdom and which was, of course, a necessary condition of the well-*ordered* republic. Thus the barony were given greater powers over their peasantry and encouraged to indulge in absurd and worthless pursuits, until finally, complained Doria, 'there remained no other virtue (if they can be called virtues) than scrupulousness in duelling and skill in arms and horseman-ship' (1973: 32–3). The middle order, the *populo civile*, were fobbed off with university doctorates, and the *populo minuto* kept busy with public festivals. These things were emptied of all political significance and each order thus became enslaved to the one above, the whole society being easily subjected to the tyranny of the Spanish crown. The status of nobility, which should have entailed an obligation to the community, conferred only ignorance and *superbia*; the doctorate of law, which should have obliged its holder to maintain justice, became merely a licence for endless and costly litigation; the public festivals, which should (like the Roman games) have encouraged a love of valour and of *patria* in the plebeians, became mere diversion and occasions for licentiousness. As a consequence, 'the superior looked upon his inferior with anger, as one who thought himself to have been cheated of the veneration he believed to be his due, the inferior looked upon his superior as one who only thought himself superior, and in this way there was neither union nor love between the various orders' (Doria 1973: 33–4). Each man became concerned, not with the welfare of his fellow citizens, but only with his own private ends or with those of his immediate kin.

As a means to undermining both the communication, *conversare*, and that other-regarding ethic which are the substance of civic life, the Spaniards also destroyed the traditional and, if we are to believe Doria, relatively free and easy relationship between the sexes which had previously existed in Naples. This relationship, in his view – and he wrote a treatise to demonstrate that women were the equal, or at least the near equal, of men – was one of the most significant in any society, since for Doria sexual relations were in the private domain what civil relations were in the public: opportunities for trust and 'conversation', which can easily collapse into honour and secrecy (1973: 48).[9]

Formerly, the Neapolitans had enjoyed free and respectful relation-ships with women. Their wives were their friends, the impartial love of friendship being the only true foundation for personal relationships within the virtuous society. The Spanish, however, set their women apart, treating them with a reverence which verged on idolatry but which also excluded respect. Like the Roman attitude towards the vestal virgins, this had the effect of destroying their gaiety, 'the spirit and the soul of their conversation', and of depriving them of all human contact outside the limits of the family, so that 'to foreigners a conversation with

[9] On the additional, and crucial, relationship between tyranny and the servitude of women, see Tomaselli (1985: 113–14).

a woman seems more like worship at a shrine than a discussion' (Doria 1973: 48–53). The Spanish treatment of women made them into objects bound not to the code of love – which is a civil virtue – but merely to the code of honour. By encouraging in the males a corresponding 'excess of gallantry' it turned their attention away from civil life into purely private concerns (Doria 1973: 56). Occupied thus, with paying grotesque compliments to women, duelling, and fighting their neighbours over imagined slights to their honour, the aristocracy of Naples, the political nation, had abandoned its role as the promoter of public welfare.

Thus, concluded Doria, by compelling men to change their customs, by making it easy for them to abandon the hard but virtuous ways of their ancestors, for the easy, unthinking, and ultimately destructive ways of the Spaniards, a society based on trust had been replaced by one based on honour, a rich and just community by an impoverished and unjust one. For the people nothing existed beyond games and ritualized devotion, for the *populo civile* nothing beyond litigation and private gain, while for the nobility there was only the interminable and profitless struggle for status.

In Doria's account the Spaniards had done to the Neapolitans exactly, and by the same means, what (according to Herodotus) Croesus had advised Cyrus to do to the Lydians: 'Make them wear tunics under their cloaks and high boots, and tell them to teach their sons to play the zither and the harp, and to start shopkeeping. If you do that, my lord, you will soon see them turn into women instead of men, and there will not be any more danger of their rebelling against you.' As Schelling observes with reference to this passage, such cultural strategies, although aimed at habits and motivations, 'at the same time deny the development of expectations and the confidence' which is the basis of trust in one's neighbour and, in the larger sense, trust in society itself (1984: 208).

The erosion of older values, the 'mutation of customs and orders' resulted, as the Spaniards had predicted, in the steady collapse of the legal system. For a society of honour is clearly not one which values or respects the impartial justice that is a necessary condition of trust.

In any well-ordered republic there must be equality before the law. Such a republic could only exist, Doria informed the president of the Magistrature of Commerce in 1740, when the city was once again living 'in the liberty of its constitution and the trust which is sustained by a rigorous and strong justice' (1953: 163). For no one will be prepared to trust another who enjoys a different legal status to himself. The positive laws of the community are also, Genovesi insisted, civil contracts, and contracts, of course, rely more heavily upon trust than they do upon the possibility – always precarious – of enforcing them. In the absence of trust, he pointed out, 'there can be no certainty in contracts and hence no force to the laws', and a society in that condition is effectively reduced 'to a state of semi-savagery' (1803: 113–16). The Spaniards had succeeded in destroying the purchase of the laws on the community by subverting the customs which sustained them; they had destroyed the *rule* of law by setting up separate courts both for the barony and for the priesthood and by allowing into the legal system entire categories of exemptions and exceptions so that no one could predict the outcome of a case or know which part of the law applied to him.

The escalation in the number of doctorates in civil law had debased the standing of the title and the social status of those who held it, while the large number of lawyers prepared to sell their services at a low cost had greatly increased the amount of litigation. This in turn, since there were insufficient controls over the grounds on which a case was entered, increased the degree of uncertainty that surrounded all early modern legal procedure and further eroded trust in the judicial apparatus of the state. Only when there were fewer lawyers and when the Dutch custom of obliging the loser to pay costs had been introduced, claimed Doria, would the courts regain some of the trust which had previously been confided in them (1953: 184–5).

IV

The degeneration of the necessary guarantors of the well-ordered community led inevitably to the collapse of the economy. Philip II's purpose, in Doria's view, had been to beggar the kingdom in order to secure its political compliance. 'For commerce', he wrote, 'is an art which unites men in civil society so that they give to each other mutual assistance . . . in such a way that neither the distance nor any other consideration can impede this mutual aid.' But trade can only flourish under two conditions, 'and these are liberty and security in contracts, and this can only occur when trust and justice rule' (Doria 1953: 162; see also 1973: 41–2). In order for these conditions to be met it was clearly necessary for the law to ensure that all trading practices – what is generally understood here by contracts – should be stable. All the Neapolitan political economists, from Antonio Serra in the early seventeenth century to Gaetano Filangieri in the late eighteenth, had criticized the laxity of the laws governing the issue of false bonds, counterfeiting (a crime of which even the viceroys were believed, correctly it seems, to have been guilty), the creation of monopolies, sudden changes in the rates of exchange and in rates of interest, and so on. Counterfeiting in particular was, Genovesi pointed out, punished with the utmost severity even among 'barbarous nations' such as the

Incas, since it threatened the social bonds which held together the entire community (1803: 102–9). In Naples, however, a man might be executed for theft, a crime whose consequences were hardly to be compared with the loss of life, but let off with a fine for an act which, in Doria's view, 'offends against public trust [*fede pubblica*] and thus against the entire republic' (1953: 180). As a result that republic had become, he claimed, 'like a merchant without trust since the slowness of the justice which is handed out to litigants breaks the trust which exists between persons' (1953: 264).

With the collapse of those conditions on which true commerce depends, trade became a question of mutual deception. Bonds and even money, since so much of it was false, were no longer freely accepted and the Neapolitans were reduced to the condition of the savages described by Genovesi who will only give with the right hand if they simultaneously receive with the left (1803: 70–1). As a consequence of massive degrees of mistrust loans were only made at exorbitant rates of interest, bankrupting all but the richest of merchants and leading to the widespread belief that a predominance of 'idle money' was the source of the kingdom's ills (see Villari 1980: 67–8; and Doria 1953: 170).

V

By destroying the Neapolitans' ability to trust each other, the Spanish crown had ruined the kingdom. The solution to this problem, offered in different forms to different rulers by both Doria and Genovesi, was, of course, to restore the well-ordered *respublica*, where the law was sovereign, where 'honour' – in any sense stronger than simple respect – would give way to public virtue, and *la fede privata* would be once again subordinate to *la fede pubblica*. Doria's and Genovesi's reflections on just what kind of society that might be, interesting though they are, do not concern me here. They inevitably fall far short of the 'non-contradictory and reasonably full description' which Dunn (in this volume) demands of any attempt to generate a structurally just society. But however inadequate as a prescription, as observations on the state of Naples in the eighteenth century, they may yet throw light on what might be regarded as some of the necessary – though by no means sufficient – conditions for social and economic growth in early modern Europe.

For Doria and Genovesi trust is the basis of the well-ordered republic. It is, in short, the motive for a man to behave towards members of the society at large in much the same way he behaves towards members of his own kin group; or, at least, it provides strong reasons why he should not – except in purely private concerns – privilege that group over any other.

The only community for Doria and Genovesi (and more widely for most Catholic political economists) in which trust was dominant, indeed the only society in which it could operate at all, was the virtuous republic exemplified by Rome and Athens and Aragonese Naples. Quentin Skinner has argued forcefully that the kind of humanistic ethics Doria and Genovesi were attempting to revive, which set this idea of the 'well-ordered republic' at the centre of all social relations, employed a similar conceptual vocabulary to Calvinism; that – to put it the other way round – the social ethos of Calvinism can be seen to constitute a special case of classical republicanism (Skinner 1974a; 1974b). If we accept this view then many of the problems historians have had with Weber's famous thesis on the association between Calvinism and the rise of capitalism disappear, since it might be maintained that it was not a specifically Calvinist or Puritan work ethic which encouraged economic take-off in the Protestant cities of the seventeenth century, or Christianity itself in the medieval cities of north and central Italy, but the secular ethic of classical republicanism.

But we still need to know just what it is about classical republicanism that makes it so peculiarly suited to capitalism or, to use the contemporary term, to the commercial society. Doria and Genovesi, in their analyses of the workings of trust, claimed (as we have seen) that the crucial fact about the virtuous and well-ordered republic – what indeed made it both virtuous and well ordered – was that by insisting on public good over private interest it enabled men from different kin groups, and hence from different societies, to trust each other; that in Weberian terms it allowed the 'out-groups' to be treated in ways similar to the 'in-groups'; and that only under such conditions was it possible to operate a properly 'commercial society'. This would seem to reinforce an aspect of Weber's work which, although it is never made much of in *The Protestant Ethic and the Spirit of Capitalism*, plays a major role in his analysis of China, namely the claim that if China had never experienced the economic growth of the West this in the end came down to the fact that in China 'the fetters of the kinship group were never shattered' and that it had been, as he said elsewhere, precisely 'the great achievement of the ethical religions, above all the ethical and asceticist sects of Protestantism . . . to shatter the fetters of the kin' (Weber 1951: 237). If we substitute 'virtuous republic' for 'ethical religions' we have a claim which looks very much like that of Doria and Genovesi. For only in the society where trust as *public* (in contrast to private) faith is held to be central, indeed the dominant social principle, will the good of the family be made subordinate to the good of society at large, and only in that kind of society will economic take-off be possible. I am not, of course, suggesting that it is *only* within the well-ordered republic, or some functional modern analogue, that capital-dependent economic prosperity is possible. The alternatives of Japan and South Korea, as described in this volume by Geoffrey Hawthorn (to give only two examples), evidently preclude any such conclusion. But it may still be the case that the problem Doria and Genovesi identified in the eighteenth century might provide some insight into why certain areas of southern Europe have singularly failed to achieve the economic take-off experienced by the north. It might, that is, lie somewhere very close to the centre of what Diego Gambetta, in the foreword to this volume, describes as 'the persistent and apparently insoluble political and economic problem Italy has faced over the century since it became a politically united nation: the underdevelopment of most of her southern regions.'

REFERENCES

Bellamy, R. 1987: 'Da metafisico a mercatante': Antonio Genovesi and the development of a new language of commerce in eighteenth-century Naples. In A. Pagden (ed.), *The Languages of Political Theory in Early-Modern Europe*, Cambridge: Cambridge University Press, 277–99.

Conti, V. 1984: *La rivoluzione repubblicana a Napoli e le strutture rappresentative (1647–1648)*. Florence: Centro Editoriale Toscano.

Doria, P. M. 1852: *Della vita civile*. Turin.

Doria, P. M. 1953: *Del commercio del regno di Napoli*. In E. Vidal, *Il pensiero civile di Paolo Mattia Doria negli scritti inediti*, Milan: Istituto di filosofia del diritto dell' università di Roma.

Doria, P. M. 1973: *Massime del governo spagnolo a Napoli*, ed. V. Conti. Naples: Guida Editori.

Duclos, C. 1820: *Considérations sur les mœurs de ce siècle*. In *Œuvres complètes*, vol. I, Paris.

Dunn, J. 1985: *Rethinking Modern Political Theory*. Cambridge: Cambridge University Press.

Filangieri, G. 1804: *Delle leggi politiche ed economiche*. In P. Custodi (ed.), *Scrittori classici italiani di economia politica*, parte moderna, vol. xxxii, Milan.

Galasso, G. 1982: *Napoli spagnola dopo Masaniello*, 2 vols. Florence: Sansoni Editori.

Genovesi, A. 1803: *Lezioni di economia civile*. In P. Custodi (ed.), *Scrittori classici italiani di economia politica*, parte moderna, vol. ix, Milan.

Nuzzo, E. 1984: *Verso la 'Vita Civile'*. Naples: Guida Editori.

Pitt-Rivers, J. 1977: The anthropology of honour. In *The Fate of Shechem or the Politics of Sex*, Cambridge: Cambridge University Press.

Schelling, T. C. 1984: Strategic analysis and social problems. In *Choice and Consequence*, Cambridge, Mass.: Harvard University Press.

Skinner, Q. 1974a: The principles and practice of opposition: the case of Bolingbroke versus Walpole. In N. McKendrick (ed.), *Historical Perspectives: studies in English thought and society in honour of J. H. Plumb*, London: Europa.

Skinner, Q. 1974b: Some problems in the analysis of political thought and action. *Political Theory* 2, 277–303.

Tomaselli, S. 1985: The Enlightenment debate on women. *History Workshop* 20, 101–24.

Villari, R. 1980: *La rivolta antispagnola a Napoli. Le origini 1585–1647*. Rome-Bari: Laterza.

Weber, M. 1925: *Wirtschaft und Gesellschaft*, 2 vols. Tubingen: Grundriss der Sozialökonomik. Abt. 3.

Weber, M. 1951: *The Religion of China: Confucianism and Taoism*. Glencoe: Free Press.

9

Trust, Cohesion, and the Social Order

Ernest Gellner

A touch of impatience can be discerned amongst realistically oriented colleagues in this series of essays: formal philosophers and economists have injected a certain *a priori* and deductive element into the discussion of trust. The description of the manner in which trust and hence economic vitality were deliberately destroyed by Neapolitan political authority is a welcome corrective (Pagden, this volume). I hope to continue in the same direction, by crossing the Mediterranean and attempting a similarly realistic analysis of a concrete society. I shall look at the way in which trust functions or fails to function in traditional Muslim society. I shall be leaning very heavily, as usual, on Ibn Khaldun (1958).

One additional, general remark must be made. The discussion in this volume fluctuates between the notion of trust as something specific within a society, one thing among others, and another, broader version of it, which makes it coextensive with the very existence of a social order. How is it possible that people actually cooperate over time when it might pay them not to do so? Trust as coextensive with *any* kind of social order is one thing, and trust as something within society, of which sometimes there is more and sometimes there is less, is another. This ambiguity may be inherent and illuminating; perhaps one way of making progress on the wider topic of the establishment of social order as such, and the diversity of social orders, is to distinguish various kinds of trust.

One other observation is addressed to political philosophers in particular: when I use expressions like Thomas Hobbes or John Locke or Plato, I don't actually mean Thomas Hobbes, John Locke, and Plato. What I mean is 'Thomas Hobbes', which is shorthand for a model constructed for purposes of exposition. The reason for this caveat is that owing to the way the modern university is organized, the history of political ideas is over-studied, and the people who study it, like the rest of us, have to practise product differentiation: otherwise their careers may suffer. Consequently there is a terrible incentive for them to write books to show that Hobbes was really liberal, and John Stuart Mill really an authoritarian, and so on. This may be fairly easy to do, but because I do not want to do it, I refrain from becoming committed to the exposition of real historic characters: I simply use their names as shorthand. And even if you suspect that privately I believe that what I refer to as 'Thomas Hobbes' is what Thomas Hobbes actually did mean, you can't actually prove it. But debate at that level takes time, and is liable to be tedious.

I

There is one point at which the conventional Hobbesian and the Ibn Khaldunian visions of the basis of social order are diametrically opposed. On the whole, the advantage lies with Ibn Khaldun.

The Hobbesian problem arises from the assumption that anarchy, absence of enforcement, leads to distrust and social disintegration. We are all familiar with the deductive model which sustains and re-enforces that argument, but there is a certain amount of interesting empirical evidence which points the other way. The paradox is: it is precisely anarchy which engenders trust or, if you want to use another name, which engenders social cohesion. It is effective government which destroys trust. This is a basic fact about the human condition, or at any rate about a certain range of real human conditions. It is the basic premise of Ibn Khaldun's sociology, which happens to be the greatest and most accurate analysis of traditional Muslim society.

The argument is that anarchy engenders trust and government destroys it; or, put in a more conventional way, that anarchy engenders cohesion. In this case, we have both an argument *and* an empirical illustration. The claim that anarchy engenders cohesion is well sustained empirically, but it can also be sustained by theoretical considerations. There is a powerful model which lends support to this contention. The model is constructed with the help of a number of factors actually corresponding to the realities prevailing in an important part of the world.

To begin with, assume the absence of any strong central authority. Secondly, add the ecological conditions which prevail in the arid zone, and which impel large and significant proportions of its inhabitants towards pastoralism. Thirdly, acknowledge the diffusion of a certain level of expectation concerning what life is meant to be like. The importance of this will emerge in due course. One might even reduce these factors to two, in so far as weak government can itself be seen as a corollary of pastoralism. Shepherds are hard to govern, because their wealth is on the hoof and they can easily escape authority. Their mobility makes it possible to avoid taxation, to raid, and to elude oppression.

If you take these three points and work out the implications, the result is that those living on such terms cannot manage without cohesion. The argument runs: pastoralism implies that the major part of wealth is on the hoof. This means that it is easy to move it, but it also makes it easy to perform acts of robbery. Pastoral work is not labour intensive. Looking after 400 sheep is not very much harder than looking after 200 sheep. But pastoralism *is* defence intensive. What the shepherd does is protect the flock from jackals, hyenas, wolves, and above all from other shepherds. And the prospects of economic growth are very remarkable: all a shepherd needs to do in order to double his wealth is ambush another shepherd.

This is quite different from the relationship between agricultural sedentary producers, who can steal the harvest but cannot easily steal the fields. If they wish to enslave the people they defeat, they land themselves with grave problems of labour management. So the appeal of aggression for agricultural producers is much less, unless they are effectively centralized and can monopolize the means of coercion, and possess the machinery for controlling the subjugated population. But for a shepherd, the temptation to rob is very strong, immediate and unconditional, *and there is only one effective means of protecting oneself against this kind of aggression.*

This method is to gang up in a group, which in effect hangs up a notice saying: anyone who commits an act of aggression against any one of us must expect retaliation from us all, and not only will the aggressor himself be likely to suffer retaliation, but his entire group and all its members will be equally liable. And this notice is in effect posted by the very culture which pervades pastoral societies. It constitutes the code of honour which is familiar to all. So the gangs themselves do not need literally to put an announcement in the press or even on their tent. The culture, or specifically the obligation of feud which is inherent in it, does it for them.

To recapitulate: because these groups are mobile and live in difficult terrain, they are very difficult to tax. Consequently there is no government, there being no resources to sustain it. Because there is no government, the groups have to look after themselves: hence they are strong, and government is weak or absent. The argument is a kind of circle, but it reflects a self-perpetuating social reality. Once this kind of system is established, it manifests itself as the highly characteristic arid zone pattern of strong, self-policing, self-defending, politically participating groups, generally known as tribes. They defend themselves by the threat of indiscriminate retaliation against the group of any aggressor. Hence they also police themselves and their own members, for they do not wish to provoke retaliation. Inside each such group, order is maintained by a similar mechanism: the group itself divides into sub-groups which each exercise restraint over the others.

This is a teleological or 'functional' argument, of course, open to the objection that the *need* for the cohesion of social groups will not automatically engender that cohesion. In the absence of a designer and creator, the favourite logical substitutes are our old friends, natural selection and rational foresight. Presumably each of them operates, though no one really knows in what proportion. All one does know is that a system corresponding to this model – a system of mutually supportive or, in the language of the present discussion, of mutually *trusting* 'kinsmen' – is conspicuously present, or was traditionally present. The 'kinsmen' need not literally be such, of course, but they do tend to be cohesive, which is a shorthand way of saying that, on the whole, they trust each other.

The argument runs thus: a single shepherd can protect himself against ambush by another shepherd only by ganging up with (say) 20 similar shepherds, and hanging out the invisible but unmistakable sign threatening retaliation against any group whose members attack any one member of the first group. Thereby the other group is forced to police and restrain its own members. This argument *applies at all levels of size*. It can be repeated at the level of the unit itself: any single such herding camp of 20 members is extremely vulnerable to any coalition of others, and the only way it can protect itself is by *also* becoming part of a coalition. The coalition itself may have to be part of a meta-coalition, and so on. The result of all this is the very characteristic 'nesting' of similar units. The similarity is vertical as well as lateral: larger units resemble their own subgroup, just as groups resemble their 'peers' on the same level of size.

These units display a number of features: above all, they have a very high military participation ratio (see Andreski 1954). Basically, all adults take part in violence. They also have a high political participation ratio. All heads of households take part in assemblies. The same is true of culture. As a Kazakh scholar writing in Russian once put it, every member of the tribe is simultaneously senator, judge, juryman, minstrel, and poet of his society (see Tolybekov 1959). Both culture and political participation are evenly diffused.

This of course makes these societies very attractive objects of romanticization by vicarious populists from other societies. But there are other, and seemingly paradoxical, cultural features that should not be overlooked. One of them is this: although they are cohesive, they are also very treacherous. Treason is built into the working of such a society and its culture and, if carried out properly and in due form, no stigma attaches to it. This kind of society could not possibly function without treason. Treason within it performs the same role that price changes perform in a market society. It helps to maintain equilibrium through realignment. Just as a rise or fall in price ideally redirects resources to the point at which they are optimally deployed, so a realignment – treason, if you will – restores balance to the segmentary tribal world. An outnumbered clan C1, unable to hold its own within tribe T1, will leave T1 and join T2. Alternatively, members of T1, if they do not wish to see themselves weakened by such a loss, will arrange an internal adjustment in numbers to ensure that C1 henceforth is on reasonably equal terms with C2 or C3.

The balancing of units requires a certain equality of size. But the accidents of birth and health and so on ensure that the groups do not in fact maintain such a neat balance of reasonably equal size. Adjustments have to be made, and a rough equilibrium maintained. The adjustments *can* of course occur through dramatic forms of betrayal, but the interesting thing is that treason can also be heavily institutionalized and ritualized. An individual or group wishing to attach itself to a new and larger grouping does so by means of a ritual. This imposes a shame compulsion on the receiving group, which cannot honourably refuse the request.

What the system does require is that people's membership of groups be very clearly defined and visible *at any given time*. The feud, that is to say genetic revenge against a whole category of people, can only work if you know who falls within a given group and who does not. In Berber customary law, there is a rule that if homicide takes place, the *ten* closest agnates are immediately at risk, because they are equally 'culpable', even though they had nothing to do with the initial act and provocation. Supposing a cousin of mine commits a murder, and I truthfully proclaim that I am eleventh in order of proximity (the eleventh claimant to his inheritance, in other words), would this protect me? This question of mine was considered extremely funny. The actual number is not to be taken literally; there is no safety in arithmetic. But the membership of the group has to be clear, and indeed it *is* clear.

None the less, you *can* change your membership. There is nothing dishonourable about changing your group membership, which of course means changing your obligation to feud, and the risk of being a victim of feud, and the participation in giving or receiving blood money. It is done simply by making a public sacrifice – and it has to be public, that being the whole point of it – to another group, which thereafter is actually obliged to accept you. The same act takes you *out* of your previous group. Such reallocation, as long as it is clear and public, is perfectly honourable.

Similarly, the feuds between these kinds of groups do not always lead to actual violence. They can be settled by collective oath. And there it is perfectly honourable, in fact it is held to be pious, to let down your side if you are not convinced of the rightness of its cause. What you are *said* to be doing is showing that your fear of the supernatural is greater than your loyalty to the clan. In practice, what you are probably doing is assessing that, in this case, it is better to let your side down, because victory at the oath might provoke too strong a coalition against it. Better pay blood money than involve ourselves in a conflict which may end badly. But, very significantly, such caution can be expressed as piety, so that in a sense morality militates against unconditioned cohesion. By reallocating yourself, by refusing to testify with your segment, you can risk splitting the group and so bring about realignment. The equilibrium-restoring mechanism works, but the calculation can be camouflaged as piety and reverence.

All this is coherent with certain well-known features of segmentary society. The great cult of hospitality, combined with a tendency to attack people, simply reflects a situation in which a stranger must be made into either an ally or an enemy. Either entertain a stranger or attack him (or perhaps both). The intermediate attitude of indifferent neutrality is not present in the logic of the situation. The result is a series of groups which are both cohesive and fragile, which perpetuate themselves by means of loyalty, and adjust to new realities by treason, whether formalized, pious, or sudden.

II

So far, I have been sketching features of the society which follow from its internal organization; they would apply to any tribal or segmentary society, irrespective of whether it is locked into a wider cultural unit, endowed with a literate civilization. So far, there is nothing specifically Muslim.

The other half of Ibn Khaldun's sociology of trust or cohesion, and of their absence, is that urban life is incompatible with trust and cohesion. Urban lineages and groups exist in name only, but Ibn Khaldun considers them to constitute a kind of sociological fraud. Urban populations may invoke a common ancestor, and say that they are of 'the house of such and such', but this is fraudulent because they are not in fact cohesive. They do not act as real corporate groups; they will not fight and feud together, and they will not defend themselves jointly. The very fact that they are urban means that they accept governmental authority, so that the vicious or beneficial circle (whichever way you look at it), which otherwise engenders cohesion and indeed also intermittent treason, does not operate amongst *them*. They are not allowed, by effective government, to act as corporate and violent bodies. They are atomized by their economic specialisms and political dependence. They have no effective groups they could betray.

Why need there be any cities, with their atomized and uncohesive, trustless populations? It is not entirely clear whether this is inherent in ecology or in culture. The standard of living to which the populations in the arid zone have long become accustomed, in the course of the last three millennia perhaps, is such that it assumes artisan production and trade. Unlike, say, East African nomads, the pastoral and rural populations of the arid zone are habituated to a certain level of equipment, from saddles and stirrups and tent equipment to decorations and carpets. But cultural equipment also counts; they also recognize, revere, and internalize a religion which involves literacy. Their entire military, productive, and cultural machinery presupposes large clusterings of artisans, plus some scribes, and the complementation of ecological diversity by trade. In brief, it presupposes *cities*.

The city is comprised of specialists. A specialist has no cousins; or rather, he does not have politically *effective* cousins. Cousin specialists stick to their lasts and do not easily combine in these self-defending, self-administering rural groups. At most, they occasionally meld into rather ephemeral urban *frondes*. They need peace to pursue their trade, and they accept oppression as the price of peace. A significant aspect of tribal culture, on the other hand, is that it despises the specialist, even (or especially) when it needs him – and even, interestingly enough, when he is held to be morally elevated. Tribesmen overtly and unambiguously despise the artisans, butchers, blacksmiths, and so on, who live amongst them, but they are also somewhat ambivalent about the religious arbitration specialists who in a sense are above them, and whom they nominally revere, not without irony.

There is an Algerian saying there is always a snake in a *zawiya*. The tribesmen look up to the holy men but they also laugh at them. Specialists *as such*, of any kind, are morally suspect. I was told in the central High Atlas that any clan which acquires the reputation of special wisdom is *therefore* deprived of the vote in tribal elections. Excellence of any kind is a form of specialization and that precludes full citizenship. The unspecialized human being constitutes the moral norm. It is he who can lose himself in a solidary unit, and gladly accept collective responsibility. By contrast, the specialists of the towns, for whom specialization is of the essence, are politically castrated and incapable of cohesion, and hence of self-government. Consequently they are also incapable of governing others.

The corollaries of this situation are worked out by Ibn Khaldun in a rather teleological but nevertheless perfectly accurate model. Given that the society as a whole needs a level of production and trade which presupposes urban centres, and given that urban centres (clusters of specialists) are quite incapable of social cohesion and hence of political and military effectiveness, what is to be done? What is done is that the tribes provide cities with rulers: the state is the gift of the tribe to the city. Economically, the tribe needs the city: politically, the city needs the tribe.

The city is made up of a market (artisans and traders), a mosque, and the citadel. The rulers in the citadel are the people who acquired the capacity or the tendency to trust each other, and hence to be cohesive, *by being ungoverned*. If you wish to govern, you must never have submitted to government yourself. Only the ungoverned condition of the savannah, desert, and mountain, engenders the kind of tribal group whose members trust each other and display cohesion.

This and this alone makes such groups capable both of government and self-government. Consequently, from time to time, some of them occupy the citadel. Once they are there, and this of course is the best known part of Ibn Khaldun's theory, they gradually lose that very cohesion they acquired when they were ungoverned, and which enabled them to rule. In his schematized version, this takes about three or four generations. They lose it in the process of governing and of benefiting from the privileges of government. After four generations or so, they are replaced by a new wave of as yet uncorrupted tribesmen, and so on for ever and ever. It is a system of rotating corporate elites, in which the personnel changes but the structure remains the same. The city provides the tribesmen with the technical and cultural equipment on which they have come to rely: the tribesmen, or rather some of them, provide the city with government and defence, whilst the rest of the tribes govern themselves, and also constitute the permanent threat which keeps the city subservient to its temporary and rotated rulers.

III

The features I have left out thus far are ideological ones. The striking thing about the arid zone during the past millennium and a half, something which was not true previously, is that the participants in the system, all or most of them, speak the same religious language. Nominally, one religion operates both among the atomized, trustless, cohesionless, *governed* urban specialists, and among the unspecialized, cohesive, participatory, self-administering groups of the countryside. The same religion is enthusiastically upheld by both elements in the system.

This was not always the case. Pastoral nomadism emerged, specialists tell us, about 1000 BC (see Shnirelman 1980). Judging from its early
documented manifestations, the Scythians had the kind of relationship
with the Greek trading cities on the Black Sea coast that pastoralists
generally have with towns: cultural inferiority, military superiority. But
the Scythians and the Greeks did not speak the same religion. Other
aspects of the model applied, but the community of moral idiom did not
(see Khazanov 1975; 1984). The achievement of Islam, in the millennium
and a half during which it has dominated the arid zone, is that the
characters in the drama have learnt to speak the same language, albeit
with very diverse accents, so that when a new dynasty arrives in the
citadel it already knows more or less how to comport itself, and others
know what to expect from it. This somewhat eases the situation. However,
the effective content of the diverse styles of this nominally single religion
is not quite identical.

One of the first persons to explore the contrast between anonymous,
doctrinal, scriptural, soteriological, unified world religion on the one
hand, and a traditional locally rooted religion which is primarily a
ratification of social segmentation on the other, was Fustel de Coulanges
(1956). But Fustel described the Mediterranean as having passed definitely
from one style to the other. The truly important thing about traditional
Islam is that within it the two styles coexist *simultaneously*, under a
single label. In the politically organized, self-administering countryside,
under the cloak of a nominal adherence to an exclusive unitarianism,
there is in fact a Durkheimian religion which works by providing social
punctuation in space and time. The sacred is incarnate, with a local
habitation and a name. It helps to define groups, define their status,
define their boundaries: it reinforces their cohesion.

In the towns, at least at the top, there is something which does more
closely approximate to the Islam of the learned theologians: an exclusive
unitarianism with a hidden deity, which proscribes mediation, and so
theoretically recognizes no clergy, and which preaches an ethic of rules
rather than of loyalty. It neither expresses the cohesion of groups, nor
provides an idiom of treachery. The difference in style is well reflected in
how you testify at court. The country folk testify in groups in collective
oath. Under proper Muslim law, you testify as an individual. The
collective oath of the tribesmen is really an expression of commitment to
the group, an expression of a willingness to bear responsibility with it. It
is not a testimony to matters of factual accuracy, which is the purpose of
the oath offered by the individual in an urban trial.

The way you marry also varies according to the nature of your social
group. If you belong to the ordinary, rural, participatory, cohesive units,
your bride price is very largely nominal and symbolic, and basically you

marry in the hallowed anthropological manner. You supply your own daughter as bride to the son of your fellow clansman, in the expectation that there will be a reciprocal payment in kind pretty soon, perhaps in the next generation. Very little money changes hands, but groups are reaffirmed and defined. One of the bonds to your group is that it not only gives you access to pasture, but also provides you with a bride for your son, and this expectation helps perpetuate the group. The preference for (in fact) classificatory parallel cousin marriages makes Muslim tribal groups endogamous. By contrast, in the urban setting, the bride price goes up. Marriage becomes a much more voluntaristic, though not an individual operation. It hinges on political and economic calculations, a forging of links in a society in which the groups are much more labile, if indeed they exist at all. The way in which religious and marital styles go with each other is well described in Vanessa Maher's (1974) book on this topic.

There is an unexplained mystery in this system. It is the moral ascendancy which the scripturalist, rule-oriented, unitarian ideology at the centre, and its scribes, have over the other half of society. Their style is recognized as morally superior, *even by those who do not practise it*. Concerning the rival claims of high and low religion, the characteristic attitude of the North African countryside was very much the same as that expressed by the pre-Islamic North African, Saint Augustine, in his famous prayer: O Lord, make me pure, but not yet.

The values of the high religions were widely recognized, but not practised. This is related to the role of high religion in state formation. The establishment of a state by cohesive, trust-endowed rural populations presupposes that they unite temporarily into a sufficiently powerful block. If, but only if, a sufficiently large number of them unite effectively, they can on occasion operate that famous rotation of the political wheel of fortune. Normally they neutralize each other of course, in endless petty feuds. And the same is true of their local incarnations of the sacred: their petty saints, mediators living on the frontiers of groups, cannot effect larger fusions, because they constitute a kind of second level of a segmentation. They are as fragmented as the tribesmen themselves. They too are engaged in rivalries with each other. The only way to beget the larger unit is in the name of something else: this higher principle is provided by 'purer' Islam.

In the course of the last few centuries, leaders have emerged in Arabia, the Sudan, Nigeria, and Algeria who united a sufficiently large proportion of tribal groups to enable them to revive the central state. But the reverence for purer Islam which makes this possible remains somewhat mysterious. It is fairly easy to document, from their own legends, that tribesmen, even when they do not practise it, nevertheless

recognize the moral ascendancy of High Islam. This becomes useful t
them, as I have explained, when they fuse a larger unit and theret
forge a state. Without High Islam they might have no idiom for thos
temporary crystallizations of a more-than-tribal unity. This late
recognition of the 'pure' version of the faith facilitates such crysta
lizations.

This is linked to the ascendancy, in the society as a whole, of th
scholar class. The scholar class is open: entry is by scholarly con
petence, not by ascription; it has no central secretariat, or even an
kind of conciliar movement; it lacks formal hierarchy, and has ver
little organizational machinery. Nor does it have any immediate po
itical power (it has no real control over the choice of governin
personnel), but is at best a sort of rubber stamp of the actual powe
situation. Yet its ethos pervades, and has enormous influence over
the moral climate of the entire society. One can theorize about how
once this becomes established, it is perpetuated: roughly speaking, an
group which dares defy the situation provides a marvellous presen
to its enemies. They can gang up against it in the name of the ortho
doxy. It is very hard to defy the central orthodoxy and its carrier
overtly.

On the Weberian theory, Protestantism in Europe made its adherent
loyal to the norms of their *calling*, irrespective of advantage. (They di
not think other-worldly advantage could be bought, and did not wish t
buy advantage in this world.) This made them *individually* an
unconditionally trustworthy and thus, according to the theory, the
made the modern world possible. In the traditional world, 'rational
economic accumulation was not rational at all: the state would depriv
you of what you had 'rationally' accumulated. But the puritans, on thi
theory, were irrationally rational. They accumulated *anyway*, to prov
their spiritual status to themselves, whether or not it was going to pay of
economically. And behold, for once it *did* pay off. Because there wer
enough of them, their mutual, spiritually motivated trustworthines
benefited them all collectively; and for once the state could not or woul
not despoliate them, or at least it did not do so everywhere. And where i
failed to do so, modern capitalism was born.

Islamic universalism has not engendered any such individual and
unconditional trustworthiness; or if it has, political conditions have no
allowed it to bear full fruit. It has, however, acted as a kind of fortifying
agent to the collective trustworthiness of clan cohesion. It thus
transmutes tribal *asabiyya* into an agency of state formation. But it doe
not seem capable of preventing that state from being patronage ridden,
and inhibiting the emergence of capitalism proper; nor does it stop it
atomized burghers from being politically supine.

IV

A number of interesting paradoxes manifest themselves when the Muslim system changes under the impact of modernity. In the traditional situation, rural political relationships are often symmetrical and participatory. There is a great deal of diffusion of power. Tribal leaders are just leaders; they are not really very distinct from their fellow members. Personal political power, when it emerges, is fragile and temporary. The social units are, in the words of a French scholar (Tillion 1966), republics of cousins; but at the same time, the spatial and temporal markers of the society are provided by inegalitarian patronage networks. Shrines and their saintly guardians mark out the boundaries of units by their own location and settlement, and orchestrate the rhythm of social time by the festivals over which they preside. The saints come in hierarchies, in organizations with great inequality of status, and with an ideology – theoretically though not in fact – of total submission and authority. Thus there are unsymmetrical, dyadic religious relationships, and symmetrical participatory political ones. Religion employs an idiom of unequal patronage; politics speaks a language of participatory brotherly or cousinly equality.

Modernity turns the system upside down. It completely changes the balance of power. The military, administrative, transport, and communications equipment available to the colonial and post-colonial state is such that, in most places, the participatory egalitarian tribal groups become weakened and eroded. They are no longer allowed to govern and defend themselves. There are one or two places where the movement has been in the opposite direction. North Yemen is one such case: the central state was probably stronger at the turn of the century than it is now. Lebanon is another: the communities are stronger, and the central state is not so much weaker as absent, having become simply the place where communities negotiate. But in general, the state is now relatively powerful and the rural groups have become debilitated, if indeed they exist at all.

Political relationships are currently a kind of shadow of the old loyalty of cousinly groups, whose idioms they continue to use. The security of men no longer lies in their cousins: the collective oath is abolished, the feud is no longer practicable. It is now easily suppressed by the gendarmerie. A person's safety no longer lies in the strength of his kin group, but rather in having a friend at the nearest district office, who in turn has a friend at the provincial capital, who has a friend at the national capital. So, a sort of dyadic unsymmetrical system of patronage relations takes over in the political sphere. At the same time, however, owing to the strengthening of the central and urbanized part of society, the need for dyadic mediational services grows weaker in the religious sphere. So the marabouts and dervishes, like the aristocracy of the French *ancien régime*, are now seen to have privileges, whilst they no longer perform essential services. They come to be castigated as pious or impious frauds. High Islam, which proscribes mediation, is now invoked more consistently. The most significant cultural event in the Muslim world of the past 100 years has been a very major Reformation, a shift from mediationist religious brokerage to a symmetrical relationship between the deity and believers in conformity with the old, but previously unpractised, high theology. Suddenly religion is egalitarian and symmetrical, centralized, with an exclusive single deity and without mediators. Believers become equals, while politics has become patronage ridden. In the past it had all been the other way round (see Eickelman 1976).

The consequence of this shift is that there are two features of the Muslim state which strike observers. They seem contradictory, but they are not. On the one hand there is the extreme addiction to patronage politics: the weak can survive thanks to protection by the strong, and everything depends on networks. There is no trust without a special relationship, and not too much even then. This is the shadow of the old style of cohesion, surviving in a modern context.

On the other hand, there is an intense moralism, an accentuation of the old unitarianism, which had always played a great part in society but is now far more effective. These two features, however, are essentially complementary. In the past, the high religion had also played a very important part in urban life. It provided a revered and permanent political constitution, and it limited political prerogatives. It supplied the law for all Muslim states. It imposed a fascinating example of the separation of powers: legislation was separated from the executive, being pre-empted by the deity. The content of divine legislation was in the keeping of the scholars. No overt legislative innovation was possible, except by analogy and interpretation of the existing legal corpus. If the deity pre-empts legislation, the executive cannot usurp it.

Secondly, the high religion provided society with a constitutional law which was the only defence of the urban population against arbitrary central power. The fusion of the moral authority of the urban scholars with a temporarily united tribal coalition *could* overturn the state. Although the urban population had no direct coercive leverage against the state, it did have this kind of moral leverage, which, in conjunction with the ungoverned countryside, constituted a kind of permanent menace for the central power. If too much indignation in the town melded with two much dissidence in the tribally cohesive countryside, the sultan was in trouble. The trust prevailing between rural cousins could fuse with the reverence always felt by the burghers, and intermittently by the tribal cousins, for Divine Law. It could engender a threat to the state from *within* society. But at present, the moralism of a scriptural religion no longer shares its influence with local, socially compromised saintly networks, whose essential role was to make concessions to the requirements of tribal life and soften the demands of a Revealed Ethic. The tribes themselves are eroded. Now, the scriptural religion can reign supreme.

The system was once based on trust between members of tribal groups; on fear of authority on the part of urban populations; and on a shared reverence for a Revelation, which restrains the arbitrariness of the urban state firstly by specifying limits to what it may do, and secondly by providing the means for activating opposition. This traditional model is worth comparing with another kind of society which has emerged, this time in the modern world, and which shares with it the opposition between trust and effective central government. In the Islamic model the central authorities were not positively hostile to trust on any theological principle, but were simply intolerant, within the very considerable limits of their capacity, of the emergence of coherent trust-engendering groups which would pose a threat to them. They would keep such groups at bay, but they could not destroy them. The central power enjoyed a symbiotic relation with urban populations which *lacked* this cohesion and trust, and was in opposition to rural populations which had it.

Something similar is a very marked characteristic of socialist societies as functioning at present. There is the systematic destruction of subordinate units, of subunits within the society, other than those which are actually part of the central machine. Civil society is pulverized and largely absent.

Socialist societies do not, like traditional Muslim ones, suffer the threat of a periphery of menacing tribes. In that sense, they are free from external pressure. On the other hand, they face other problems. Like all industrial societies, they live under the requirement of ensuring a high economic performance and economic growth. They are dependent on the administrative, managerial, educational, intellectual clerisy of their own society. In other words, the *ulama* of the socialist world are not only secretaries, judges, administrators, and legitimators of the social order, which is what they were in Islam. They play a far greater part. They are crucial in *production*, not just in administration. And although you can do unpleasant things to some of them all the time, and to all of them some of the time, you cannot do unpleasant things to all of them all the time without incurring economic catastrophe.

This is one of the basic dilemmas of socialist policy. Politically it needs to atomize society; economically, it needs autonomous institutions. The systematic atomization of society from above has interesting parallels, *and* contrasts, with elements of the traditional Muslim case. In Islam, the productive system contained no menace. It was the most docile element. It could be atomized without economic catastrophe. But the principles of cohesion which had engendered the state, or rather had trained its rulers, at the same time also threatened it: rival would-be rulers *also* possessed such cohesion.

In conclusion, cohesion and trust contribute not merely towards the establishment of a social order as such, but also towards the establishment of checks on government. In traditional Islam, the market or urban element of society aided political centralization by its own weakness, but was devoid of trust and cohesion: but the countryside – cohesive, endowed with fragile trust, and self-governing – did provide a check on central power, in alliance with urban-based scripturalist moralism. Tribal life, conditioned primarily by lack of government and the consequent need for cohesion, was the only source of a certain kind of trust, which bound men in groups, even though it was also haunted by the possibility of treachery. In the towns, there was specialization, no trust, and order based on fear. Religion provided an idiom in terms of which the various elements of the total society could communicate with each other. It provided the terminology for both tribal trust and urban fear. It could intermittently help tribal cohesion to extend its scale, and to revitalize the polity by providing a new set of rulers. Modern conditions have played havoc with this system, and have in part turned it upside down.

REFERENCES

Andreski, S. 1954: *Military Organization and Society*. London: Routledge and Kegan Paul.
Eickelman, D. F. 1976: *Moroccan Islam*. Austin, Texas.
Fustel de Coulanges, N. M. 1956: *The Ancient City*, trans. W. Small. New York: Doubleday Anchor Books.
Ibn Khaldun 1958: *The Muqaddimah*, trans. F. Rosenthal. London: Routledge and Kegan Paul.
Khazanov, A. M. 1975: *Sotsialnaia Istoria Skifov* (Social history of the Scythians). Moscow: Nanka.
Khazanov, A. M. 1984: *Nomads of the Outside World*. Cambridge: Cambridge University Press.
Maher, V. 1974: *Women and Property in Morocco*. Cambridge: Cambridge University Press.
Shnirelman, V. A. 1980: *Proiskhozhdenie Skotovodstva* (The origins of pastoralism). Moscow: Nanka.

Tillion, G. 1966: *Le Harem et les cousins*. Paris.
Tolybekov, S. E. 1959: *Obshohestvenno-ekonomicheskii stroi Kazakhov v XVII–XIX vekakh* (Socio-economic structure of the Kazakhs in the 17th–19th centuries). Alma-Ata.

10

Mafia: the Price of Distrust

Diego Gambetta

There is a number of places around the world where three unfortunate sets of circumstances coexist: where people do not cooperate when it would be mutually beneficial to do so; where they compete in harmful ways; and, finally, where they refrain from competing in those instances when they could all gain considerably from competition. There are probably not many, though, where such a powerful combination has lasted for centuries. Southern Italy – especially the Tyrrhenian regions of Campania, Calabria, and Sicily – is conspicuous among them, in spite of the fact that Italy as a whole is now one of the most successful of industrial countries.[1]

It is tempting to conclude, therefore, that people in the south are either stubbornly irrational or entertain masochistic preferences. While the possibility cannot be excluded that they may have evolved such preferences as a means of reducing the cognitive dissonance caused by prolonged exposure to such an environment, the overall aim of this paper is to reconcile individual rationality with protracted collective disaster. If anything, in this case, the latter results from an excess of individual rationality. This paper is an account of the remarkable responses to a generalized absence of trust and of the mechanisms by which such responses, while reinforcing distrust, have none the less brought about a relatively stable social structure. Its major underlying assumption is that the *mafia* – although by no means its only element – represents the quintessence of this structure, in which all the crucial behavioural patterns converge to form an indissoluble but explosive mixture. In addition, the mafia is exemplary of those cases where the public interest

[1] I wish to thank Keith Hart, Geoffrey Hawthorn, and Anthony Pagden for their helpful and penetrating comments on an earlier version of this paper.

lies in collapsing rather than building *internal* trust and cooperation (Schelling 1984).

In the first section I shall consider the historical background by looking at the effects of Spanish domination in southern Italy and by following Alexis de Tocqueville in his journey to Sicily. In the second, drawing on the classic study by Leopoldo Franchetti ([1876] 1974), I shall outline the causes and long-lasting features of the Sicilian mafia. In the final section I shall consider some of the intended and unintended mechanisms whereby the mafia, while exploiting and reinforcing distrust, has been able to maintain itself for over a century.

I

Anthony Pagden (this volume), standing on the shoulders of two Neapolitan thinkers, Paolo Mattia Doria and Antonio Genovesi, articulates a plausible and enticing account of how a generalized sense of distrust might first have spread under the Habsburg Spanish domination. Most of the component strategies of *divide et impera* were adopted by the Spaniards: a bewildering and sophisticated array ranging from discouraging commerce and the production of wealth to the manipulation of information; from fostering religious superstition to establishing vertical bonds of submission and exploitation at the expense of solidarity between equals; from destroying equality before the law to overturning the relationship between the sexes. As Pagden argues, much of what they did can be seen as the promotion and selective exploitation of distrust.

We do not know whether the accounts of Doria and Genovesi were set against a trust-based society which existed under an allegedly less disagreeable rule – that of the Aragonese – or against the virtues of an ideal society with which southern Italy had never been blessed.[2] We do know, however, that there is something very striking in Pagden's account, something analogous to discovering the first steps in the childhood of an adult we know and whose behaviour has remained something of a mystery to us. We discover that that behaviour has a *genesis*, that the seemingly intractable backwardness of southern Italy emerges from a plausible history. But knowing something of the causes which generate a state of affairs is quite different from understanding how such a state can outlast those causes. The mechanisms of reproduction or – to switch to the language of game theory – the enduring convergence of expectations, constraints, and individual interest on a particular *equilibrium*, must

---

[2] If Thucydides is right, we should certainly consider going back quite some time. He said of Sicilians that they were 'sui commodi quam publici amantiores' (quoted by Fazello 1558: 28).

have a force of their own, and must lie more in the *adaptive responses* selected by the subjects of the Spanish domination and by their successors than in the strategies of domination themselves. The type of behaviour of which the mafia represents the most radical, aggressive, and perfected expression has been subject to a wide range of mutations and instability, but at a certain level of abstraction it has never been transformed into something radically different; if anything, its essential peculiarities have been strengthened. The use of the term *equilibrium*, therefore, is not just an analogy but is adopted here in the sense of a state of affairs in which all or most agents, in spite of what they may think of the collective outcome, have not found adequate incentives to behave differently and to change that outcome in any significant way. How was it, then, that a social system centred around such notions as *fede privata* and public distrust maintained its equilibrium?

In 1827, approximately 100 years after Doria and 50 after Genovesi, Alexis de Tocqueville, then a young man, undertook the first of his renowned travels and went to Naples and Sicily. Let us leave Naples then, and follow him further south. Most of *Voyage en Sicile*, the first long essay he ever wrote, is lost, and only 30 pages survive.[3] There is an imaginary dialogue, in these few pages, between two fictional characters: one a Sicilian, Don Ambrosio, and the other a Neapolitan, Don Carlo. In spite of their differences, Tocqueville writes, 'tout deux semblaient avoir fait de *la duplicité* une longue habitude; mais chez le premier, c'était plutôt encore un fruit amer de la nécessité et de la servitude; on pouvait croire que le second ne trompait que parce que *la fourberie* était le moyen le plus court d'arriver au but' (1864–67: 154; my italics).

Don Ambrosio blames Don Carlo and his fellow citizens for doing to the Sicilians pretty much the same things that Doria and Genovesi blamed the Spaniards for having done to the Neapolitans: 'Notre noblesse . . . elle n'est plus sicilienne. Vous lui avez ôté *tout intérêt dans les affaires publiques*. . . . Vous l'avez attirée tout entière à Naples . . . vous avez abâtardi son coeur en substituant *l'ambition de cour* au désir de l'illustration, et le pouvoir de *la faveur* à celui du mérite et du courage' (pp. 157–8; my italics). Don Carlo, embittered by the violence of the attack, returns the challenge by asking the Sicilian why it is then that the Sicilians have adapted to rather than rebelled against such an unbearable yoke. To this Don Ambrosio replies that 'dénaturée par l'oppression, [l'énergie] cachée [de notre caractère national] ne se révèle plus que par des *crimes*; pour vous, vous n'avez que des vices. En nous refusant la

---

[3] Its loss is reported by J. P. Mayer, the editor of the 1957 edition of Tocqueville's complete works. A search I conducted at the Bibliothèque Nationale in Paris was equally unfruitful.

justice, en faisant mieux, en nous la vendant, vous nous avez appris à considérer *l'assassinat comme un droit*' (p. 59, my italics).

Through this fictional account, by which Tocqueville manages to convey his reflections on the journey, we begin to grasp some of the elements of the peculiar process of adjustment to – rather than rebellion against – domination which to different degrees involves both Naples and Sicily: the absenteeism of an aristocracy lured by the pleasures and servility of the court; the predominance of private over public concerns, of duplicity, cunning, and favour over merit; and the fashion for crime and murder, which have become habitual and are even felt to be legitimate rights.

Moreover, not only did the Spaniards exploit distrust for the purpose of domination, but they taught some of their subjects to do so too and to pass it on to others. The Bourbon Spanish domination, which replaced the Habsburgs in 1724 and, except for a brief interval, lasted until the Italian unification in 1861, continued to pursue the policy of *divide et impera* and took particular care to foster the hatred between Neapolitans and Sicilians: so much so that, as the Tocqueville dialogue shows, 'in the minds of Sicilians the Bourbon and the Neapolitan domination became the same thing' (Franchetti [1876] 1974: 79).

Yet the diffusion throughout southern Italy of the characteristics of the Spanish rule and of the peculiar responses it received do not tell us how and why some features of this system, *mutatis mutandis*, have endured until the present day. It is probably not a coincidence, though, that only 11 years (1838) after Tocqueville wrote his account, we read for the first time in an official report of the existence of a thing called *the mafia* (Hess 1986: 114); and, what is more, we read of it as an already established social force. The sketchy historical account given thus far does not amount to an analytical exposition of the causes that generated the mafia or its less renowned but equally fierce twin entities, the *camorra* (Naples) and the *'ndrangheta* (Calabria).[4] But on intuitive grounds, it makes a criminal response plausible. Most of the ingredients were there. How they merged into a coherent structure is something we shall consider below.

II

In 1876 Leopoldo Franchetti – a Tuscan landowner who travelled in Sicily and was animated by a strong degree of civil passion – wrote what, still today, remains one of the most coherent and comprehensive accounts of the Sicilian mafia and its surroundings. His study – *Condizioni*

4 On the *camorra* see Walston (1986); on the *'ndrangheta* see Gambino (1975).

politiche ed amministrative della Sicilia – has much the same quality as some of the best nineteenth-century classics in the social sciences.[5] What is striking is not only the freshness of style and the bold disregard of disciplinary boundaries – typical of those (in this respect) happy days – but the fact that he was in a position to come up *then* with remarks which make considerable sense *now*. In other words, Franchetti's book constitutes indirect evidence that the mafia in the nineteenth century has characteristics which are still present today, and makes it possible to think of this phenomenon as something arching over no less than 100 years.[6] Virtually everything Franchetti wrote is supported by the evidence which has since emerged, and what we know about the way the mafia has evolved is largely consistent with his analysis.

Franchetti essentially identifies two related sets of causes for the emergence of the mafia. The first is eminently political and has to do with the absence of credible or effective systems of justice and law enforcement. From at least the time of the sixteenth century (Cancila 1984), Sicilians were able to trust neither the fairness nor the protection of the law.[7] This pre-existing state of affairs caused considerable difficulties to the newly formed Italian state, which, in spite of its weakness and its mistakes, might otherwise have claimed the right to a far higher degree of legitimation than any of the previous regimes (I shall return to the role of the democratic state below).

The second set of causes concerns economic rather than political trust. As Gellner shows (this volume), the lack of a central agency is not in itself an explanation of social disorder: on the contrary, social cohesion and acceptable rules of collective conduct may emerge across a multiplicity of local clusters. Even the presence of an *untrustworthy* central agency – although of course different from the complete lack of one – is not quite sufficient to explain the emergence of the mafia. The untrustworthiness of the state, by interacting with economic relations, sets another process in motion: as Dasgupta and Pagden both argue (this volume), distrust percolates through the social ladder, and the unpredictability of sanctions generates uncertainty in agreements, stagnation in commerce and industry, and a general reluctance towards impersonal and extensive forms of cooperation. Sicilians – as everyone knows – do

[5] Unfortunately it has only been translated into German, and is semi-forgotten or superficially understood in Italy. An exception is providded by Pezzino (1985), who takes Franchetti's arguments seriously, especially those about the role of the then newly formed Italian state.

[6] See Cancila (1984) for interesting evidence suggesting that some elements of mafioso behaviour were already present in the sixteenth century.

[7] There were not just deliberate intentions on the part of the rulers behind the unpredictability and unfairness of the law, but also objective conditions, such as the isolation of Sicily and the scarcity of internal roads, which made other than local law enforcement far from easy (see Pezzino 1985).

not trust the state: beyond the boundaries of limited clusters, they often end up distrusting each other as well.

In turn, economic backwardness 'closes off a multiplicity of channels which could give vent to the activity of private citizens. . . . In such a state of affairs, the only goal one can set for one's activity or ambition [is] to prevail over one's peers' (Franchetti 1974: 71): 'your enemy is the man in your own trade', claims a Sicilian proverb (Gower Chapman 1971: 65). The desire to prevail over one's peers, combined with the lack of a credible central agency, does not lead to ordinary 'market competition: instead of outdoing rivals the most common practice becomes that of doing them in. Individual improvements are seen as desirable and possible, but social mobility is and is believed to be a zero-sum game.

The opportunities for social mobility should be considered as a third concomitant cause. Franchetti does not do so explicitly, yet evidence suggests that the areas in southern Italy where organized crime has traditionally evolved are those where for different reasons social mobility was feasible. As well as in the large urban concentrations such as Naples and Palermo, it emerged in the *latifondo* of western Sicily where landowners were absenteeists (Blok 1974), but not in other parts of Sicily (Franchetti 1974: 53–6), or in Calabria (Crotonese) and Puglia, areas where the presence of landowners left no opportunity open to the rural middle class (Arlacchi 1980; Cosentino 1983). It also developed in those small farming areas which manifested a thriving agriculture, but not in those based on a subsistence economy (Arrighi and Piselli 1986). Lack of trust, matched by heavy constraints on social mobility – such as in the case of the depressing village studied by Banfield (1958) – does not offer sufficient incentive to 'specialize' in prevailing over one's peers, but simply leads to a deeply fragmented social world and to the reproduction of wretchedly poor economic conditions.

By contrast, in a politically and economically untrustworthy world which is not lacking in scope for social mobility, and where *le pouvoir de la faveur* prevails over justice and merit, the sole remaining merit is in fact that of seeking *la faveur* from those above, extorting it out of one's equals, and distributing part of its fruits – the smallest possible part (Franchetti 1974: 27) – to a select group of those below. Here, people cluster in groups, take shelter behind the men who make themselves respected (p. 38). Associations and clusters involve persons of all classes and occupations (p. 38), and only personal relations – where distrust is less threatening – count and are believed to count as means of social mobility (p. 36; see also Pezzino 1985: 49–50).

In this context, we may begin to understand why mafiosi do not emerge as ordinary criminals, acting in isolation as individuals (Franchetti 1974: 101). Or, at least, why they are not perceived as such: the *pubblica opinione* in Sicily sees them more as men capable of enforcing privately that public justice the Spaniards had eroded (p. 93) and that nobody could trust. And this is still the way they see themselves today (Arlacchi 1983: 151). To Don Ambrosio, 50 years earlier, recourse to *l'assassinat* still seemed appalling. At the time when Franchetti is writing, it is taken as sign of the capacity to protect (p. 108), as the foremost sign of reputation (pp. 9, 33).[8]

The mafia at any one time can thus be seen as a successful cluster or coalition of clusters. It is successful not just at coping defensively with lack of trust – as in the case of weaker and non-violent forms of association such as clienteles and patron–client relations – but at turning distrust into a profitable business by a relentless, and if necessary violent, search for *exclusivity*. Its single most important activity is the enforcement of monopolies over the largest possible number of resources in any given territory.[9] Each mafioso is either a monopolist or the acolyte of a monopolist. 'Cosa nostra' – as members apparently call it (Staiano 1986) – means that the thing is ours, *not* yours; it stresses inclusion, and inclusion can only subsist by simultaneously postulating exclusion. The long-lasting specificity of the mafia is that it tolerates no competition, and it probably tends to engage precisely in those types of activity and transaction which most lend themselves to monopolization (Schelling 1984: 184): land, cattle, sources of water in a dry land, markets, auctions, ports, building, transport, and public works are all areas which, for different reasons, can be easily controlled, where exclusivity is relatively easy to enforce.

Historically, the *crime* most characteristic of the mafia is the use of violence to enforce the monopoly of otherwise legal goods. As we shall see in the next section, even the profitable practice of extortion in exchange for protection does not always take on the features of an entirely criminal exercise: it is not just applied to recalcitrant victims, and a clear demarcation line between protection against true and protection against deliberately generated threats is often very hard to draw.

The mafia, moreover, is not – as has recently been claimed (see Blok 1974) – something which originates only in the countryside. Since its inception (Franchetti informs us) it has been an urban as well as a rural phenomenon. Prominent mafiosi often belong to *la classe media*, to what elsewhere has managed to become the bourgeoisie (p. 97). The difference is this: that whereas in other places this class has succeeded in guaranteeing a 'legislazione uguale per tutti', in this area, where private

---

[8] For a bitter satire of the 'right' to murder in Sicily see Anonimo del XX secolo (1985).

[9] Some of the literature on the subject has confused a change in the field of undertaking with a change in the specific ubiquitous component of mafioso behaviour (see Gambetta 1986).

power dominates and even 'the mind cannot tell the difference between the public interest and immediate personal interest' (p. 35), it is inevitable, wrote Franchetti, that villains and *classe media* should find themselves in close connection and that they should exchange services (p. 108). But the middle class can sustain the search for exclusivity with the same personal gifts which in other circumstances it invests in peaceful business: order, foresight, caution, and cunning (p. 97). They go so far as to practise understatement about their real power, a style they ostensibly share more with the British than the Italian mentality. This style, moreover, has won them reputation and trust. ('It is strange', wrote Alongi in 1887, 'that in that hot and colourful country where ordinary speech is so honey-sweet, hyperbolic and picturesque, that of the mafiosi is curt, restrained and decisive'; quoted by Hess 1973: 52).

In more recent periods the mafia may have approximated the status of a formal organization,[10] but initially it was probably an uncertain and erratic coalition of local monopolies which cooperated at some times and ignored each other or fought bloody wars at others. The only limit to the expansion of monopoly, wrote Franchetti, is the challenge of 'another coalition, not less strong, bold and fierce' (p. 10). Indeed, one of the theoretical reasons which most strongly suggests that the mafia of any one period is likely to be more or better organized than previously is that competition for monopoly is likely to weed out the less organized clusters. But even if the mafia has evolved into a more organized entity, it has not managed to reach a stage at which stable cooperation can be sustained for any length of time. The reasons, both theoretical and historical, have yet to be properly understood, but the evidence suggests that neither has the mafia evolved towards a single monopoly successful in submitting all others, nor has it dissolved. The characteristics of its persistence suggest those of a turbulent equilibrium.[11]

To the extent to which one cluster does not triumph over all others, and all clusters do not melt peacefully into the fabric of the democratic state, the solution to the problem of trust that mafioso behaviour offers will remain at once individually rational and collectively disastrous. Trust – as we shall see in the next section – here displays the features of a positional good (see Pagano 1986), for one can trust others and be

[10] Here I shall not address the question – which I have addressed elsewhere (Gambetta 1986) – of whether the mafia has been able to develop as a proper organization. However, I believe that there is enough evidence (Staiano 1986: 55–61), as well as sufficient theoretical grounds, to think that such an organization – somewhat like a confederation of local governments not always at peace with each other – has indeed existed. What is more difficult is to say whether such a confederation is still capable of operating now, after several years of internal conflict and state repression.

[11] The notion of equilibrium does not, that is, apply to any one cluster or coalition of clusters in particular, but to the fact that, in spite of its internal wars and those intermittently waged against it by the state, *a* mafia has so far always managed to re-emerge.

trusted by them only to the extent that trust is subtracted from somewhere else: more trust on one side means less on another. This is a kind of trust that is in endemically short supply and that, unlike the trust which Hirschman (1984), Dasgupta and I myself explore (elsewhere in this volume), does not increase with use. After all, it is perhaps no trust at all, but rather the segmentary and patchily organized exploitation of distrust. The corollaries of distrust – and indeed its self-reinforcing behavioural expressions of secrecy, duplicity, information intelligence (Franchetti 1974: 30), and betrayal – all feature prominently in the lives and careers of mafiosi. Today, as much as 100 years ago, the minds of mafiosi are constantly occupied by thoughts of risks and traps, populated by a threatening array of 'traitors, spies and torturers' (Arlacchi 1983: 151). As an old *capo-mafia* wrote to a young member: 'I beg you to be careful, for the world is all infamous.' Indeed, there is no one we can trust in this world.

                                        III

We have described the causes that may explain the emergence of the mafia. We still have to consider the mechanisms by which it has managed to maintain itself over such a long period.[12] These mechanisms are a combination of intended and unintended consequences. Let us begin with the latter.

Franchetti says that in Sicily those who are clever, energetic, and ambitious can only find a way to improve their social position by dedicating themselves to the 'industria della violenza' (p. 97). If one does not want to have anything to do with the mafia, then, in the absence of a legitimate authority in which to take refuge, the only alternatives are those of migrating and lying low ('se ne stanno neghittosi', p. 109). Both have been widely pursued, thereby – indirectly and unintentionally – enhancing the sense of distrust on which the force of the mafia thrives: as a result of migration and withdrawal into private life, the proportion of 'well-adjusted' or complacent people increases and the system is reinforced. A wide range of evidence (Arlacchi 1983) suggests that, on the margin, people who migrate do so also because of the mafia. Given that 'mafia-averse' people tend to migrate more frequently, the degree of opposition is likely to decrease and the power of the mafia to increase. The effects of migration are clearly unintended, because those who migrate do not do so *in order to* enhance the force of the mafia (although they may of course recognize those effects).

---

[12] For an account of the continuity of the mafia see also Catanzaro (1985).

The second, partially unintentional, mechanism which explains the successful survival of the mafia has to do with the democratic state, which while hostile to such an alternative power as the mafia has also to depend on its capacity to mobilize votes. Geoffrey Hawthorn, elsewhere in this volume, argues that there might be two ways to undermine or override 'vicious circles' such as the mafia: one consists in the emergence of a predictable environment, the other in 'a power which is *independent* of the interests that maintain them'. The former, through the example Hawthorn gives of changing relationships on the land in the western Gangetic plain, consists essentially in the emergence of a reliable market for credit and produce, and is largely unintentional. As I shall argue below, in the world of the mafia monopoly a reliable market is a contradiction in terms and is not likely to come about, or at least to spread, 'naturally'. The latter, through the example Hawthorn gives of South Korea, consists of an authoritarian and military rule which, in itself monopolistic, would not tolerate local monopolies. In a sense, this implies that in order to get rid of the mafia, what we need is simply another – bigger and better – mafia.

Italy did once have a power which was largely independent of the mafia, or at least of the social strata supporting it, and which did contribute to a partial undoing of the mafia (Duggan 1985): this was of course the Fascist regime. In contrast, democracy, by its very nature, has to rely for consensus on larger parts of the population. Thus the temptation to come to terms with those who hold a monopoly of people's votes, regulate the dispensation of political trust, and somehow guarantee local 'law and order', has been strong, and in several instances has proved irresistible. This, of course, has not enhanced the already fragile trust in central authority in Sicily or the country as a whole. Here, it is not possible to go into details. Suffice it to say that it is unlikely that democracy's complicity with the mafia, at least at the national level, has been consistently intentional and conspiratorial, even though there are clearly cases in which this has been so. And as the majority of Italians would certainly agree: 'better the mafia than fascism!' Still today, any attempt to eradicate the mafia is caught between two extremes: that of using too little force and thereby remaining ineffective, and that of using too much, putting civil liberties at risk.

The aggregate and unintended effects of migration go some way towards explaining the lack of opposition to the mafia and its consequent capacity to survive. So does the intrinsic, and otherwise beneficial, weakness of democracy. But the weakness of the state – which has never fully succeeded in acquiring legitimation in the south – can only be measured in comparison with the strength of the local social structure (Franchetti 1974: 101) and its capacity to foster cooperation through intentional action.

The mechanisms which motivate cooperation in any form of human endeavour, as Bernard Williams explains elsewhere in this volume, comprise four basic elements: coercion, interests, values, and personal bonds. People, that is, may decide to cooperate (1) for fear of sanctions; (2) because cooperation enhances their mutual economic interests; (3) because they have general reasons, whether cultural, moral or religious, to believe that cooperation is good irrespective of sanctions and rewards; and finally (4) because they are related to one another by bonds of kin or friendship.[13]

Even without having read Williams's essay, the mafia learnt this lesson well, and relies on *all four* mechanisms simultaneously.[14] Owing to constraints of space, I shall limit myself to detailed consideration of only the first two: coercion, and especially economic interests.[15] Their combination, within a world of deep distrust, is itself a robust pillar of mafia business for, irrespective of values and cultural codes, the force of constraints and opportunities can bring about rational adaptation on the part of people living in proximity with mafioso networks, even if they are not related by kin or do not entertain strong beliefs about the social importance of adhering to the code of honour or that of silence.

> It so happens that a person who would be prepared to make very great sacrifices in order to stop the domination of violence, is compelled to support it, strengthen it and associate with it . . . . He cannot think to resort to the law, because the probability of being shot for those who do so is far too high for him to expose himself lightly . . . . External circumstances impose themselves on everyone, irrespective of the inclinations of his mind (Franchetti 1974: 106–7).

The ability to use violence, whether direct or in the form of a credible threat, is a generalized ingredient of mafioso behaviour. It is the feature which most radically distinguishes the mafia from other forms of southern Italian cluster (see Gribaudi 1980: 69–75). Having recourse to

[13] Although the four basic mechanisms can be usefully distinguished for analytical purposes they are unlikely to represent four distinct motivational sets in people's minds all the time: we cannot always be sure whether our cooperation is motivated by fear of retaliation, economic advantage, or faith in the code of silence, or, finally, because it is our 'friend' who is asking us to cooperate. Within each cluster all possible reasons operate simultaneously to discourage the temptation to defect.

[14] To draw a map of the extent to which organizations of whatever sort rely on the four motivational sets would be well beyond the scope of this paper. Intuitively, however, there do not seem to be many which rely on all four at the same time. This may go some way towards explaining the relative success of organized crime of Italian origin in the United States with respect to other ethnic groups. While all rely on coercion and interest, the Italians probably have a more perfected tradition of suitable values and well-oiled codes of friendship and kinship.

[15] Several other authors have devoted a great deal of attention to the other mechanisms: for the code of honour and instrumental friendship see, for instance, Catanzaro (1985); for the importance of kinship and its manipulation see Arlacchi (1983: 154–64).

private violence is valuable outside as well as inside the cluster: outside, against unyielding victims, rival mafiosi groups, recalcitrant cooperators, and officials loyal to the state; inside, to punish defectors, discourage internal competitors for the leading positions, or, conversely, to challenge the leaders. Many mafiosi have begun their careers with violent acts (Hess 1973; Arlacchi 1983), but have subsequently relied on the reputation with which such acts provided them: 'basta la fama' wrote Franchetti (p. 104), in line with some of the most advanced game theory (see Milgrom and Roberts 1982, who show that, contrary to the standard economic claim, 'predatory practices' to maintain a monopoly are not irrational if reputation and future challengers are taken into account). They become persons with a reputation and are trusted, and, if interests diverge, they are trusted, in a limited but effective sense, to resort to violence without a second thought.

The relationship between violence and the other mechanisms suitable for inducing cooperation is threefold. First of all there is the relationship of *substitution*: violence substitutes for and can be substituted by (1) values – larger doses of *omertà* ensure lesser ones of violence; (2) interests, which can encourage cooperation and dispense with the need for violence; (3) personal bonds – relatives and friends are by definition more likely to cooperate, and hence there is a lower demand on violence to keep them under control. Next, there is the relationship of mutual *reinforcement*: greater quantities of *omertà* diminish the risks attached to the use of violence; at the same time, the higher the expectation that violence will be used, the higher the likelihood that silence will be scrupulously observed, to the point that it becomes impossible to say whether *omertà* is maintained out of faith or fear (Franchetti 1974: 31). Similarly, a greater capacity to satisfy mutual economic interests within the network, while offering a greater incentive to aggression from rival groups, may call for a more widespread use of violence in protection and at the same time act as an insurance against the undesirable consequences of its use. Conversely, a greater capacity for violence increases the capacity to satisfy mutual economic interests, thereby reinforcing the bonds of economic cooperation.

As I explain in the conclusion to this volume, there are also instances of a third, *contradictory* relationship between coercion and cooperation. An exaggerated use of violence – besides engendering paranoia in the users – can lead to revenge and the breach of *omertà*, as in the case of Tommaso Buscetta who, in 1983, decided to confess all he knew after half of his family was murdered. His confession brought to trial in Palermo nearly 500 persons suspected of a large number and variety of crimes (Staiano 1986).[16]

---

[16] Most cases of defection to the police involve the widows of mafiosi killed by other mafiosi.

Violence by itself, however, will not do. It is risky, costly, and generates instability and conflict: explaining the persistence of the mafia simply by its capacity for coercion would be nearly as limited as explaining the persistence of capitalism on the same basis (see Przeworski 1985). The promotion of cooperation must also rely on a more powerful weapon: the satisfaction of economic interests. Mutual interests are served in a variety of ways, both within and without the immediate mafioso networks. Within the network, solidarity in case of arrest or death 'in the field' acts as insurance against the risks attached to illegal activities (Schneider and Schneider 1976: 189). Outside it, a wide range of economic bonds are formed: they can involve the corruption of civil servants, the exchange of favours for electoral support, or the handling of labour disputes for the benefit of landowners and entrepreneurs. But they may also be remote and aseptically insulated from the violent core of mafia activity: when private citizens, for instances, are offered extremely high interest rates to invest their money in informal banking systems without needing to know, like most investors, whether that money will be spent in financing philanthropic enterprises or drug trafficking. Thus the network of interests that mafiosi form around themselves can be widely ramified, ranging from active criminality, through corruption, to rational adaptation on the part of ordinary citizens (Franchetti 1974: 101).

Even the fundamental and time-honoured practice of extortion can be so deeply entrenched that it becomes difficult to distinguish between victims and accomplices, for the extortion bonds may take on rather ambiguous connotations. Franchetti's account is striking:[17]

> The distinction between a damage avoided and a benefit gained is up to a point artificial. [In most cases] the line that separates them is impossible to determine, or rather it does not exist in human feeling. When evildoers intrude on and dominate most social relationships, . . . the very act that saves one from their hostility can also bring their friendship with all its associated advantages (p. 129).

The violence of extortion and the self-interest of the 'victim' tend to merge and to provide an inextricable set of reasons for cooperation: the advantage of being a 'friend' of those who extort one's money or goods is not therefore simply that of avoiding the likely damages that would otherwise ensue, but can extend to assistance in disposing of competitors, or protection against the threats of isolated bandits, and against the risk of being cheated in the course of business transactions.

---

[17] Over a century after Franchetti wrote his account exactly the same notions are being expressed by the prosecutors in the current trial in Palermo (see Staiano 1986: 82–3).

The latter risk is particularly interesting with respect to the problem of trust, and worth pursuing in more detail, for it allows us to explore more analytically, if as yet tentatively, the economic heart of mafioso behaviour. We know that the absence of trust in business has a devastating effect: a high expected probability of being cheated (of being saddled with a 'lemon') may lead to the non-emergence or even to the collapse of market exchange, especially in those cases where asymmetric information – concerning the quality of the goods exchanged – is relevant (Akerlof 1970; Dasgupta, this volume). Within the cluster of people they protect, mafiosi offer a peculiar solution to the problem raised by the market of 'lemons'. On this issue, a Neapolitan coachman in 1863 had the following to say (consider that bad used horses were then the counterpart of the bad used cars of today):

> I am a murdered man. I bought a *dead* horse who does not know his way around, wants to follow only the roads he likes, slips and falls on slopes, fears squibs and bells, and yesterday he fledged and crashed into a flock of sheep that was barring the way. A *camorrista* [the Neapolitan version of a mafioso] who protects me and used to control the horse market, would have spared me from this theft. He used to check on the sales and get his tip from both buyers and sellers. Last year I wanted to get rid of a blind horse and he helped me to sell it as a good one, for he protected me. Now he is in jail and I was forced to buy this bad horse without him. He was a great gentleman! (quoted by Monnier [1863] 1965: 73–4)

There are several illuminating points in this amusing yet perfectly realistic account, the substance of which is confirmed by evidence from several other sources referring to more recent times (Arrighi and Piselli 1986: 399–404; Galante 1986: 97). The coachman willingly pays the protection money in compensation for an actual defensive task performed by the mafioso, and he bitterly regrets the latter's forced absence. The mafioso, by means which are left unclear but which presumably involve his reputation for toughness, seems capable of deterring the seller from handing over a 'lemon'. Without that protection the coachman is truly at risk, for he is indeed, as it were, saddled with a bad horse.

More difficult to interpret is the fact that the seller too gives the mafioso a tip. This could suggest, in line with Dasgupta's argument (this volume), that with respect to that particular transaction the protection the mafioso offers is really a *public* good which benefits both sides. If he did not act as guarantor the exchange would not take place at all, for the potential buyer would be deterred from entering the transaction for fear of getting a bad deal. The seller's tip, in other words, might reflect the price he is prepared to pay to be trusted. If the world were made up of only three agents – seller, coachman, and mafioso – the transaction would leave everyone better off: transaction costs would be higher than in a trustworthy world, but returns too would be higher than those yielded by no transaction at all.

If there is not just one seller on the market, however, the seller may also pay the mafioso for a service that has nothing to do with trust: for directing the customer to *him* rather than to another seller, for helping him to fend off the competition.[18] If all sellers look equally untrustworthy, and the mafioso can enforce honest behaviour from and signal *any one* of them to the buyer, then he must find some additional incentive to choose *one* in particular for whom to act as guarantor. Thus the seller's tip to the mafioso might reflect both the price of being considered trustworthy *and* the extra price of being *chosen* from among other potential sellers.

One might ask why the mafioso should not offer his 'mark of guarantee' to all sellers on the market and then let customers choose on the basis of taste, price, and the detectable quality of the goods. He would thus effectively offer trust as a public good: all sellers could chip in to pay him his due for making them appear trustworthy, and transactions would then take place in an 'ordinary' market. The available evidence suggests that this is not the case and that the mafioso tends to guarantee, *and* therefore to select, only a limited number of sellers *at the expense* of others.

One reason the mafioso might prefer to offer trust *in conjunction with* discouraging competition is that if that trust were *too* public he would then be unable to enforce the collection of his fee from all sellers, who would find free-riding particularly easy. He might also find it difficult to check on all transactions carried out by those sellers he guarantees, with the risk of losing his reputation if a 'lemon' were to be sold behind his back. A further reason why his intervention as guarantor must always be identifiable – linked, that is, to specific transactions – is to make sure that the buyer knows that if he gets a good deal this is due to the mafioso's protection and not to the independent honesty of the seller, which could foster the growth of trust directly between buyer and seller and put the mafioso out of business.

This is a crucial point, for it is by acting in such a way that the mafioso ends up selling trust as a positional good – a good, that is, that one seller can 'consume' only if other potential sellers do not (Pagano 1986). And this is presumably why competition develops in harmful ways, for in

---

[18] Here I do not discuss the problem of whether the mafioso is paid in actual cash or, as often happens, in other forms: presents in kind, credit for future transactions, or the exchange of favours. Although scholars have repeatedly stressed its importance, this problem is analytically irrelevant to my purpose.

order to stay in – or enter into – business, other potential sellers are forced to rely less on improving the quality of their goods and the competitiveness of their prices, than on developing those (ultimately 'military') skills which might subtract monopolistic power from the mafioso and his cluster. In other words, they have either to become mafiosi themselves or to ask for the protection of other mafiosi.

From what the coachman says we also learn that, on another occasion, the mafioso succeeded in helping him to sell a blind horse as a good one. This indicates that the mafioso is not offering his protection to *all* buyers on the horse market: he is not really, in other words, dispensing a public good to the buyers either. We are not told, however, why the mafioso on one occasion satisfies the interests of both buyer and seller, while on this occasion he takes care only of those of the latter, at the expense of those of the former. It could be that the victim is an occasional buyer to whom it is not worth offering protection for just a single transaction, whereas on the other hand it would be advantageous to promote the (in this case dishonest) interests of his coachman friend.

A more subtle interpretation might be that the mafioso, by 'guaranteeing' the sale of a blind horse to a victim who for whatever reason is not under his protection (or indeed under that of any more powerful mafioso),[19] is performing a demonstrative action: reminding everyone that without his protection it is not just likely but 'guaranteed' that cheating will occur. The mafioso himself has an interest in *regulated injections of distrust* into the market to increase the demand for the product he sells – that is, protection. If agents could trust each other independently of his intervention he would, on this score at least, be idle. The income he receives and the power he enjoys are the benefits to him of distrust.

Thus coping with, and at the same time re-creating, distrust would seem to be the means by which the power of the mafiosi has endured so long. No matter how distrust is generated, once it has been generated the important thing from the point of view of the individual buyer is to find a way of riding away from the market with a good horse rather than a bad one. From the point of view of the seller, the first priority is to be able to sell a horse; better still, a bad one. To choose to obtain the mafioso's protection can hardly be considered irrational. The collective disaster that is likely to follow from these individually rational premises – sky-high murder rates, higher transaction costs, lower incentives for technological innovation other than 'military' innovation, migration of the best human capital, higher cheating rates, poorer quality of goods and services – is the sad and largely unwanted result which has kept southern Italy the way it is.

[19] If the victim has been under more powerful protection this would be another typical case for the emergence of violent retaliation. It is clear that, in order to prevent tragic mistakes, it is essential to know who is who.

REFERENCES

Akerlof, G. 1970: The market for 'lemons': qualitative uncertainty and the market mechanisms. *Quarterly Journal of Economics* 84, 488–500.

Anonimo del XX secolo 1985: *Una modesta proposta per pacificare la citta' di Palermo*. Naples: Qualecultura.

Arlacchi, P. 1980: *Mafia, contadini e latifondo nella Calabria tradizionale*. Bologna: Il Mulino.

Arlacchi, P. 1983: *La mafia imprenditrice*. Bologna: Il Mulino.

Arrighi, G. and Piselli, F. 1986: Parentela, clientela e comunità. In *Storia della Calabria*. Turin: Einaudi, 367–492.

Banfield, E. 1958: *The Moral Basis of a Backward Society*. Glencoe: Free Press.

Blok, A. 1974: *The Mafia of a Sicilian Village, 1860–1960*. Oxford: Basil Blackwell.

Cancila, O. 1984: *Come andavano le cose nel sedicesimo secolo*. Palermo: Sellerio.

Catanzaro, R. 1985: Enforcers, entrepreneurs and survivors: how the mafia has adapted to change. *British Journal of Sociology*, 35, 1, 34–55.

Cosentino, F. 1983: Imprenditori sociali e processi di cambiamento nella Sicilia occidentale. Università degli studi di Modena: Tesi di Laurea.

Duggan, C. 1985: Fascism's campaign against the mafia. Oxford: doctoral thesis.

Fazello, T. 1558: *De rebus siculis decades*. Palermo.

Franchetti, L. [1876] 1974: Condizioni politiche ed amministrative della Sicilia. In L. Franchetti and S. Sonnino: *Inchiesta in Sicilia*, vol. I. Florence: Vallecchi.

Galante, G. 1986: Cent'anni di mafia. In D. Breschi et al., *L'immaginario mafioso*, Bari: Dedalo.

Gambetta, D. 1986: La mafia non esiste! Cambridge: unpublished paper.

Gambino, S. 1975: *La mafia in Calabria*. Reggio Calabria: Edizioni Parallelo.

Gower Chapman, C. 1971: *Milocca: a Sicilian village*. Cambridge, Mass.: Schenkman.

Gribaudi, G. 1980: *Mediatori*. Turin: Rosenberg and Sellier.

Hess, H. 1973: *Mafia and Mafiosi: the structure of power*. Lexington, Mass.: Lexington Books.

Hess, H. 1986: The traditional Sicilian mafia: organized crime and repressive crime. In R. J. Kelly (ed.), *Organized Crime: a global perspective*, Totowa, New Jersey: Rowman and Littlefield.

Hirschman, A. O. 1984: Against parsimony: three easy ways of complicating some categories of economic discourse. *American Economic Review* Proceedings, 74, 88–96.

Milgrom, P. and Roberts, J. 1982: Predation, reputation and entry deterrence. *Journal of Economic Theory* 27, 280–312.

Monnier, M. [1863] 1965: *La camorra*. Naples: Arturo Berisio Editore.

Pagano, U. 1986: The economics of positional goods. Cambridge: unpublished paper.

Pezzino, P. 1985: Alle origini del potere mafioso: stato e società in Sicilia nella seconda metà dell'ottocento. *Passato e Presente* 8, 33–69.

Przeworski, A. 1985: *Capitalism and Social Democracy*. Cambridge: Cambridge University Press.

Schelling, T. 1984: *Choice and Consequence*. Cambridge, Mass. Harvard University Press.

Schneider, J. and Schneider, P. 1976: *Culture and Political Economy in Western Sicily*. New York: Academic Press.

Staiano, C. (ed.) 1986: *L'atto d'accusa dei giudici di Palermo*. Rome: Editori Riuniti.

Tocqueville, A. de 1864–67: *Voyage en Sicile*. In *Œuvres complètes*, vol. VI, Paris.

Walston, J. 1986: See Naples and die: organized crime in Campania. In R. J. Kelly (ed.), *Organized Crime: a global perspective*, Totowa, New Jersey: Rowman and Littlefield.

11

Kinship, Contract, and Trust: The Economic Organization of Migrants in an African City Slum

Keith Hart

PROBLEM

This paper[1] is based on fieldwork done 20 years ago in the slums of Accra, Ghana's capital city.[2] For two and a half years I lived among migrants from north-east Ghana called Frafras who included the Tallensi, the object of a classic study by Meyer Fortes (1945; 1949; see Hart 1978). At home these were a traditionally stateless people, huddled together in densely packed egalitarian settlements, millet farmers and raisers of livestock. In 1960 only 1 in 16 was Muslim or Christian; fewer adults had even a modicum of schooling. Their political organization and religion were based on descent ties, neighbourhood (manifested as an earth cult), ritual specialization of clans, and marriage exchange. The largest corporate units (patrilineages) were linked to the constant flux of self-reproducing domestic groups by a common ideology of kinship and the practice of ancestor worship. Age and genealogical seniority conferred office and stewardship of collective assets, principally cattle for bridewealth, on an informal gerontocracy. But individual mobility and small-scale accumulation were widespread; and the frequency of raiding between quite close neighbours lent considerable uncertainty to the social life of these fighting hill tribesmen.

[1] I am grateful for their comments on earlier drafts of this paper to Ray Abrahams, Eduardo da Fonseca, Tanya Luhrmann, Alan Macfarlane, Anthony Pagden, Johnny Parry, and especially to Diego Gambetta and Geoff Hawthorn.
[2] The fieldwork took place in 1965–68 and is embodied in a Cambridge PhD thesis (Hart 1969). There are many reasons why I balked at publishing the enthnography in subsequent years, most of them to do with my criminal associations.

By the 1960s the Frafras were dispersed throughout Ghana as unskilled labourers, petty traders, soldiers and, in popular repute, thieves. They circulated between town and countryside, being usually linked to an extended family network based on their home village. When I first went there maybe 10,000 Frafras (out of a total of a quarter million) were living in Accra, many of them in a sprawling slum called Nima. This was a migrant shanty town, the chief red light district of the city's lower classes, and a criminal 'badlands' only sporadically policed from the outside. I lived with a Frafra 'fence' (receiver) and before long became involved in a series of criminal and semi-legitimate enterprises which formed the backbone of my fieldwork. Having intended to study political and associational life, I found the focus of my research gravitating towards the self-made economic activities which sustained Nima's inhabitants. Many Frafras had poorly paid wage jobs, many had none. Virtually all of them derived income from what I later (Hart 1973) came to call the 'informal economy': a sphere of self-employment, casual labour, petty accumulation, and illegal transfers defined at its apex by the corruption of public life. I concentrated on the few successful Frafra entrepreneurs to be found in Accra and scattered elsewhere throughout Ghana (about 70 cases in all);[3] but I also tried to capture the style of economic life for the mass of transients and longer-term residents who made up the migrant community, one of scores of ethnic groups retaining a distinctive identity in Nima's melting-pot.

I was captivated by what seemed a paradox: on the one hand the banality of a barely differentiated Dickensian mob, of water carriers, bread sellers, shit shovellers, taxi drivers, pickpockets, and prostitutes; on the other the communal spirit of hill tribesmen whose fathers were earth priests and who expected to end their days as custodians of ancestral shrines. I was impressed by the energy and ingenuity of their efforts to enrich themselves and by the inevitability of long run failure for all but a handful. It seemed as if the economy was being made, unmade and remade from day to day. The central task for everyone was to find a reasonably durable basis for livelihood and even for accumulation, a stable core in the chaos of everyday life. That was why even a poorly paid job was valued: it was an island of regularity and predictability in a sea of ephemeral opportunities. I now think of this as the search for economic *form*, the search for the invariant in the variable, for rules and regularity in a world constituted by flux, emergence, informality.

The Frafra migrants were doubly hampered in this task. Firstly, they lacked effective legal sanctions; the state's presence in the slum was intermittent and punitive (occasional police raids). They knew well

---

[3] Details of the entrepreneurs' sample may be found in Hart (1969). Another paper (Hart 1975) discusses a number of issues germane to the present enquiry.

enough about the contractual ethos of bourgeois civil society, but it was not evident how such an ethos could be translated into the social conditions typical of Nima. They were in many ways pre-adapted to the statelessness of the slum, less suited perhaps than migrants from the savannah's Islamic civilization to the emergent mercantile society which was growing up in the interstices of state rule. Secondly, even as many aspects of their traditional mores were reinforced by slum conditions, it was not easy to transfer their customary rural institutions to the city. At home kinship is structured by lineage organization, lending the full authority of ancestors to fathers, husbands, and senior brothers. Away from home the migrants abjured any simulation of this religion of descent. Genealogical differences of generation were collapsed into a single conceptual brotherhood; ancestor worship could not be practised since the structure of home groups necessary to make up a sacrificial congregation could never be replicated. The sheer unequal power of parenthood writ large was mainly absent in the slums, where ethnic solidarity found expression in beer talk and kinship was a domestic relationship of uncertain moral provenance.

To summarize, Frafra migrants were faced with the need to build economic relations from scratch in a world lacking both orderly state regulation and the segmentary political structure of their customary society. I shall argue that they had three basic models for such relationships, none of them unproblematic. One, *kinship*, is an extrapolation from statuses typical of traditional ideology and practice; its antithesis is the legally sanctioned *contract* of the modern state and civil society. There remains the zone of free-floating social relationships formed by choice in the expectation of mutuality. The most neutral term for this zone is *association*, but its strongest form of expression is *friendship*, the negotiated order of free individuals joined by affection and shared experience rather than by legal sanction or the ties of blood. It is in this third area of social life that trust plays so prominent a role, relatively unmediated by the formal obligations of kinship and contract.

The remainder of the paper is divided into three sections. Only in the last of these ('Argument') will I return to explicit consideration of the issues raised here. The main problem I address is the basis of durable economic relations in an environment that is marginal to both traditional and modern society. The section on ethnography is primarily concerned with indicating, by way of examples, the tenor of commercial life and petty enterprise in Accra's slums. It is not structured explicitly to highlight specific points about trust. This description is contextual to the later analysis of the significance of trust in migrants' attempts to build viable patterns of enterprise. The third section of the paper ('Definition') prepares the ground for such an analysis by exploring the semantics of trust and cognate terms.

ETHNOGRAPHY

My main concern is with the difficulties Frafras faced in trying to establish enterprises; but firstly we should consider the more diffuse issue of commodity exchange, the ordinary business of buying and selling. Most sellers in Nima are women, although the upper echelons of trade in Accra are dominated by men, often European or Lebanese men. There is a general lack of liquidity, that is the women's customers generally run out of cash before each montly pay period is half over. Indeed budgeting is extremely rare, especially for single men. Expenditures are normally erratic, even when individuals succeed in stabilizing some part of their income by earning wages. In this situation continuous commerce would be impossible without a high level of credit. Credit is thus the most prominent feature of buyer–seller relations; and you do not bargain if each side has a long-term arrangement to protect. This is particularly true of the purchase of daily comestibles, less so of occasional deals involving consumer durables like items of furniture. The higgling or sliding price mechanism that Westerners imagine is endemic to foreign bazaars is absent from large sections of Nima's market.

Prices normally vary by volume for a fixed price. Thus a woman will buy her goods from a wholesaler, often on a daily basis, take out a third of the total quantity to give away as sweeteners to preferred customers, and divide the rest into equal piles sufficient to give her a profit if sold for a standard sum. The customers always buy, say, a shilling of yams; what they get for it varies. The interdependence of both parties is based on the fact that sellers are subject to unpredictable shortages and gluts of supply and must have a steady clientele, while the buyers of course need to eat when they have no cash. Since bargaining depends on the ability of each party to walk away from the deal, this pervasive structure of credit and clientelistic particularism restricts the scope for such behaviour. It is not accidental that game theorists talk about used cars and 'lemons'. The rational negotiation of risk is less appropriate when most purchases go on the slate.

The problem of default was omnipresent. The women were usually illiterate and relied on fantastic memories to keep a register of customers' debts. If challenged they could always list each purchase over several weeks, persuading the client by sheer power of mental arithmetic. This reliance on memory placed an upper limit – perhaps eight to ten – on the number of debtors each trader could support. Capital shortage was another restrictive consideration, of course. As partial defence against default, traders of a given commodity would stick together where possible and share information on their clients' trustworthiness. They could also ostracize persistent offenders and avoid being played off against each other. Interest rates in Nima were high, 25 to 50 per cent per month, and outstanding debts at the end of the month would often be increased by such an amount. The high price of money reflected not just the obvious risk of default, but rather its extreme scarcity and the inefficiency of commercial institutions.

I noticed that something like chains of debt were commonplace. Each migrant made and received loans (including traders' credit). If a man came into a windfall – a stolen wallet or a back-dated pay rise – he was as likely to lend the money as to pay off existing debts. This meant that when he was being dunned by a creditor, he could pass on the pressure to one of his debtors. There is an analogy with traditional bridewealth transactions where in-laws typically chase an infinitely regressive chain of debt in order to retrieve an outstanding cow. Another metaphor for this process, besides that of a chain, might be the ripples caused by a stone dropped into a pool. Beer drinking (a traditional millet beer from the north) is the main activity of Frafra men at weekends. I calculated that women beer brewers generally sold a volume valued at five to six times their initial production costs. But they gave away a third, and most of the rest was sold on credit; so that they often had difficulty finding the cash to start off another three-day brewing cycle. Every now and then a major millet trader would arrive to collect on credit sales to the brewers. These impressive ladies would sit in the courtyard of their principal customer, for all to see. The brewers would put the squeeze on their clients, the clients would turn to their debtors, and so on.

The sanctions available to traders when dealing with defaulters were weak. One woman was reduced to entering a client's room at 4 a.m. to steal his only pair of trousers, which she then waved triumphantly in the courtyard while shouting out his crimes: 'You think Alhassan is a big man because he walks around in trousers and white shirt, but he won't pay a poor woman for the bread and cola he eats!' Public humiliation of this sort is a poor substitute for legal sanctions. But, as we know, small debt settlement is hard to secure anywhere. Although Nima was beyond the law and a violent place to live in, traders rarely if ever resorted to force in settlement of debts incurred by legitimate commerce. Usury and criminal enterprise were often a different matter, but even in the area of casual sex, pimps were rare and most women relied on informal moral sanctions to extract money from their lovers, so that prostitution as we know it was not common. That is to say that what Durkheim ([1893] 1933) called the 'non-contractual element of the contract', the non-rational conditions for rational negotiation, assumed a dominant role in shaping commercial life in Nima. Markets were normally far from competitive, and price-setting mechanisms were governed by relatively long-term considerations of credit that helped to stabilize turnover and to regulate the erratic fluctuations which buffeted parties on both sides.

Frafra migrants were well aware that much of this commercial activity depended on the establishment of trust between free agents whose scope for default was palpable. The protagonist in the following example laid great stress on the importance of a personal style capable of winning and sustaining the friendship and trust of strangers. His conversation often turned to episodes such as the time when, as a house servant, he refused to steal from his white employer, with beneficial long-term results. He had once been a part-time photographer, and his account of that period of his life epitomizes the precarious, highly individuated casual enterprises which many Frafra migrants sought to combine with wage employment.

Atia had been hawking a camera around with intermittent success: the problem was that it was 35 mm and his customers were often unwilling to wait until the film was used up. His breakthrough came when he went to a girls' secondary school with 600 pupils and persuaded the principal to allow him to take the girls' photographs at weekends. Many others had tried and failed; but, as he put it, his sweet approach worked. He spent over £10 on chickens, eggs, and gifts of money before she agreed and gave him exclusive photographic rights in the school.

Trade was brisk: every weekend he got through two or three films 'cutting' the girls. Whenever they saw him, they all wanted photos to send to their boyfriends and families. Some asked to be taken in the nude: 'I was trusted by all of them; they knew that I was there for the money, that's all. If one asked me to stay and do something, another will call for photo before.' He used to try to get an advance where possible, usually half. Those who gave him an advance were asked to write their names in a book, although he was himself illiterate. This was to stop any false claims; but in general he worked on a degree of mutual trust. If no advance had been paid and he made two copies which were refused, he couldn't force them to pay. If he had tried force, he said, maybe they would have ganged up against him and stopped buying his pictures altogether. So he relied on goodwill. Some girls would pay for a bad photo and later tear it up. If he heard of this, he would do them a new set free. Sometimes he 'fell down' when he spoiled the whole negative and had to refund all the advances. Atia claims his average profit was 50 per cent. Good photos fetched more or less what he asked for. If a customer was pleased, she might not ask for change from a banknote. By buying wholesale from one man and using another individual for enlarging, Atia could often get his production costs reduced. So the profit from two films over one weekend, although highly variable, could be substantial, more than a week's wages for steward work.

Later he had to give up photography after joining the army; he was put on a charge for spending too many weekends out of barracks. Despite

the doubling of army pay after the 1966 coup and the benefits of being a
regularly paid soldier, Atia was chronically indebted and looked back on
his work as a weekend photographer with some nostalgia, as a time when
he was free. Be that as it may, Atia's enterprise was short-lived and
unstable. He depended on the patronage of a headmistress and on his
ability to step through a minefield of adolescent girls. Having failed to
place his enterprise on a more durable basis, he fell back on a securely
paid job. His willingness to invent the conditions of his participation in
the market economy, rather than accept passively whatever its formal
institutions had to offer, was typical of Frafra migrants. A few of them
were more successful.

In the space of two and a half years, I built up case records on 71
Frafra entrepreneurs living in southern cities and their homeland
(including both villages and the main town of Bolgatanga). One in five
had assets worth more than £10,000 in the mid 1960s; half had accumulated £2,000 or more. These were substantial sums by Frafra standards,
but only three were rich on a national scale. Men outnumbered women
four to one. They usually maintained a diverse portfolio of investments;
few were committed to managing a single enterprise. They were part-time
petty capitalists: in the south, a third were still employed for wages and a
further half had been employed fairly recently. The most common medium
for investment was housing for rent (three-quarters of the sample); next
in priority (each being an interest of half the sample) were trade –
wholesale, retail, and commodity speculation; bars – beer and gin, food
(most of the women were traders or caterers); machinery and plant
producing services – flour mills, water supplies; and crime, including
money lending at usurious interest rates. A third of the sample owned
one or more commercial vehicles; transport was the riskiest but most
lucrative form of investment. In addition, some Frafras were contractors
in the construction industry.

Many of these activities belong to the sphere of circulation – rent,
interest, trading profit, theft – which make few labour demands. But
half of the entrepreneurs employed five or more workers and 80 per cent
at least two. For most of them the key problem of accumulation was that
of organizing a labour force in such a way as to secure routine transfer of
surplus value to the owner of an enterprise. Trust enters into this issue,
but it was much more prominent in the sphere of circulation, where
economic organization is shaped by credit and debt and the partnership
of equals rather than by productive hierarchy. I will return to this
question in the concluding section. Half the sample neither spoke nor
wrote any English (Ghana's official language) and only one in six was
literate. Yet, as a group, they were remarkable for having made a break
with traditional religion; whereas more than nine out of ten Frafra

migrants were pagans, 21 per cent of the entrepreneurs were Muslim and 18 per cent were Christian or some agnostic mixture, a total of almost 40 per cent in the Ghana sample. This figure rose to near 50 per cent in urban areas and 60 per cent in the southern cities of Accra and Kumasi.

As an example of enterprise involving the hierarchical organization of labour, I will briefly describe transport operations. The richest Frafra entrepreneurs all owned commercial vehicles, but the risks of failure were very high; the abandoned hulks which litter Ghana's roadsides offer silent testimony to the idea that transport is an entrepreneur's graveyard. In their home town of Bolgatanga, several Frafras ran long-distance trucking firms, mostly using 7 ton lorries. In the south, it was more common for individuals to operate small vehicles on a part-time basis: taxis, intercity estate wagons ('Peugeot') and minibuses ('Benz').

If you buy a car or lorry, there are three things you can do with it: drive it yourself, hire a driver, or sell to a driver on a hire purchase basis ('work and pay'). No one who spends his days behind a wheel is in a position to accumulate. Most naïve operators opt for hiring a driver for fixed wages, since the prospective profit is greater. This is why they usually fail: a wage employee has no incentive to maintain the vehicle or to be honest with the takings. One alternative is to make a driver pay the owner a fixed sum daily; but again, he has no stake in the vehicle and there is nothing to stop him making common cause with a crooked fitter to supply inflated repair bills or to certify that the vehicle was legitimately off the road for several days owing to breakdown. The most secure method is to sell the vehicle to the driver on an instalment plan and make him responsible for maintenance, a method pioneered in Ghana by Lebanese traders. Some owners would run the risk of hiring a driver for the first trouble-free year of a new vehicle and then sell it second-hand on the work-and-pay basis.

One Tallensi entrepreneur, after several false starts, evolved his own method of running a transport enterprise. He would buy driving licences for young men from his home area and let them serve an apprenticeship on someone else's taxi until he was convinced they were a good risk. When he had enough cash in hand to buy a vehicle for £2000–£3000, he would pick out one from his pool in reserve (many of whom lived in his household of some 80 persons). He would then write up a contract, adding £1000 to the sale price, selling it to the driver at £10 a day, with a clause giving him the right to seize the bus if the driver missed three successive days' payments. The driver is responsible for maintenance, but if he is in difficulties the entrepreneur pays for the repairs and adds the cost to the total to be repaid. In the interest of quick turnover, he is anxious that the vehicle should not lie idle for long. Most drivers take one to one and a half years to buy their bus or taxi. This case is remarkable for being largely independent of the Muslim-controlled lorry-park system in Ghana. It is also worth noting that kinship, self-reinforcing agreements, and legally binding contracts played a more important part in his enterprise than friendship and trust. He was not a trusting man – in contrast to Atia, the unsuccessful photographer – and this was reflected in his preference for hire purchase agreements over direct employment for wages.

On the face of it, another alternative to wage employment is family labour. Many small enterprises – a bar, a flour mill, a market stall – are well suited to family labour. But in practice it often turned out differently. Many of the catering and retail entrepreneurs were single women; and few of the men had conjugal relations which allowed them to enter into partnership with their wives, since the traditional role pattern is typically both patriarchal and segregated. Few had children old enough to be much help, and most of those were busy acquiring the qualifications for a career of literate employment. The fact that descent organization did not travel to the south meant that kinship ties were much more fluid and the authority of household heads was frequently weak. Here the contrast is with Asian minority communities whose tight cohesion provides patriarchs with external support to domestic hierarchy. Frafra migrants were mostly an undifferentiated brotherhood of mobile single men, linked to a few prominent married men by ties of patronage and pseudo-kinship or descent. Such a community did not lend support to domestic hierarchy. Consequently, family labour was problematic. One significant exception consisted of a group of Christian entrepreneurs for whom marriage meant an egalitarian partnership with a wife conceived of as friend.

Employment of workers involves supervision, delegation, and control on a scale which many enterprises in the sphere of circulation largely avoided. Usury, speculation, landlordism, and theft are usually inter-mittent activities, lacking the routinized preoccupations of most productive enterprises. Here the main problems concern extraction of rents or debts from clients, establishing cooperative relations with partners, and negotiating obstacles imposed by public authorities. In a place like Nima, even more than in Ghana generally, legal sanction for contracts is weak or non-existent, so that most activities are outside the law, whether or not they self-consciously infringe it. Rates of return are nominally very high, interest rates of 25 to 50 per cent per month being normal as against the legal maximum of 30 per cent per annum and current bank lending rates of under 10 per cent per annum. On the other hand, default may be as high as four loans out of five, an expression both of the general lack of trust and of the value attached to trustworthy relationships. Recalcitrant tenants are hard to budge; and market fluctuations trap all but the most expert speculators. Rational calculation of profit under these circumstances is virtually impossible, leading to an atmosphere of windfall and catastrophe which is not conducive to sustained accumulation.

My field notes are full of unexpected deductions from profits that had been calculated on paper. My landlord and I once speculated in the grain market by buying 50 bags of maize in anticipation of a substantial price rise before the next harvest. Not only did many hidden expenses arise (a bag shortage, the market porters' union, pesticide for the insects), but the USA flooded the market with a donation of surplus maize. This left us scrambling to sell on credit as our only chance of making a small profit; and it took us a lot of effort to get our money back.

This raises the question of what takes the place of law as the major source of sanctions in economic relations. From where do the forms of economic life draw their effectiveness? Clearly force was far from centralized; but systematic use of violence to enforce payment was relatively rare in Nima, as I have already indicated. Criminals used force in their relations with each other and with the police but not normally on the local public, from whom they expected and received a considerable measure of communal support. Reputation, name, honour, the macho complex offered much more scope for creditors and rentiers hoping to shame their clients into payment. Of course, successful entrepreneurs did use forms of contractual agreement; for example, a client might agree to sign a document for a loan of £150, when he had in fact received only £100, thereby evading the law on usurious interest rates. Pawnbrokers acquired real assets and thereby reduced risks. Above all, economic life depended on the discovery of complementary or shared interests which might make commercial agreements self-reinforcing in the short and medium term.

Nevertheless, a significant part of all this wheeler-dealing hinged on friendship, on the trust generated by shared experience, mutual knowledge and the affection that comes from having entered a relationship freely, by choice rather than status obligation. Whenever my landlord introduced me to one of his 'good friends', I knew that he was almost certainly a crook, probably from another ethnic group, a member of a criminal fraternity stretching back decades with a common background of gambling dens, police raids, gaols, diamond smuggling, drug rings, and all the rest. These were the men he turned to when he needed to trust someone, not his family or his fellow tribesmen. Elsewhere in Nima these friendship networks were solidified into more corporate brotherhoods by religious organization, especially by Islamic control of the cattle trade and long-distance transport. And in West Africa, but not for the Frafras, such informal organization was often provided by secret societies. Meyer

Fortes (1969) argued that kinship carries an 'axiom of amity' and perhaps it does; but another Tallensi proverb says *maalong gaat soog* 'familiarity is better than kinship' (literally 'making sweet', the experience of being treated well). In the fourth section the contrast between kinship and friendship lies at the core of an attempt to assess the significance of trust in Frafra economic relations.

DEFINITION

I study dictionaries. Our words contain a sort of archaeological stratigraphy representing great historical shifts in society *and* the continuing evolution of meaning and usage. Words do not stand still, and any attempt to fix them will fail. Some words change fast (compare Jane Austen's 'economist', an efficient housekeeper, with today's academic fraternity); others less so. Perhaps *trust* belongs to this latter category.

The Germanic stratum of English stresses the active voice of *ich*; it is personal and transitive. Latin-based constructions yield agency to abstractions, camouflage the speaker's voice in passive or intransitive verbs. Beyond this ancient distinction, modern society has exposed us to mass anonymous phenomena like markets and states which have removed from sight the intermediate pattern of human interdependence that give rise to the words we now use. In particular, modern English usage frequently collapses the distinction between persons and things, so that trust can refer equally to a person, an idea, or an object. Nothing stands between the individual subject and a depersonalized, abstract world; and our words reflect this fact. But in origin they referred to another world explicitly founded on concrete human relationships, on activities and passions: love, persuasion, coercion.

The discovery of such a world depends heavily on the achievements of British social anthropology. By investigating societies without states in Africa and Oceania, my predecessors revealed patterns of social organization and human interdependence that we had forgotten and could not recreate in our philosophical speculations. Hence the power of *African Political Systems* (1940) and of monographs on the Nuer and Tallensi. Unfortunately the lessons Fortes and Evans-Pritchard taught are easily lost. We need this knowledge if we are to escape the tyranny of modern conceptions of the world. For this reason, I wish to distinguish carefully between trust in persons and more abstract understandings, so that we can contrast what we are with what we are not.

The set of synonyms to which *trust* belongs is unusually confusing.[4] Faith, trust, and confidence all express belief. *Belief* is originally

[4] The principal sources for the etymological argument are the appendix on Indo-European roots in the *American Heritage Dictionary* (Morris 1969: 1505–50) and Buck's

something held dear (compare with *love*). To believe is to accept something as *true*. To *believe in* is to have *faith*, *trust*, or *confidence* in someone or something. Faith and confidence both come from Latin *fides*, which is the nearest thing to the Germanic *trust*. Since the Middle Ages, faith has replaced belief as the strongest word for trust placed in a person or thing. To cut through the detail, I wish to propose a continuum of words connoting *belief* based on the degree to which they rest on evidence of the senses. Faith requires no evidence; trust is an expectation based on inconclusive evidence, is tolerant of uncertainty or risk; confidence is a strong conviction based on substantial evidence or logical deduction. These are all subjective attitudes.

The notion of *reliance* expresses complete confidence, a presumptively objective state where belief is no longer necessary. To rely on something is to be tied to it, bound (compare with *religion*), as to an objective condition of existence. When there is no choice, *reliance* become *dependence*. Belief, by contrast, connotes freedom of the subject to make commitments in the absence of full knowledge. Belief is a feeling that a person or thing will not fail in performance. Feeling varies inversely with evidence or proof. Thus *faith* is an emotionally charged, unquestioning acceptance. *Trust* implies depth and assurance of such feeling, with inconclusive evidence or proof. *Confidence* involves less intensity of feeling, being based often on good evidence for being sure. *Trust* thus stands in the middle of a continuum of words for belief mixing extremes of blind faith and open-eyed confidence. Its etymology shows trust to be *true* like a *tree*, firm, steadfast, and loyal; not impervious to the evidence of the senses, but founded on a willingness to endure risk and uncertainty.

I wish to suggest that *Trust* has been historically associated with the notion of friend. Modern usage restricts the number of our friends to a narrow circle of intimates, narrower by far than those whom we might occasionally be inclined to trust. But among the Frafras of my study – and perhaps for medieval Englishmen – trust was closely bound up with an idiom of classificatory friendship which had a relatively broad range of application. One definition of *friend* (*American Heritage Dictionary*) is 'a person whom one knows, likes, and trusts'. This is superior to the *Oxford English Dictionary*'s retention of Johnson's definition: 'one joined to another in mutual benevolence and intimacy'. A *friend* is someone to whom one is not bound, and hence etymologically speaking *free*, based on choice not status obligation. A friend is not a kinsman. Friend is free and analogous to *wife* in some Germanic dialects (Frigg, Friya – wife of Odin), someone chosen. If friendship no longer means to

Dictionary of Selected Synonyms in the Principal Indo-European Languages (1949). Much of this work is highly speculative, even poetic.

us what it used to, neither does trust, when we can place trust in persons and things with no semantic discontinuity.

Social relations have generally evolved from a concrete, interpersonal basis to the abstract mass anonymities of political economy, an evolution obscured by a modern usage which tends to objectify persons as abstractions, much as pre-industrial cultures personify objects. Social theorists perennially ask how qualities of trust, fairness, and cooperation which belong naturally to intimate social worlds might be projected on to the modern stage of markets and states. Neoclassical economists, however, by basing their most general propositions on a formal rational calculus of individual decision-making, have tended to obscure the sociological distinction on which this paper hinges.

I agree with the emphasis placed by both Partha Dasgupta and Niklas Luhmann (in this volume) on the importance of personal agency in defining trust. Thus Dasgupta identifies trust as an expectation about another *person*'s actions which influences our own actions before we have full knowledge of the outcome; and Luhmann exposes to full view the distinction between personal and impersonal social organization. Clearly trust is the predication of one's own actions on actions of others which bear an identifiable risk of turning out unfavourably. The problem is to control extrapolation from a theory of rational choice to the larger frameworks of modern mass society.

To some extent, the institutions of industrial society justify a theoretical stance in which the personal–impersonal distinction remains blurred. But a study such as this one, of life on the margins of the modern state, requires that the difference between levels of social experience be kept in sharp focus. A similar problem arose when anthropologists turned to the analysis of kinship in stateless societies. Here the largest political groups, such as clans, are often represented as being *like* families. Yet Fortes (for example 1958) showed that the political and domestic levels were often contradictory and should be kept analytically separate. An anthropological approach to the problem of trust would insist on no less a degree of analytical discrimination. To summarize, I situate the notion in a set of belief concepts bounded at the extremes by faith and confidence, where the variable significance of evidence or proof is matched by a compensating level of affectivity. As such, trust is located in the no man's land between status and contract, the poles of primitive and modern society in evolutionary theory (Maine 1861).

ARGUMENT

The specific sociological analysis goes something like this. The Frafra migrants face the problem of establishing economic forms, durable relations of partnership and hierarchy, in the city slum. Three basic models for how to go about this present themselves. The most obvious and apparently profitable of these is the contractual ethos of the civil society they think they have joined, that is individualism, rationality, market, impersonal law – the bourgeois package of city life. Here economic relations are in principle entered into freely and by choice, but the contract imposes binding obligations sanctioned by state law. There are several reasons why this does not generally work. State law does not apply except in the form of occasional punishment. Markets are erratic and the substantive conditions of rational calculation are largely absent. The Frafras have not been socialized to make and keep contracts of this sort (they are, for instance, rarely on time), and the impersonal disciplines involved have to be invented from scratch. They lack education. They have no grounds for *confidence* in outcomes established by contract.

Looking for some alternative form of guarantee, the migrants turn to the antithesis of modern civilization, their own customary moral institutions founded on the identities of kinship, descent, and family, reinforced as they are by a common language and religion, by the certain obligations of birth and community. This option too is fallible. The institutions do not travel *en bloc* to Accra, and some of the important public sanctions of domestic hierarchy are missing: lineages, ancestor worship, the security of their homeland. The migrant community is an egalitarian brotherhood of floating young men anchored in the patronage of a few resident big men. It is not closed or powerful enough to shore up the authority and reliability of kinsmen. In any case kinship is a poor foundation for the reckoning of two-sided economic relations, especially unequal relations, since its central postulate is identity, sameness, a collective self defined by opposition to the generalized other. The idea of shared but separate interests cannot be expressed through a kinship idiom. Not surprisingly, Frafra migrants lose *faith* in their traditions as a viable framework for urban economic life.

Almost *faute de mieux*, denied the opportunity to rely on the poles of primitive and modern society, they fall back on the sphere of social life that people, perhaps friends, make out of their free-floating association. This, as Mauss (1967) argued most cogently, is the true locus of society, where self and other meet in some reciprocal understanding, where interests and risk are negotiated within relations formed by shared experience (even secrets), by love, knowledge, choice. Friends are free, and they remain free or they are no longer friends. Society in this sense is always personal, active, concrete: perhaps inevitably charismatic or magical, straddling as it does the abstract tyrannies of nature and reason, of totality and isolation.

Does friendship work for the Frafras? In a way it has to work, although rarely without the reinforcement of some other social interest. The case of money lending illustrates the point. Loans in Nima are never made to strangers. Landlords lend to tenants, patrons to clients. The borrower often invokes friendship as a way of soliciting a loan; the pretension of familiarity is the normal rhetoric of economic life in a place like Accra. Kinsmen make poor borrowers since they equate their interests with those of the lender. Again, small traders sell to strangers for cash. Once their customers become more familiar, they grant them special privileges (extras and, more important, credit), engendering trust by means of the gift and making a kind of friendship between buyer and seller, even when it was not a precondition for their association. Regular clients with substantial debts are few, and the traders must pick them carefully: in this respect they are as selective as we are with our personal friendships. But this does not prevent Frafras and others like them from invoking friendship quite casually in their economic relations, a sort of inflation of the social currency that members of our civil society would be likely to resist.

Most migrants fail to transcend the mores of fighting hill tribesmen in the social chaos of the slum. But some of them do. They are aided in this process if they make a break with traditional religion, for both negative and positive reasons. They need some social and cultural distance from the axioms of a society where personal freedom is hedged in by kinship obligations on all sides. World religions also confer membership of new associations which lend organization and sanctions to negotiated social relations. Similar claims could be made for secret societies and criminal fraternities. In Accra, Islamic brotherhoods controlled much of the intermediate level of business between the state-made corporate zone and its amorphous hinterland. They did so in informal ways which have been documented brilliantly by Cohen (1969) for the Hausa trading diaspora. Christians, at least the few Frafra Christians, did not join organizations relevant to their enterprise, such as Masons, Rotary, Lions etc. But they were encouraged to elevate their wives to the position of friend, partner, and equal, just as Anthony Pagden tells us (in this volume) Neapolitan social theorists (and, for that matter, a long list of more familiar thinkers) argued we all should, if we are to break down the wearing inertia of familism and segmentary politics which finds expression in the macho complex of public rivalry and private partiarchy. And the idea of two working as one, the ancient but often abused notion of wife as friend, is surely a recurrent theme in the history of enterprise.

Some Frafra migrants learnt to *trust* those whom they chose as friends, especially if they could draw on associations or on conjugal partnership. Impersonal pieces of paper were largely worthless. But personal relationships are created over time; so that exchange relations in Nima were above all a *learning* process. People found out by trial and error what worked for them; and the failure rate was very high. Accordingly, the problems of managing information and developing effective social tactics severely restricted ease of entry into the sort of market that most economists would characterize as competitive. The contrasting case studies presented in the second section make it clear that no easy correlation can be drawn between entrepreneurial success and an ability to make friends or engender trust. Indeed the highly successful transport entrepreneur relied on kinship and contract, while the hustler made more of the need for trust.

Frafras relied on trust as a last resort, for good reasons. Trust is essential to dealing, as is known by the diamond traders and by the game theorists, with their suckers, free-riders, and lemons. But the routines of productive organization are not easily managed by an ethos of personal freedom. Kinship and contract each offer a durable model for hierarchy and control: parental and legal sanctions respectively. This is why traditional rural society has room only in the margins for achieved relations of friendship and why trust accumulates in the interstices of mass societies organized by markets and states. Trust is central to social life when neither traditional certainties nor modern probabilities hold – in weak states or relatively lawless zones of public life, and in the transition to capitalism, especially in the mercantile sphere of circulation where credit is so important – but not as a basis for industrial production and division of labour. In other words trust is the negotiation of risk occasioned by the freedom of others, whom we know personally, to act against our interests in the relative absence of constraints imposed by kinship identity or legal contract. Domination and interest offer a more pervasive and durable basis for society than friendship and trust.

The list of triadic word sets shown in table 11.1 captures some of this argument. Like all words, these are ideal types: they either make for good communication and rational insight or they do not. Real people and societies do not conform to these types: empirical life is always a mixture, and our interest is in the varying emphasis of different arrangements. The most important observation is that, whereas many languages have words which identify some of the conceptual oppositions in the table, such as kinship and friendship, confidence and trust, it is normal for cultural categories and social organizations to be formed out of hybrid constructs. This was pointed out by Pitt-Rivers (1973) in his excellent paper 'The kith and the kin', written for Fortes's Festschrift.

Starting from the premiss that Fortes's link between kinship and the 'axiom of amity' was odd in view of the conceptual opposition most cultures make between kinship and friendship, Pitt-Rivers went on to

TABLE 11.1 *Elements of a triadic model of social organization*

KINSHIP	ASSOCIATION	CIVIL SOCIETY
Status	Relation	Contract
Family	Personal	Impersonal
Community	Network	Individual
Nation/descent	Social life/alliance	Market/state
Nature	Love/friendship	Mind
Self	Self/other	Other
Same	Like/analogous	Different
Custom	Experience	Law
Habit/conviction	Sentiment	Calculation
Traditional	Charismatic	Rational
Religion	Magic	Science
Language	Poetry	Logic
Closed	Secret	Open
Obligatory	Free	Free/obligatory
Certainty	Risk	Probability
Long term	Medium term	Short term
No evidence	Some evidence	Strong evidence
High feeling	Intermediate	Low feeling
FAITH	TRUST	CONFIDENCE

argue that, in the Mediterranean region at least, the key social relations are a fusion of the two polar types, both obligatory and free, a sort of pseudo-familism of the kinsman-friend: patron, godfather, brother-in-law, indeed affinal relations in general. Something similar can be discerned in religious brotherhoods and in the sworn secrecy of associates who take on the symbolic attributes of blood and common substance in their rituals. We can go further. A familiar critique of utilitarianism is that the contract rests on a non-contractual element which is both prior and irreducible to its logic. Hence capitalist firms are organized not just by a state-made legal sanction for exploitation, but by having recourse to the ideology of paternalism and mutual trust. Real social organization depends on creative combinations of the types, and successful mixtures will vary according to their situational effectiveness. It is the intellectuals who suppose that modern society could ever be founded on rational choice alone or that the simple-minded identities of primitive kinship-based societies have no room for person or the individual, as in practice all societies must.

My most general point has been made several times in this paper. Our modern English usage, inured as it is to the abstractions of mass society, makes no systematic discrimination between persons and things. But, if we rely on the language and ideology of our times alone, we will fail to understand a social evolution which crucially entails a shift in emphasis from personal to impersonal relations as a function of society's greater size and complexity. The value of the Frafra case study is that it forces us to conceptualize social life on the margins of the industrial world; and to concede that 'trust' may occupy a rather different place in the spectrum of social organization there than it does in the imagination of economists.

REFERENCES

Buck, C. S. 1949: *A Dictionary of Selected Synonyms in The Principal Indo-European Languages*. Chicago: University of Chicago Press.

Cohen, A. 1969: *Custom and Politics in Urban Africa*. London: Routledge and Kegan Paul.

Durkheim, E. [1893] 1933: *The Division of Labour in Society*. Glencoe, Ill.: Free Press.

Fortes, M. 1945: *The Dynamics of Clanship among the Tallensi*. London: Oxford University Press.

Fortes, M. 1949: *The Web of Kinship among the Tallensi*. London: Oxford University Press.

Fortes, M. 1958: Introduction. In J. Goody (ed.), *The Development Cycle in Domestic Groups*, Cambridge: Cambridge University Press, 1–14.

Fortes, M. 1969: *Kinship and the Social Order*. London: Routledge and Kegan Paul.

Fortes, M. and Evans-Pritchard, E. (eds) 1940: *African Political Systems*. London: Oxford University Press.

Hart, J. K. 1969: Entrepreneurs and migrants: a study of modernization among the Frafras of Ghana. Cambridge University, PhD thesis.

Hart, J. K. 1973: Informal income opportunities and urban employment in Ghana. *Journal of Modern African Studies* 11, 61–89.

Hart, J. K. 1975: Swindler or public benefactor? The entrepreneur in his community. In J. Goody (ed.), *Changing Social Structure in Ghana*, London: International African Institute, 1–35.

Hart, J. K. 1978: The economic basis of Tallensi social history in the early twentieth century. In G. Dalton (ed.), *Research in Economic Anthropology*, vol. 1, Greenwich, Conn.: JAI Press, 185–216.

Maine, H. S. 1861: *Ancient Law*. London: Murray.

Mauss, M. 1967: *The Gift*. New York: Norton.

Morris, W. (ed.) 1969: *The American Heritage Dictionary of the English Language* (first college edition). Boston: Houghton Mifflin.

Pitt-Rivers, J. 1973: The kith and the kin. In J. Goody (ed.), *The Character of Kinship*, Cambridge: Cambridge University Press, 89–105.

12

Neither Friends nor Strangers: Informal Networks of Subcontracting in French Industry

Edward H. Lorenz

Economists as a rule have attached little importance to the role of such social ties as trust and friendliness in market exchange. As Albert Hirschman (1982) has observed, this can be explained by the fact that the ideal market upon which claims of allocative efficiency rest involves large numbers of price-taking anonymous buyers and sellers supplied with perfect information. With such markets there is no room for bargaining, negotiation, or mutual adjustment, and the operators that contract together need not enter into a recurrent or continuing relationship.

   This paper considers a case which does not conform to the economist's competitive ideal, that of continuing and recurrent relations between French firms and their subcontractors.[1] These are relations involving mutual dependency, where each firm's actions influence the other. The situation by its very nature calls for cooperation, and it is reasonable to ask whether trust plays a role in this process.

   In order to motivate the discussion, I will first describe the context in which I decided to focus on the theme of trust and subcontracting. In 1985 I began a study of the introduction of new technology in small and medium French engineering firms.[2] This was prompted by a number of intriguing bits of evidence. From 1975 firms in this category had improved their performance relative to large firms in terms of profitability and rates of growth of output and employment. Further, in terms of the

[1] I would like to thank Diego Gambetta, Frank Wilkinson, Willy Brown, and Christina Ocampo for their interest in and suggestions for improving this paper. I also benefited from the comments of the participants in the trust seminar.

[2] The small and medium category (*petites et moyennes entreprises* or PME) refers to enterprises employing between 20 and 499 employees.

latter two criteria, the smaller firms in this category (between 10 and 100 employees) had outperformed the larger (Delattre 1982). Secondary sources also showed that small and medium firms had been some of the most dynamic investors in advanced computer-based technology, primarily NC and CNC machine tools (Cavestro 1984).

This picture of comparatively rapid growth and technological sophistication contradicted established views of the role of small firms in the French economy. In particular, it was inconsistent with the dualist model which predicted technological backwardness in accordance with the confinement of small firms to unstable portions of the product market. In order to come to some understanding of these unorthodox shifts in relative performance, I decided to investigate the process of mechanization in a selected number of mechanical engineering firms in the Lyons conurbation.

Preliminary visits to firms with 200 to 500 employees revealed that most had substantially reduced their employment levels since 1980. The value of their sales, however, had in most cases increased after a dip in 1982–83. This could be explained in part by improvements in their productivity, but also by a substantial increase in their use of subcontracting for intermediate component production.

To some extent, of course, the firms had used subcontracting before; few were of sufficient scale in their operations to warrant investing in plant for such specialized tasks as gear grinding or heat treatment. And they all made use of subcontracting to meet temporary capacity constraints.[3] What I was observing, however, was different. It was a shift to subcontracting on a permanent basis for such standard operations as turning, milling, and drilling. It allowed the firms to avoid making investments in up-to-date machine tools and was frequently the occasion for a reduction in capacity, with some existing plant being sold off. While the general type of operation subcontracted was not specialised or specific to the particular firm in question, the design and specifications of the components were. Thus it was not a case of substituting in-house production for standardized components available in the market: rather, components were being machined (turned, milled, etc.) by subcontractors according to firm-specific plans produced in the design offices of the client firm.

What appeared to be taking place, then, was a process of industrial disintegration similar to the well-documented Italian *decentramento*

---

[3] This form of subcontracting is encouraged by the rigid restrictions French legislation places on laying off workers. During the 1970s these restrictions spawned a proliferation of temporary help agencies whose employees do not benefit from the same protective legislation. Another common arrangement is the use of so-called *intérimaires*, permanent employees of one firm with an excess supply who are loaned on a temporary basis to a firm facing a capacity constraint.

(Piore and Sabel 1984; Sabel and Zeitlin 1985). The small-firm sector was benefiting from large firms hiving off some of the activities formerly undertaken in-house. When I questioned management about these policies, they generally attributed the decision to increase subcontracting to the 1981–82 depression in engineering together with the tremendous improvements in productivity then being made possible through the introduction of the CNC machine tools. Most argued that given the slow-growing and uncertain markets in which their firms operated, it would be impossible to amortize investments in CNC equipment. They were not in a position to continuously operate the equipment for the 12 to 16 hours a day required to achieve a satisfactory return on the investment. Smaller specialists, on the other hand, were in a position to do this, in part because they aggregated demands from multiple clients, and in part because of their greater internal flexibility in terms of shift work and overtime. In short, subcontractors could do it more cheaply.

Cost considerations, then, dictated the initial switch from in-house production to reliance on the market. Further discussion showed, however, that these evolving market relations were a far cry from those of the standard textbook, where 'faceless buyers and sellers meet for an instant to exchange standardized goods.' By 1984–85 the firms had begun to use a suggestive word to describe their relationship to these new subcontractors: partnership (*partenariat*). In the course of conversations in which I myself participated, other equally emotive terms evoked the nature of interfirm relations: the importance of loyalty (*fidélité*); the existence of a moral contract (*contrat moral*); and the need for mutual trust (*confiance mutuelle*). This language suggests a certain anxiety inherent in subcontracting, and the need for something like trust if the relationship was to work smoothly. Such considerations led me to structure my interviews around the following set of questions:

1 What risks does subcontracting pose, and what safeguards do firms make use of to minimize these risks?
2 What are the mutual obligations implicit in the relation of partnership?
3 What is the role of reputation in ensuring that contractual obligations are met?
4 How does a firm decide if it can trust another, and can this trust be intentionally created?

The remainder of the paper will be concerned with these issues, both at the analytical and the empirical level. I begin with some general remarks on the meaning of trust.

I

From my introductory comments it is no doubt evident that my notion of trust has something to do with relations of mutual dependency. I will now give a more precise definition of trusting behaviour in social relations.[4] This will clarify at least some of the semantic difficulties involved in employing a word with such varied usage. I will then turn to a discussion of the theoretical literature on vertical integration and subcontracting which shaped my empirical investigation. In the process, the relevance of the general definition of trust to subcontracting relations in particular will be made clear.

Trusting behaviour consists in action that (1) increases one's vulnerability to another whose behaviour is not under one's control, and (2) takes place in a situation where the penalty suffered if the trust is abused would lead one to regret the action. In economic terms this implies that the action would not be taken in the absence of trust because the expected net benefit is lower than if some alternative is chosen. In short, there is no best strategy independent of trust.

It is perhaps worth while to elaborate further on the implications of this definition. Firstly, trust presupposes decision-making in a situation of risk, where the risk is attributable to the strategic behaviour of others or to the possibility that they will behave opportunistically. By opportunistic behaviour I have in mind not only such blatant forms as stealing and lying, but also more subtle techniques such as withholding information in an effort to confuse. As Dasgupta (this volume) has noted, the possibility of such behaviour is a necessary condition for the question of trust to arise. If all people are invariably honest, doing their best to fulfil their commitments, then there is no problem of trust as I have defined it.

Secondly, the action and hence the risks are avoidable: one does not have to engage in trade with another firm (although this implies forgoing the potential benefits of trade). Being able to avoid the relation is fundamental. If you could not, you might say something like: 'I have no choice but to trust this person, institution, etc.' Clearly, there being no choice, we need not invoke trust to explain our behaviour. Of course, as Luhmann (this volume) points out, whether or not a relation is seen to be avoidable is often highly subjective, and presumably varies in accordance with the structure of institutions and political power.

Thirdly, it is useful to distinguish between risk associated with the behaviour of others and the risk of what economists call uncertain or exogenous events, such as acts of Nature or unpredictable changes in

[4] In common with Luhmann (this volume), I draw on the psychological literature, particularly Deutsch (1973).

consumer demand and prices. Trust in this context is unrelated to our concerns of possible opportunism and the violation of commitment.

II

Hirschman (1982) suggests that recent approaches in economics can address the role of social ties such as trust in market exchange. These approaches are concerned to explain the existence of continuing relations between economic actors by placing stress on such factors as transaction cost, limited information and imperfect maximization.

I would like to suggest that the transaction cost literature (associated notably with Williamson 1975; 1985) can tell us something about the role of trust in the economy. As the term 'transaction cost' suggests, this literature is concerned with the organizational implications of the costs of making a transaction. This includes not only the cost of reaching an agreement satisfactory to both sides, but also that of adapting the agreement to unanticipated contingencies and of enforcing its terms. Enforcement refers not only to potential litigation, but also to the use of private safeguards to prevent violation, a point I discuss in some detail in the empirical section below. The relation of transaction costs to the economy parallels that of friction to a physical system: it is often ignored in formal models but is none the less of great practical significance.

How does this relate to our concern? Trust enters into the argument because the presence of these costs is directly linked to the possibility that economic actors will be have opportunistically. This is obvious enough in the case of contract enforcement, but perhaps less so in those of negotiation and adaptation. Surely these latter costs are attributable to the time and expense of drafting a comprehensive agreement that attempts to account for all possible contingencies. But Williamson (1985) has made the point that in the absence of opportunistic behaviour there would be no need to attempt such costly planning: it would suffice for the two parties to agree always to adapt output to unanticipated contingencies in a jointly optimal way and always to share profits according to some general rule established in advance. Sequential adaptations would not pose risks if one could trust the other to behave honestly.

The tenor of my argument is probably becoming clear. If transaction costs are thought of as friction in the economy, then trust can be seen as an extremely effective lubricant. To quote Arrow (1974: 23): 'It saves a lot of trouble to have a fair degree of reliance in other people's word.'

I should emphasize that my use of the legalistic term 'contract' does not imply a comprehensive written agreement. In the subcontracting cases in question, agreements are never written. The only written document is the order form. Certainly there is no effort to engage in comprehensive planning. The initial agreement is a reference point, the gaps in planning being intentional, and it is understood that adaptations will have to be made if the relation is to continue. This incompleteness of contracts is one of the reasons (though not the only one) why, to my knowledge, there is no use of the courts to resolve disputes. It requires both subcontractor and client to engage in an ongoing process of discussion in order to resolve misunderstandings and ambiguities and arrive at acceptable terms. The court system is simply not designed to provide these services is an efficient manner.

Given the possibility of opportunistic behaviour, trust is an essential ingredient in intermediate product subcontracting in so far as the two firms are locked into the relation. By lock-in effects I mean not only that the mutual benefits will be achieved only if trade takes place, but that the identity of the partners counts. Switching partners involves a loss for both sides. As Klein, Crawford, and Alchian (1978) have argued, firms become locked into a relation when investments in specific assets have been made. This results in a bilateral monopoly. Specific assets are those whose value is less if switched to alternative transactions and consequently whose value is not fully salvageable if the relation breaks down. This situation would arise, for instance, if a subcontractor invested in machinery dedicated to the production of a specific component for a particular client and if the subsequent use of the machinery to service other clients' needs then entailed a costly retooling process.

An example may help to illustrate my point. Suppose a subcontractor invests in specialized fixtures and tooling to grind gears specific to a particular product. The amortized fixed cost of the tooling is £1000 per day and the daily operating costs are £200. Any contract price above £1200 per day for the subcontractor's services will allow a positive return on the investment. Suppose further, because the tooling and fixtures can only be adapted to other requirements at considerable cost, that the salvage value of the equipment if sold is £500 (daily rental equivalent). Consequently, if the contract is prematurely terminated the subcontractor faces a daily equivalent loss of £500. On the other hand, the client faces a potential loss associated with having to pay more for the components to be produced elsewhere with general purpose – and hence less efficient – equipment. He may also face costs due to the disruption of production while a replacement subcontractor is being found. The situation clearly calls for discussion and understanding, since without cooperation either side can block trade, thereby incurring mutual losses.

There is a large game-theoretic literature on such bilateral monopolies, concerned to find 'solutions' in terms of a determinant price for the supplier's services and hence for a division of joint profits (Rapoport

1970; Shubik 1959). The outcome is indeterminate in the sense that individual profit-maximizing decisions by the supplier and the buyer lead to an impasse. This is partly resolved in some models by explicitly taking into account the relative bargaining power of the two actors, represented by the magnitude of the loss each faces if the other carries out the threat to block trade.

My concern here is less with the terms of the original bargain than with the possibility of *ex post* opportunism: either reneging on the agreement or using the occasion of unanticipated contingencies to try to shift the distribution of joint profits in one's favour.[5] Returning to our example, suppose the subcontractor and the client agree on a contract price of £1200, allowing the subcontractor to break even on the proposed investment. Once the investment is made, however, the subcontractor's vulnerability is increased. The client is in a position to appropriate the subcontractor, demanding a new contract price slightly greater than £700 (the £500 salvage value if the assets are sold off and the £200 daily operating costs). He may justify this in the name of unexpected financial difficulties, which the subcontractor is generally not in a position to verify. Conversely, the subcontractor, realizing that the client faces stiff penalties for late delivery of the product to the final customer, may opportunistically use his bargaining power to push up the contract price, similarly claiming unforeseen costs. Verification may again be both difficult and expensive.

The main point is that even a situation of *ex ante* competitive supply, with a large number of subcontractors tendering bids for the contract, can be transformed into one of bilateral monopoly due to investment in specific assets. Once this occurs there is scope for opportunistic behaviour. If assets are general and products standardized, on the other hand, there is not. In this case the identity of the partners is not important, since if problems develop each can go his own way and fully redeploy his assets in other transactions without loss of value.[6]

---

[5] This is not to preclude the possibility of opportunism at the negotiation stage. Less trust implies that each side will take more costly measures to ensure that the other is truthfully disclosing their costs and revenues.

[6] This precludes the special hazard of fly-by-night firms. Suppose a subcontractor agrees to invest in a quality-improving asset (say a high-precision inspection device) for the purpose of a particular client's order. They agree on a price per component that allows the subcontractor a certain percentage return on the investment. The subcontractor, who has no intention of maintaining the relation, dishonestly avoids the investment, delivers a product below the specified quality, and receives the agreed price. The problem is discovered only when the component is assembled in the final product, whereupon the client responds by terminating the relation. The subcontractor gains from cheating and faces no loss associated with having invested in a specific asset that is not fully salvageable. The argument rests, of course, on asymmetric information, the subcontractor knowing more about the quality of the component than the client. In the empirical section below I discuss the safeguards whereby firms seek to protect themselves from such hazards.

The implication of this discussion is that the problem of trust in economic exchange is raised by the potential for opportunism inherent in investment in specific assets. Arguably, the contracting parties would avoid this problem if they could reach self-enforcing agreements. An agreement is defined as self-enforcing if the threat to terminate transactions (with a subsequent loss of business) if one party is caught cheating is sufficient to deter opportunism and ensure that contractual obligations are met. If such threats were sufficient, this would appear to resolve the problem of trust since each side would then be certain of the (rational) behaviour of the other.

The necessary conditions for self-enforcing agreements to be feasible have been enumerated in an interesting article by Telser (1980). His conclusions conform to the familiar results for infinitely repeated games which are discussed in this volume by Dasgupta.[7] Firstly, the sequence of transactions must be open-ended. There must always be a positive probability of continuing the sequence or else the relation will unravel. Secondly, for each player the discount rate has to be low enough for the one-off gains from cheating to be less in value than the expected net benefits that will be lost as a consequence of termination. Thirdly, the common knowledge assumption must hold. The players must share the knowledge that they share this ranking of the respective gains to be had from either violating or upholding the agreement.

There are two reasons why I believe this argument does not circumvent the need for trust. First of all it confuses information and trust. Clearly it is not enough for two firms to come together and share information on their costs and revenues. They also must trust each other's word. In other words, for common knowledge to play its assigned role in self-enforcing agreements there must exist a prior bond of trust between the contracting parties. Secondly, it does not adequately address the probability that unexpected developments in an unforeseeable future will trigger opportunistic responses. Trust will be essential to reassure those contemplating a long-term relation that adaptations to such future contingencies will be made in a jointly optimal way. The problem of trust in this context could only be avoided by making one of the following highly implausible assumptions about the nature of economic agents or the economic environment respectively. One could assume perfect rationality on the part of the actors: unlimited and costless ability to collect and process information. This would allow them to fully anticipate all relevant future eventualities. Alternatively one could simply assume what economists call a static world: a world without uncertainty due to exogenous events.

---

[7] See also Klein and Leffler (1982) for the case of quality assurance in final product markets.

In fact, with either of these admittedly unrealistic assumptions, it can be argued that the need for self-enforcing agreements would be eliminated due to the efficiency of third-party assistance in dispute resolution. If there were no limits to rationality, the two firms could costlessly negotiate a comprehensive agreement accounting for all possible circumstances. As Meade (1971) suggested, the world would be reduced once and for all to a giant higgle-haggle. Any subsequent efforts to alter the terms of the agreement could easily be rejected by the courts or by a third party as necessarily an effort to shift the distribution of joint gains to the favour of one side.[8] Much the same conclusion follows if we assume a world without uncertainty. In such a world, lacking in unanticipated contingencies, it would likewise be easy to negotiate a comprehensive agreement which the legal system could efficiently enforce.

In conclusion, then, once firms are locked into a relation, trust is essential. The need for trust can be circumscribed through the efforts of the parties to engage in comprehensive contracting. But the limits to our rationality in a world where surprise is inevitable ensure that such efforts will be imperfect at best. Trust cannot be disposed of entirely. The implications of this for economic exchange are threefold:

1 The right sort of investments may not be made, since actors do not trust each other to refrain from abusing their bargaining power to renege on contract terms or to use a shift in circumstances to shift the division of profits in their favour.
2 A considerable amount of expense may go into fashioning safeguards designed to minimize the risks of being a victim of opportunistic behaviour. These expenses could be avoided if there were mutual trust.
3 More subtly, those in a bilateral monopoly may hesitate to demand legitimate adaptations to changed conditions, fearing such demands may cause conflict owing to a suspicion that they are in fact illegitimate, and intended only to change the agreed distribution of profits.

III

The theoretical discussion implies that given plausible assumptions about the economic world, trust has an important role to play in facilitating efficient contractual relations. Is this borne out in practice? I now turn to

---

[8] This of course assumes that the courts are trustworthy. I make this assumption in the empirical section which follows, and I think it is a reasonable one. The French firms I interviewed never suggested that a concern over honesty prevented them from using the courts.

an interpretation of the empirical results, addressing in turn each of the questions raised in the introductory section. These results are based on interviews conducted with the managerial personnel of ten client firms, all located in the Lyons conurbation.[9] The firms include the following subsectors of mechanical engineering: machine tools, textile machinery, packaging machinery, mining equipment, and industrial filters. They are not mass producers: their products are large, complex, customized, and expensive. As production is to order they find it difficult to predict their requirements with any accuracy beyond a horizon of six months to a year.

The size of the firms varies between 100 and 400 employees. In most cases, as noted, employment levels have declined since 1980, owing in part to improvements in productivity and in part to increased use of subcontracting. Even those firms with expanding sales are not taking on additional labour. With one exception the firms experienced a decline in sales between 1980 and 1982 and subsequently have recovered to varying degrees. The size of the subcontracting firms they use, with few exceptions, is between 3 or 4 employees and 60. The average is between 10 and 20.

The first point to be made is that there is extensive use of safeguards by client firms to minimize the possibility of being the victim of opportunistic behaviour and hence the need to rely on trust. There is an Italian saying which captures much of the sentiment: 'It is good to trust but it is better not to trust.' First, client firms prefer to solicit tenders from a minimum of three subcontractors in order to preclude an opportunistic distortion of production costs. They also prefer to split an order between a minimum of two subcontractors so that if difficulties develop with one it is possible to switch to the other. This practice may, of course, entail a loss of potential scale economies depending on batch size.

Once firms are locked into a relation owing to investment in specific assets, such policies no longer apply. It is then impossible to refer to the market to ensure competitive pricing. In the case of physical assets (machine tools etc.) it is extremely rare for subcontractors to invest in machinery specific to a particular client's requirements. I only came across one significant example. The problem potentially arises in the case of tooling, that is specialized dies and moulds for forging and casting, and specialized fixtures and cutting tools for component machining. But

[9] The firms were initially visited in 1985. Five were revisited approximately one year later. In each case the production manager responsible for the firm's overall subcontracting policy was interviewed and in most cases so too was the buying agent. While these interviews constitute the principal source of information for this study, I also visited five subcontractors who work for three of the client firms. In each case I spoke to the owner or managing director. These interviews were less systematic than those conducted with the clients. The aim was simply to check for major discrepancies between the two sides' characterization of the subcontracting relationship.

risks are easily avoided: these physical assets are mobile and the client purchases them and retains control. If problems develop with one subcontractor the tooling is recovered and transferred to another. The rule is that subcontractors invest only in general purpose equipment. It is unclear whether this entails significant losses, however, since the more specific the machinery the less the sacrifice in scale economies from retaining production in-house. More suggestive of loss is the fact that when production of a particular type of component is carried out both in-house and externally (which does occur), the in-house machinery tends to be more specific.

Specific investment can take other forms, for example in training and skills. In the case of component machining this is relatively unimportant. As one production manager observed, 'nobody has a monopoly position in turning or milling.' There is a degree of skill specificity in the case of assembly work, and the general policy is that employees of the subcontracting firm undergo a period of on-the-job training in the assembly shops of the client firm before undertaking subcontracting on their own premises. In short, the costs of training in specific skills are borne by the client. The hazards implicit in such an arrangement no doubt help explain why so little assembly work is contracted out.

Assembly subcontracting poses a further hazard of the fly-by-night kind through private information on quality. In the case of individual component production, quality can be readily controlled. The client firm is as technically knowledgeable as the subcontractor. As a rule individual components are inspected on delivery and payment is made only after ascertaining that they meet the stipulated standards. In the case of subassemblies or entire machine assemblies, however, it is impossible to check the individual components, and problems due to poor workmanship may appear some time after the machine has been sold to the final customer. According to the client firms, it is primarily this problem of quality assurance which discourages them from resorting to assembly subcontracting on a regular basis.

Quality can pose a serious problem when components are delivered at the last moment, thus holding up completion of the machine and its delivery to the customer. This is costly since firms face severe penalties for late delivery on contracts which can sometimes amount to over £1 million. The risk of late delivery, accompanied by poor quality or not, is apparently the most difficult to safeguard against. Bear in mind that we are not talking about standardized components. The market cannot supply an instantaneous replacement; nor can the component easily be produced in-house.

In such cases, how is the firm to interpret a request from the subcontractor for an extension on delivery? Is it a legitimate request due to an unanticipated machine breakdown or some other unfortunate difficulty? Or is it opportunistic, the work having been taken on in the full knowledge that the capacity to complete the order on time was lacking? Given the difficulties of verification, repeated problems of delivery lead to the latter conclusion, with the subcontractor being dropped. When client firms say a subcontractor is trustworthy they invariably have in mind the question of prompt delivery as well as quality and price.[10]

Even when a subcontractor takes the precaution of investing solely in general purpose equipment it is possible to be locked into a relation. This occurs when a generalized capacity expansion is made only because of the prospect of selling a large amount of a particular product to a particular client. If the contract is then prematurely terminated the subcontractor is left with a large overhang of excess capacity that can only be sold off at distress prices. This clearly was recognized as a problem by the subcontractors interviewed, though they had varying degrees of success in coping with it. One quite successful subcontractor, for example, stated that occasionally it found it necessary to refuse orders from established customers so as to avoid the risks of a high degree of dependency. Others, who had grown up in close association with individual firms, had over 50 per cent of their sales directed to a single client. In such cases the loss of that client could prove crippling.

One of the most interesting results of the study is that not only do subcontractors seek to diversify their clients in order to reduce the risks of dependency, but so too do client firms. The accepted rule among the engineering employers of Lyons is that orders should be limited to between 10 and 15 per cent of a subcontractor's sales. The maximum figure is set to avoid the possibility of one's own market difficulties having a crippling effect on the subcontractor. Any figure less than 10 per cent, however, would imply too insignificant a position in the subcontractor's order book to warrant the desired consideration.

Effectively, then, clients put themselves in the position of the subcontractor in determining the optimal level of orders, much as game theorists have argued they should. From the subcontractor's perspective a reliable client is one who maintains a level of work. If a client firm wants a subcontractor to take its interests into account on recurrent contracts regarding quality and delivery, it is simply not acceptable to pull the work back in-house (assuming this were possible) whenever the firm faces a fall in final demand. Quantity adaptations also pose a trust

[10] Another potential hazard is that the subcontractor, recognizing his enhanced bargaining power at such times, will demand an increase in the contract price, claiming perhaps exceptional breakdown costs. In the short run the client may have no choice but to accede to the demand. A number of firms described such instances. There do not appear to be any effective safeguards. The only response is to seek an alternative supplier while completing the contract and subsequently break off the relation.

problem. How is a subcontractor to interpret a decline in the level of work from a particular client? Is the client facing legitimate difficulties, or is it opportunistically pulling work back in-house having first encouraged a capacity expansion? In the case of dedicated capacity expansions of a general purpose nature, quantity adaptations can be quite as contentious as price adaptations.

The 10 to 15 per cent figure seems to represent an optimum. It allows the client a degree of flexibility without undermining the viability of the subcontractor, and at the same time ensures the client is considered sufficiently important to make a continuing relation of interest.

This brings us to my second point, the meaning of the term 'partnership' or the expectations implicit in the moral contract. Partnership clearly implies something more than what is stated on the order form. It is not merely a question of not buying more than you know you can pay for. It seems rather to involve the following: in exchange for improved performance by the subcontractor on quality and delivery, the client firm will make every effort to guarantee a level of work; furthermore, any adaptations to price, quantity, and delivery are to be made in a non-opportunistic way by both sides, with full disclosure of the relevant information. In particular, this implies that the subcontractor will not be unconditionally dropped if a differential in terms of price or quality emerges with respect to competitors. Rather, clients stated that they operate a system of advance warnings; a reasonable period is allowed to their partner to match the competition. It also implies that clients will not pull back work in-house each time product demand falls. A number of firms observed explicit sharing rules to resolve problems associated with uncontrollable fluctuations in demand. A typical procedure was to guarantee that a constant fraction of work would be produced both in-house and by subcontractors regardless of the absolute level of output.

To sum up, partnership entails a long-term commitment and reflects a condition of mutual dependency where both client and subcontractor are in a position to influence the other by their behaviour. Partnership is a set of normative rules, determining what behaviour is permissible and what constitutes a violation of trust. The rules are designed to facilitate exchange in a situation otherwise open to exploitation.

The third point under consideration is the role of reputation in assuring compliance with the terms of the 'moral contract'. To put this question in another way: do firms rely on reputation alone in determining whether to trust each other? The evidence suggests that reputation is important but no substitute for experience. My information pertains primarily to the client's perception of the subcontractor and I would not want to exclude entirely the likelihood of asymmetry here. The client firms are comparatively visible, being prominent members of the Lyons engineering community and in most cases larger than the subcontractors. My interviews suggested that they are acutely aware of their reputation for reliability. When asked how they signalled their trustworthiness to potential subcontractors, they invariably referred to this.

But let us consider the conditions necessary for reputation effects to deter defection, here defined as violating the implicit terms of the partnership relation:

1 Common knowledge: all defections have to be made public. This does not simply mean a public announcement. It has to be possible to distinguish between real and bogus claims, to know who really was the offending party. This is frequently impossible.
2 The defector has to pay the full penalty: the firm cannot simply change its management team and ask for and receive forgiveness from the community.[11]

These are stringent conditions. In general, it is clear that client firms do not rely solely on reputation to determine the trustworthiness of a sub-contractor, in the sense of his willingness to uphold the terms of the moral contract. To know whether a subcontractor is trustworthy (and this is my fourth point) they rely additionally on their own experience. One manager said a minimum of a year and a number of contracts was required, though he claimed that after three months he had an intuitive sense of how things would turn out based on personal contact with his opposite number. Another firm gave the figure of two to three years. During this period they operated a conscious testing process. Initially short-term contracts were given, it being understood that renewal would depend on performance. Once satisfied, a one-year contract was offered in which for a fixed price they guaranteed a level of work. At this point, according to the manager, the two firms were partners.

Time and experience were critical elements in deciding whether or not to trust. This suggests, much along the lines of Good's argument (this volume), an incremental notion of trust, of trust being built up in success-ive stages. It should be stressed, however, that it is not simply a question of registering performance on successive contracts and assigning a probability of trustworthiness on that basis. Invariably interviewees stressed the need for personal contact, and a number of firms stated that geographical proximity was desirable because it facilitated this. Thus one manager observed: 'It is important to visit and to talk, to know each other. This is partnership. If we know each other it is easier to resolve problems and to

---

[11] One client firm, close to bankruptcy in 1980 and now supported by the state, was actively trying to improve its reputation for reliability. Management spoke as if the world began in 1983. The success of the publicity campaign was not entirely clear, but there was no evidence that this firm experienced greater problems with subcontracting than others in the region.

adjust. So the closer we are to each other the easier it is. The Rhône-Alpes has an advantage owing to the availability of subcontractors.

How are we to interpret this stress on the importance of personal relations? Is this evidence that friendship or caring is involved in efficient economics? Are we to conclude that trust between firms depends on bonds of friendship between the respective employers or managers? From the structure of this paper you can probably foresee that my answer is negative. It would be difficult to explain how trust could be present as often as it is in subcontracting if it were to depend on sentiments of friendship. If this were true, we would have to adopt in the economic sphere Hawthorn's (this volume) conclusion in the political: that any ·attempt to produce trust which was not in fact an attempt to produce something else, something self-reinforcing, must fail. It seems implausible to entertain feelings of friendship for someone when it is realized that he or she is acting in a friendly way solely for the purpose of facilitating an economic transaction.

I interpret the stress on personal contact in a different way and as primarily to do with a pervasive problem in continuing economic relations: the need to adapt to contingency. Personal contact facilitates this by allowing for an easier exchange of information. You learn about the other person's idiosyncracies and together you forge a special language which permits more sensitive interpretation. In short, you develop what might be called an understanding.

This is what I take the French managers to mean when they say they know each other and are partners. Perhaps this relation can best be conceived as an intermediate level between friends and stranger, for which capitalist societies have developed a distinctive tolerance. Of course, nothing I say precludes the possibility that those involved in recurrent economic relations may develop deeper personal bonds and that this may also become a reason for trusting. But the evidence of French subcontracting shows that such bonds are not a necessary precondition for trust. If this interpretation is correct, then there is nothing to prevent firms (if they consider it worth while) making a concerted effort to inspire confidence. Certain types of behaviour, certain types of personal contact involving the exchange of information and the giving of mutual assurances, plus a considerable time for the consistency of one's behaviour to be observed and tested: an effective combination of these things will surely enhance a reputation for trustworthiness.

IV

Economists generally assume that the narrow pursuit of interest results in efficient economic exchange. The aim of this paper has been to dispute this assumption.

The theoretical section addressed two issues: to determine the conditions under which the need for trust develops in relations of economic exchange, and to show that business interests cannot negate that need because human rationality is limited and the environment is uncertain. Trust is crucial when contracting parties invest in specific assets, locking them into a relation. Limited rationality means that efforts to protect ourselves from opportunism through comprehensive contracting will inevitably be deficient. Rational comprehensive contracting is impossible. Trust is expedient.

The empirical investigation of machinery producers and their subcontractors in Lyons illustrates these themes. Firstly, it indicates that promoting trust is costly. In addition to the time it takes to establish a personal rapport between client and subcontractor, it involves a set of policies referred to as partnership. Client firms offer substantial guarantees on the level of orders and prices in exchange for improved performance on quality and delivery. Secondly, it demonstrates that while trust is costly, lack of trust is more costly still. Without the long-term commitment of partnership, the client's use of subcontractors is dictated by the changing demands of his market. This makes the subcontractor's orders volatile. Volatility inhibits quality-improving investment in up-to-date technology. It discourages flexibility in recontracting terms. Competitive success increasingly depends on cooperation as requirements for quality have escalated internationally and markets have become more uncertain. Clients should be called upon to recognize their dependence on subcontractors in this respect. Thirdly, it is apparent that where possible clients and subcontractors limit the dependence that creates the need for trust in the first place. Subcontractors avoid investing in capital equipment or skills specific to the client's needs. For similar reasons, clients avoid subcontracting final assembly operations. These are general rules with few exceptions: the exceptions that occur do so within trust.

Finally, the broader implication of this research is that trust can be created intentionally. This is not to preclude multiple mechanisms. Trust between firms in Lyons may have resulted in part from the shared values of community members. Yet it is clear that trust was more than a by-product of actions directed towards other ends. This was amply demonstrated in the practice of partnership, which sacrifices short-term gains for the long-term benefits of mutual cooperation.

REFERENCES

Arrow, K. 1974: *The Limits of Organization*. New York: Norton.
Cavestro, W. 1984: L'automation dans les industries de biens d'équipement. II.

Collection des Études. Paris: Centre d'Études et de Recherches sur les Qualifications.

Delattre, M. 1982: Les PME face aux grandes entreprises. *Economie et statistique* 148, 3–19.

Deutsch, M. 1973: *The Resolution of Conflict: constructive and destructive processes*. New Haven: Yale University Press.

Hirschman, A. O. 1982: Rival interpretations of market society: civilizing, destructive, or feeble? *Journal of Economic Literature* 20, 1463–84.

Klein, B. and Leffler, K. B. 1981: The role of market forces in assuring contractual performance. *Journal of Political Economy* 89, 615–41.

Klein, B., Crawford, R. A., and Alchian, A. A. 1978: Vertical integration, appropriable rents, and the competitive contracting process. *Journal of Law and Economics* 21, 297–326.

Meade, J. E. 1971: *The Controlled Economy*. London: George Allen and Unwin.

Piore, S. and Sabel, C. 1984: *The Second Industrial Divide*. New York: Basic Books.

Rapoport, A. 1970: *Two-Person Game Theory*. Ann Arbor: University of Michigan Press.

Sabel, C. and Zeitlin, J. 1985: Historical alternatives to mass production: politics, markets and technology in nineteenth-century industrialization. *Past and Present* 108, 133–76.

Shubik, M. 1959: *Strategy and Market Structure*. New York: Wiley.

Telser, L. 1980: A theory of self-enforcing agreements. *Journal of Business* 53, 27–44.

Williamson, O. E. 1975: *Market and Hierarchies: analysis and antitrust implications*. New York: Free Press.

Williamson, O. E. 1985: *The Economic Institutions of Capitalism*. New York: Free Press.

Part III

Conclusion

13

Can We Trust Trust?

Diego Gambetta

In this concluding essay I shall try to reconstruct what seem to me the central questions about trust that the individual contributions presented in this volume raise and partly answer.[1] In the first section, I briefly qualify the claim that there is a degree of rational cooperation that should but does not exist, and I shall give a preliminary indication of the importance of the beliefs we hold about others, over and above the importance of the motives we may have for cooperation. In the second section, I define trust and the general conditions under which it becomes relevant for cooperation. In the third, I discuss the extent to which cooperation can come about independently of trust, and also whether trust can be seen as a result rather than a precondition of cooperation. In the final section, I address the question of whether there are rational reasons for people to trust – and especially whether there are reasons to trust trust and, correspondingly, distrust distrust.

I

The unqualified claim that more cooperation[2] than we normally get would be desirable is generally sterile, is often characterized by irritating

[1] In this essay converge not just several of the ideas which contributors have published in this volume but also those which were patiently expressed in conversation, and thanks to which my reflections on trust were shaped and reshaped. I am intensely grateful to all of them. Throughout the seminar, I relied constantly on the invaluable help of Geoffrey Hawthorn. The essay also benefits from exchanges with several other people at different stages of the seminar. In particular, I would like to express my appreciation to Luca Anderlini, Elisabetta Galeotti, Albert Hirschman, Caroline Humphrey, Alan Macfarlane, Andy Martin, Paul Ryan, Hamid Sabourian and Allan Silver. I am also particularly grateful to Heather Pratt for helping me to edit this volume as well as for polishing my awkward English.
[2] In this essay 'cooperation' is meant in the broad sense of agents, such as individuals, firms, and governments, agreeing on any set of rules – a 'contract' – which is then to be

rhetorical flabbiness and, if preached too extensively, may even have the effect of making cooperation less attractive (Hirschman 1984a). Such a claim can be and is disputed in a variety of ways. Let us begin by considering whether we necessarily need more cooperation, keeping, for the moment, the distinction between cooperation and trust blurred and their relationship implicit.

'According to the trite observation' – Adam Smith wrote – 'if there is any society among robbers and murderers, they must at least . . . abstain from robbing and murdering one another' (Smith [1759] 1976: 86; see also Saint Augustine in Dunn, this volume). This 'trite' observation serves a double purpose: it reminds us that basic forms of cooperation are inevitable if a society is to be at all viable, but it also points out, perhaps unwittingly, that there are instances of cooperation – notably those among robbers and murderers – that we may want to dispose of rather than improve. We may want *less* cooperation (and trust) rather than more, especially among those who are threatening us, and whose cooperation is a hindrance to ours. *A priori*, we cannot always say whether greater trust and cooperation are in fact desirable (Schelling 1984: 211).

The problem, however, is not only that we may want less of it among our enemies, but also that we may not want it among ourselves, at least not all the time.[3] And it is not just that we may lazily wish not to have to cooperate, but that we may wish for something else instead, notably competition. The ideological stance which holds competition and the 'struggle for survival' to be the texture of life is largely inadequate: in so far as it draws upon analogies with the animal world for its legitimation it is quite simply wrong (Bateson 1986 and this volume; Hinde 1986) and if taken literally there is no need to go back to Hobbes to realize that it would make social life impossible, or at least utterly unpleasant. Yet a certain dose of competition is notoriously beneficial in improving performance, fostering technological innovation, bettering services, allocating resources, spreading the fittest genes to later generations, pursuing excellence, preventing abuses of power – in short, in enriching the human lot. The rationale for this view is that not only those who succeed in competition benefit, but that the positive influence of competition is likely to be more generally felt.

---

observed in the course of their interaction (cf. Binmore and Dasgupta 1986: 3). Agreements need not be the result of previous communication but can emerge implicitly in the course of interaction itself, and rules need not be written but can be established as a result of habit, prior successful experience, trial and error, and so on.

3 There are also cases where we may not want universal cooperation for, beyond a certain threshold, additional cooperators could jeopardize the effectiveness of cooperation (cf. Elster 1986).

Even if we believe both that there are people whose cooperation we would wish to diminish and that the arguments in favour of competition are empirically as well as theoretically valid in a sufficiently large number of instances to make them relevant, it does not follow that, thus qualified the claim that there is a wide variety of cases where it would be desirable to improve cooperation is thereby invalidated. On the contrary, this claim holds in the relationships between as well as (to differing degrees) within countries, whether socialist or capitalist, developed or underdeveloped. The problem, stated in very general terms, seems to be one of finding the optimal mixture of cooperation and competition rather than deciding at which extreme to converge. Cooperation and competition are not necessarily alternatives; they can and do coexist in both the animal and the human world. Very few people, however, would venture so far as to claim that in the world as it is we have managed to get that balance right. Neither the Invisible Hand nor, as far as humans are concerned, natural evolution seems to help in selecting optimally between these two states, and we still seem profoundly ignorant of the ways in which we might master the causality that brings them about.

More important still, the possibility of competition may depend upon cooperation to a much larger extent than is generally acknowledged, especially in capitalist countries (Hirsch 1977): the most basic form of human cooperation, abstention from mutual injury, is undoubtedly a precondition of potentially beneficial competition.[4] As Robert Hinde (1986) has pointed out, there is a difference between outdoing rivals and doing them in, and within species, competing animals are considerably more inclined to the former than the latter. Even to compete, in a mutually non-destructive way, one needs at some level to *trust* one's competitors to comply with certain rules.

This applies equally to political and economic undertakings, and the awareness of such a need is not, of course, particularly novel. In spite of the fact that Hobbes has come down to us as the theorist of the inevitability of coercion in the handling of human affairs, he himself was conscious of the decisive role of the growth of trust among political parties for building viable societies (see Weil 1986). So was Adam Smith with respect to economic life. His notion of self-interest is not only contrasted from 'above' with the absence of benevolence, as is predominantly stressed, but also from 'below' with the absence of predatory behaviour (Smith [1759] 1976: 86; see also Hont and Ignatieff 1983). And, finally, in a characteristically historical remark Weber observed that the universal diffusion of unscrupulousness in the pursuit of self-interest

---

4 This does not entail a causal relationship whereby cooperation generates beneficial competition. It is more likely to be the reverse, i.e. harmful competition may be a motive for seeking cooperation.

was far more common in pre-capitalist societies than in their supposedly more competitive capitalist counterparts (1970: 17ff.).

The point, though, is not only that we may lack that basic form of cooperation which nurtures beneficial competition, as is often the case in underdeveloped countries. Nor is it just that we have competition where the majority would prefer cooperation, the international relations between superpowers being the foremost example (Hinde 1986). We may simply have the lack of mutually beneficial cooperation, with nothing to replace it. Game theory has provided us with a better understanding of why cooperation may not be forthcoming even when it would benefit most of those involved. As Binmore and Dasgupta put it in their survey of the subject: 'It is a major and fundamental error to take it for granted that because certain cooperative behaviour will benefit every individual in a group, rational individuals will adopt this behaviour' (1986: 24). Irrespective of individual rationality and motivation, cooperation may still fail to take place.

In this respect, one of the most interesting as well as threatening lessons of game theory is that even if people's motives are not unquestioningly egoistic, cooperation may still encounter many obstacles. This is a much more striking result than that which shows that rationality in the pursuit of self-interest may not suffice. Consider, for instance, the well-known case of the Prisoner's Dilemma and related games: the mere expectation that the second player might choose to defect can lead the first player to do so, if only in self-defence. The first player's anticipation of the second's defection may be based simply on the belief that the second player is unconditionally uncooperative. But, more tragically, it may also be based on the fear that the second player will not trust *him* to cooperate, and will defect as a direct result of this lack of trust. Thus the outcome converges on a sub-optimal equilibrium, *even if* both players might have been *conditionally* predisposed to cooperate (cf. Williams, this volume). The problem, therefore, is essentially one of communication: even if people have perfectly adequate motives for cooperation they still need to know about each other's motives and to trust each other, or at least the effectiveness of their motives. It is neccessary not only to trust others before acting cooperatively, but also to believe that one is trusted *by* others.

The lack of belief should not be confused with the lack of motive for cooperation. Motives for cooperation are of course crucial (see Williams, this volume). Yet, the mirror image of the 'major and fundamental error' of taking rational cooperation for granted is another fundamental error: that of inferring, if cooperation does not come about, that there are no rational motives for cooperation, and that people actually *prefer* the lack of it. For example, the ubiquitous problem of traffic jams in cities is often taken as a sign of the predominance of poisonous preferences for travelling by car over travelling by other mens. Although to some extent this may be so, there are also strong grounds for believing[5] that the motives for cooperation – that is, using bicycles and public transport –are not absent. What is lacking is the belief that everybody else is going to cooperate, which generates the fear of being the only 'sucker' around to sweat on the pedals, and the corresponding unwillingness to cooperate oneself. Thus, rationally motivated cooperation may not emerge and, if it does not, it does not follow that rational motives compatible with an increase in collective welfare are absent, but more simply that not enough people trust others to act by those motives. Revealed preference may simply reveal the fact that they are conditional on our beliefs: if the latter change, the former may change accordingly.

Here, traditional game theory does not help, for it considers beliefs to be far more undetermined than they are in reality, and further assumes that they are common knowledge. As a result, game theory loses predictive power, for it can 'find' more equilibria – usually more uncooperative ones[6] – than in fact there are in the real world. But 'why should beliefs held by different individuals (or types of individual) be commonly known? The fact is that our understanding of human psychology . . . is hopelessly imperfect. In particular, we have little idea of how individuals actually acquire beliefs' (Binmore and Dasgupta 1986: 11). Among these beliefs, trust – a particular expectation we have with regard to the likely behaviour of others – is of fundamental importance.

II

In this volume there is a degree of convergence on the definition of trust which can be summarized as follows: trust (or, symmetrically, distrust) is a particular level of the subjective probability with which an agent assesses that another agent or group of agents will perform a particular action, both *before* he can monitor such action (or independently of his capacity ever to be able to monitor it) *and* in a context in which it affects *his own* action (see Dasgupta and Luhmann in particular, this volume). When we say we trust someone or that someone is trustworthy, we implicitly mean that the probability that he will perform an action that is beneficial or at least not detrimental to us is high enough for us to consider engaging in some form of cooperation with him. Correspondingly, when

[5] This suspicion is backed by evidence: in a recent referendum held in Milan nearly 70 per cent of the population – many more than the number of unconditional pedestrians – indicated a preference for closure of the city centre to private and non-residential traffic.

[6] Thus Woody Allen, in *Hannah and her sisters*, says that the reason we cannot answer the question 'Why the Holocaust?' is that it is the wrong question. What we should ask is 'Why doesn't it happen more often?' Somewhat similarly, we should ask why uncooperative behaviour does not emerge as often as game theory predicts.

we say that someone is untrustworthy, we imply that that probability is low enough for us to refrain from doing so.

This definition circumscribes the focus of our interest in trust in several ways.[7] Firstly, it tells us that trust is better seen as a threshold point, located on a probabilistic distribution[8] of more general expectations, which can take a number of values suspended between complete distrust (0) and complete trust (1), and which is centred around a mid-point (0.50) of uncertainty. Accordingly, *blind* trust or distrust represent lexicographic predispositions to assign the extreme values of the probability and maintain them unconditionally over and above the evidence[9]. Next, the definition stresses the fact that trust is particularly relevant in conditions of *ignorance* or uncertainty with respect to unknown or unknowable actions of other (see Hart's definition of trust as something suspended between *faith* and *confidence*, and Luhmann on the distinction between the latter and trust, this volume). In this respect, trust concerns not future actions in general, but all future actions which condition our present decisions. Thirdly, by postulating that our own actions are *dependent* on that probability, it excludes those instances where trust in someone has no influence on our decisions. Finally, it limits our interest to trust between agents and excludes that between agents and natural events. At this level of abstraction, the definition could reflect trust in the intentions of others not to cheat us and in their knowledge and skill to perform adequately over and above their intentions.[10] The essays in this volume refer to both, although the former is generally more prominent.

The condition of ignorance or uncertainty about other people's behaviour is central to the notion of trust. It is related to the limits of our capacity ever to achieve a full knowledge of others, their motives, their responses to endogenous as well as exogenous changes. Trust is a tentative and intrinsically fragile response to our ignorance, a way of coping with 'the limits of our foresight' (Shklar 1984: 151), hardly ever located at the top end of the probability distribution. If we were blessed with an unlimited computational ability to map out all possible contingencies in enforceable contracts, trust would not be a problem (see Dasgupta and Lorenz, this volume).

Trust is also related to the fact that agents have a degree of freedom to disappoint our expectations. For trust to be relevant, there must be

---

[7] For an interesting review of different views on trust in the social sciences see Mutti (1987).

[8] The probability distribution of expectations can also be seen as expressing the *reputation* of others (cf. Dasgupta, this volume).

[9] *Loyalty*, in this context, can perhaps be seen as the maintenance of *global* trust – in a person, a party, an institution – even in circumstances where *local* disappointments might encourage its withdrawal.

[10] For a discussion of these distinctions cf. Barber (1983) and Luhmann, this volume.

the possibility of *exit*, betrayal, defection. If other people's actions were heavily constrained, the role of trust in governing our decisions would be proportionately smaller, for the more limited people's freedom, the more restricted the field of actions in which we are required to guess *ex ante* the probability of their performing them. Trust can be, and has been, more generally defined as a device for coping with the freedom of others (see Luhmann 1979; Dunn 1984).

The rulers of a slave society – assuming that they do not mind what slaves *think* – can restrict their trust in the slaves and in the viability of their society to the belief that the slaves are not going to commit mass suicide. They simply trust to the fact – not invariably borne out by historical evidence – that most humans, even under extreme conditions, have a preference ordering which ranks life before death. Here, trust must be understood in the limited sense of trusting the effectiveness of coercion as a motive for cooperation (see Williams, this volume). By contrast, trust becomes increasingly salient for our decisions and actions the larger the feasible set of alternatives open to others.

The freedom of others, however, is not by itself sufficient to characterize the conditions in which the issue of trust arises. Our relationship with people who are to some extent free must itself be one of *limited freedom*. It is a freedom in the sense that we have to have a choice as to whether we should enter into or maintain a potentially risky relationship: it must be possible for us to refrain from action. If it were only others who enjoyed freedom, while we had no alternative but to depend on them, then for us the problem of trust would not arise: we would hope rather than trust (see Hart's discussion of *reliance*, and Luhmann's of *confidence*, this volume). The freedom is limited in the sense that if our feasible set of alternatives is *too* large the pressure to trust anyone in particular tends to be lower (see Lorenz's discussion of exit options in markets, this volume).

In conclusion, trusting a person means believing that when offered the chance, he or she is not likely to behave in a way that is damaging to us, and trust will *typically* be relevant when at least one party is free to disappoint the other, free enough to avoid a risky relationship, *and* constrained enough to consider that relationship an attractive option. In short, trust is implicated in most human experience, if of course to widely different degrees.

Cooperation frequently makes some demand on the level of trust, particularly of mutual trust (for the conditions under which this occurs cf. Williams, this volume). If *dis*trust is complete, cooperation will fail among free agents. Furthermore, if trust exists only unilaterally cooperation may also fail, and if it is blind it may constitute rather an incentive to deception. However, depending on the degree of constraint, risk and interest involved, trust as a precondition of cooperation can be subjected to demands of differing intensities: it may be *needed* to varying degrees, depending on the force of the mechanisms that govern our cooperative decisions in general and on the social arrangements in which those decisions are made.

When considered prescriptively, this conclusion further suggests that we can circumscribe the extent to which we need to trust agents or cope with them in case of distrust. A wide variety of human endeavour is directed towards this end: from coercion to commitment, from contracts to promises, with varying degrees of subtlety, mutuality, legitimation, and success, men and women have tried to overcome the problem of trust by modifying the feasible set of alternatives open not only to others, but also to themselves.

Coercion, or at least its credible threat, has been and still is widely practised as a means to ensure cooperation; in its extreme form, to ensure submission and compliance. But it falls short of being an adequate alternative to trust; it limits the extent to which we worry about, but does not increase trust. On the contrary: coercion exercised over unwilling subjects – who have not pre-committed themselves to being prevented from taking certain courses of action or who do not accept the legitimacy of the enforcement of a particular set of rights – while demanding less of *our* trust in others, may simultaneously *reduce* the trust that others have in us.[11] It introduces an asymmetry which disposes of *mutual* trust and promotes instead power and resentment. As the high incidence of paranoid behaviour among dictators suggests, coercion can be *self-defeating*, for while it may enforce 'cooperation' in specific acts, it also increases the probability of treacherous ones: betrayal, defection, and the classic stab in the back.[12] (A more subtle way of constraining agents against their will is to enhance and exploit *their* mutual distrust. This has been known since antiquity as *divide et impera*, and is here explored in rich historical detail by Pagden; some of its consequences are taken up in my own paper on the mafia.)

Coercion does not have to be illegitimate, and may be employed for the purpose of enforcing rights which are commonly shared. In this case, instead of a unilateral action, coercion may itself be part of those cooperative arrangements intended to reinforce and reproduce a degree of trust in the observance of agreements previously reached with respect to those rights. But even if the controlled exploitation of coercive power

[11] This may establish some limit to the benefits of coercion to those who practise it, for as Veyne (1976) and Elster (1983) suggest, extremely successful and ubiquitous coercion can lead people to the extreme of making myths of their rulers.

[12] As I explain in my paper on the mafia, in spite of their constant efforts to over-determine the motives for cooperation, mafiosi are often obsessed with betrayal and deception.

were considered legitimate, it would not generally constitute an exhaustive 'functional equivalent' of trust. It would still be true that societies which rely heavily on the use of force are likely to be less efficient, more costly, and more unpleasant than those where trust is maintained by other means. In the former, resources tend to be diverted away from economic undertakings and spent in coercion,[13] surveillance, and information gathering, and less incentive is found to engage in cooperative activities.[14]

Constraint is relevant not only for us in deciding how far we need to trust others, but also for others to decide how far they can trust *us*. It is important to trust, but it may be equally important to *be trusted*. *Pre-commitment*, in its various unilateral and bilateral forms, is a device whereby we can impose some restraint on ourselves and thus restrict the extent to which others have to worry about our trustworthiness (see Dasgupta, this volume). In the case of Ulysses it may have been used to combat lack of self-trust (Elster 1979; Dasgupta, this volume), but it is generally invoked to weaken the demand that our trustworthiness places on others. How effective it can really be is particular in the extreme, and the range of possibilities is far too wide to attempt to apply any general principle. Certainly pre-commitment can be positive if it sets external causes in motion: when two individuals keep keys to the same safe, for instance. But it can also be costly, and a cause of bitter regret: when one decides to wear a chastity belt and throw the key into the river. In general, pre-commitment acting on external causes might be defined as the mirror image of coercion, in that it more or less significantly shifts the problem of trust towards a small subset of options: the banker need *only* trust his partner not to murder him or rob him of his key, and the departing lover need *only* be convinced that there *is* no second key.

Contracts and promises represent weaker forms of pre-commitment, which do not altogether rule out certain actions, but simply make them more costly. Contract shifts the focus of trust on to the efficacy of sanctions, and either our or a third party's ability to enforce them if a contract is broken. Promises are interesting in that the sanctions they imply may themselves take the form of trust: 'When a man says *he promises any thing*, he in effect expresses a *resolution* of performing it; and along with that, by making use of this *form of words*, subjects himself to the penalty of never being trusted again in case of failure' (Hume [1740] 1969: 574).

---

13 See Brenner (1986) for an account of the reasons why in pre-industrial societies the economic surplus tended to be invested in improving extra-economic coercion.

14 Some of the cumbersome aspects of Italian *vis à vis* British bureaucracy can be explained by the fact that the former invariably starts from the assumption that the general public are an untrustworthy lot whose every step must be carefully checked. Quite apart from the likely effect of self-fulfilment, there is the suspicion that the cost of running such a system may far outweigh the cost of even a large amount of cheating.

As contracts and promises suggest, the relevance of trust in determining action does not only depend on constraint; it is a matter, in other words, not just of feasible alternatives, but also of *interest*, of the relative attraction of the feasible alternatives, the degree of risk and the sanctions they involve. The importance of interest is twofold: it can be seen to govern action *independently* of a given level of trust, but it can also act on trust itself by making behaviour more predictable. The former applies when we consider trust – in the sense of a given value p of the probability – as an assessment prior to an assessment of other people's interests, while for the latter to hold there has to be some degree of information about the interests of others. Here I shall engage in a preliminary consideration of the first case, postponing the more complex second case to the next section.

If we assume an *a priori* estimate of the probability that a person will perform a certain action – which is to say a given degree of trust, predicated on whatever evidence (friendship, membership of a group, style of clothing) other than the interests of that person – the question is: how high does that probability have to be for us to engage in an action the success of which depends on whether the other person or persons will act cooperatively? The answer is that the *optimal threshold* of the probability of believing we trust someone enough to engage in such action will not be the same in all circumstances. In this sense, actions which are dependent on other people's cooperation are *independent* of trust: for any given level of trust, they may or may not be initiated depending on our particular predispositions and interests. That is, we can not only expect the threshold to vary *subjectively*, as a result of individual predispositions (one's inclination to take risks or degree of tolerance of potential disappointment); we can also expect it to vary in accordance with *objective* circumstances (Good, Luhmann, this volume). For example, it will be higher when the costs of misplacing trust are potentially higher than those of not granting it at all and refraining from action: to walk about in a trench in sight of the enemy (to pick up the example discussed by Axelrod 1984) requires an extremely high degree of trust that the enemy will observe the implicit truce, and the costs of being wrong may prove much more serious than those of lying low. We may attach a certain value p to the probability that someone is trustworthy, but if he has a gun – or the atomic bomb – this will make a considerable demand on the value of p for us to act. Here the pressure *not* to trust, to let only a very high threshold of trust govern our action, is strong (see Good, this volume). By contrast, if we expect an action – subject for its success to a cooperative response – to yield higher returns than the alternative options, what we stand to lose from 'playing defection' may be great enough for us to proceed even when p is small.

Here the pressure to accept even a low level of trust as the basis of cooperative action is stronger. We may have to trust *blindly*, not because we do not or do not want to know how untrustworthy others are, but simply because the alternatives are worse.

An interesting case arises where there is *tension* between the intensity of our interest in acting and the value of p. We may either not know whether to trust, or even know that we distrust somebody, but if we were to refrain from engaging (or attempting to engage) in cooperation, our losses could nevertheless be unacceptably high: opting out is a feasible option, but we would pay for it dearly. The option of avoiding or exiting from a relationship, for instance, may be present with respect to any one individual agent, but not when considered in aggregate terms: we may have a choice as to which restaurant we assign a high enough probability of not giving us food poisoning, but there are circumstances in which we can hardly afford to distrust *all* restaurants without perhaps suffering unpleasant consequences. The pressure to lower the trust threshold and pick *one* of them is substantial. Moreover, if we do not have any firm idea as to whether we can trust a particular individual – the probability is set at 0.50 – we may do away with the problem by choosing at random. This too, as in the case of forced reliance on someone else, is more a matter of hope than trust – at least in the first instance, when we have no evidence either way.

If the pressure to act is great even when the trust threshold is lower than 0.50 – when we verge, that is, on distrust – the tension between action and belief can generate, by means of wishful thinking and the reduction of cognitive dissonance, a deceptive rearrangement of beliefs. Thus there are those who distrust entire categories of people except the member of that category with whom they have a special relationship. Da Ponte makes this point clearly in Mozart's *Così fan tutte*. Don Alfonso claims: 'E'la fede nelle femmine come l'Araba Fenice, che vi sia ciascun lo dice, dove sia nessun lo sa.' And the lovers respectively reply: 'La Fenice è Dorabella' and 'La Fenice è Fiordiligi'. They both boldly and in mutual contradiction claim that all women are unfaithful except their fiancées.

In conclusion, the above examples tell us not *how* a certain level of trust is reached, but only that once reached it may be effective for action yielding potential cooperation, in different ways depending on the constraints, and on the costs and benefits presented by specific situations. Clearly, the higher the level of trust the higher the likelihood of cooperation, but cooperative behaviour does not depend on trust alone, and the optimal threshold of trust will vary according to the occasion. In addition, the last example indicates that the tension between what we need and what we believe may be strong enough to generate irrational, fideistic responses. Confidence, in the sense defined by Luhmann in this volume, might be described as a kind of blind trust where, given the constraints of the situation, the relationships we engage in depend or are seen to depend very little on our actions and decisions. In other words, confidence may also issue from wishful thinking and the reduction of cognitive dissonance; it would then be more akin to hope than trust. We still know little, though, about how a certain level of trust is or can be achieved and promoted.

III

The first question is, why bother? Why should we bother about trust at all when cooperation can be generated by other means? One solution is in fact that of not bothering, and concentrating instead on the manipulation of constraints and interests as those conditions of cooperation on which we can intentionally and most effectively operate. We can aim to promote as much cooperation as possible by deploying some reasonable degree of coercion and by supporting arrangements which encourage cooperation through self-interest, thereby making small demands on trust (for a successful case see Hawthorn, this volume and for the limits of this approach see Dasgupta, Dunn, Lorenz, Hawthorn, and Williams, this volume). If we are lucky enough to live in a society which holds some moral and religious beliefs – a side effect of which is to motivate cooperation for its inherent virtues – we can make good use of them. But we cannot count on these being readily available.

This is not just *a* solution: it is possibly *the* standard solution, which, filtered through Machiavelli, Hobbes, Hume, and Smith, has been handed down to the present day as the most realistic, economical, and viable. Trust – like altruism and solidarity – is here deemed a *scarce resource*. Elster and Moene make extremely clear the argument for this solution with respect to economic reform (1988):

> Indeed, some amount of trust must be present in any complex economic system, and it is far from inconceivable that systems with a higher level of general trust could come about. It would be risky, however, to make higher levels of trust into a cornerstone of economic reform. We may hope that trust will come about as the by-product of a good economic system (and thus make the system even better), but one would be putting the cart before the horse were one to bank on trust, solidarity and altruism as the preconditions for reform.

There is much to be said for this strategy – which might come under the heading of *economizing on trust* – and on the whole the papers in this volume are not opposed to it, nor do they necessarily say that it does not work. They do, however, raise three important points which diverge from this approach. The first is that trust is *not* scarce in the sense of a resource that is depleted through use; the second that although it is often a by-product, this is not always so; and the third that there are extremely important cases where self-reinforcing arrangements acting on interests are either too costly (or unpleasant) to implement, or unavailable in the first place because trust is in excessively short supply. I shall expand these points shortly, but first we need to take a step backward.

The most economical strategy of all is not that of not having to bank on trust, but that of not even having to bank on manipulating cooperative arrangements, on the assumption that rational – in the sense of optimal – cooperation evolves by itself. Pat Bateson's contribution to this volume explores some forms of cooperation in the animal world. The existence of cooperation among animals seems to suggest that cooperation may evolve without necessarily postulating trust, a belief which animals are unlikely to entertain. As Bateson argues, the emergent behaviour of social groups may contribute to their success: some of the features which make individuals successful in evolution may do so by working in conjunction with features developed by other individuals in the same group. Whether or not a group survives, in other words, depends on the emission and reception of signals which foster cooperation, in so far as cooperation improves the adaptive features of a particular group.

When transferred to the human world, the evolutionary approach might *a fortiori* suggest that trust would be better understood as a result rather than a precondition of cooperation. Trust would exist in societies and groups which are successful because of their ability to cooperate, and would consist in nothing more than trust in the success of previous cooperation. Cooperation could be triggered not by trust, but simply by a set of fortunate practices, random at first, and then selectively retained (with varying degrees of learning and intentionality).[15]

The idea that trust might follow rather than precede cooperation is reinforced by work in game theory, such as that of Axelrod (1984), which shows that even where trust is very limited and the chance of communication very slim – as between enemies facing each other across the trenches – cooperation may still evolve if other conditions obtain. The conditions Axelrod indicates with reference to a repeated Prisoner's Dilemma are (a) that the parties involved cannot escape confrontation

---

[15] Hayek (e.g. 1978) should probably be regarded as one of the theoretical fathers of this view. Nelson and Winter (1982) too, though they do not mention trust as a feature of the economic success of individual entrepreneurs, would probably agree that cooperative arrangements and trust might at times be among the successful entrepreneurial practices positively selected by markets.

(they have a choice only as to whether they cooperate or compete); (b) that they know they will be locked in this situation for a long period, the end of which is unknown; and finally (c) that they have a low enough discount rate of future benefits. Under these conditions – even if the parties involved cannot commit themselves in advance, cannot monitor the relevant behaviour of the other party before the event, and do not have the slightest prior notion of whether and to what extent they can trust each other – cooperation may still be triggered by a random 'signal' which is then retained due to the success of its consequences.

Take, for instance, the cooperation of 'live and let live' which flourished between enemy soldiers in the First World War (Axelrod 1984). This might be accounted for in various ways. It may have arisen as the result of a soldier shooting – out of distraction, boredom, or nervousness – at some clearly non-human target in the opposite trench. Or it may be that soldiers on both sides stopped shooting at regular intervals because they happened to have their meals at the same hours of the day. Such random signals may eventually have been 'interpreted' by one side as an incli-nation on the other towards an implicit truce, and they may have responded with other signals; first just to test for possible misunder-standings, then with increasing conviction, until the exchange slowly assumed the features of a stable cooperative abstention from mutual injury. Furthermore, what may have emerged accidentally can sub-sequently be *learned*, and soldiers apparently learned several ways of signalling to the 'enemy' their predisposition to cooperate.

It is not so much that trust is not involved here, as that it would not seem to be a precondition of cooperation. In essence, the conditions lie partly in the objective circumstances, and partly in the accumulation of knowledge with reference to mutual interests and the potential satisfaction of those interests through cooperative behaviour. The probability that the other party will not act in a harmful way is raised by the understanding that mutual interest makes defection costly enough to be deterred. The soldiers' belief that they can trust each other results from an inference concerning the effectiveness of their interests as a motive for rational action in initiating and maintaining cooperation. Thus p is raised in the course of cooperation itself, without any assumption being made as to prior levels: 'The cooperative exchanges of mutual restraint actually changed the nature of the interaction. They tended to make the two sides care about each other's welfare' (Axelrod 1984: 85). In the previous section we saw that interest, irrespective of trust, could make cooperation more likely simply by making action more pressing. On closer inspection we find that when that pressure is commonly shared *and* this fact is known to both sides, then cooperation is motivated and trust itself may increase as a result.

Hume made the case for this process absolutely clear:

> When each individual perceives the same sense of interest in all his fellows, he immediately performs his part of any contract, as being assur'd that they will not be wanting in theirs. All of them, by concert enter into a scheme of actions, calculated for common benefit, and agree to be true to their words; nor is there anything requisite to form this concert or connection, but that every one have a sense of interest in the faithful fulfilling of engagements, and express that sense to other members of the society. This immediately causes that interest to operate upon them and interest is the *first* obligation to the performance of promises.
>
> Afterwards a sentiment of morals concurs with interest, and becomes a new obligation upon mankind (1969: 574).

Axelrod's work suggests that this 'concert' may issue even from the most minimal chance 'to express that sense of interest', in a situation as apparently unconducive to cooperation as that of war, where agents, if anything, are more likely to distrust each other.

There are several problems with respect to generalizing the evolutionary approach. By this I do not mean the objection that it is difficult to generalize from experiments where each agent is represented by one computer strategy, or that the conditions fostering a cooperative outcome – such as having some knowledge of each other's interests – are sometimes hard to meet (cf. Williams, this volume). Even discounting these, I would still argue that – with respect to the time span of reasonable relevance to any given generation – the spontaneous evolution of a cooperative equilibrium among humans is only *just as likely* as that of a non-cooperative one, unless some restriction is imposed on agents' beliefs.

Although Axelrod claims that cooperation can evolve without trust, the strategy of tit for tat (according to his experiments the optimal one in playing the Prisoner's Dilemma) is inconceivable in relation to humans without at least a predisposition to trust: when the game has no history a cooperative first move is essential to set it on the right track, and unconditional distrust could never be conceived as conducive to this. If one group of soldiers for some reason believes itself to be facing a mob of unrestrained warriors and trusts neither the latter's time preferences nor their rationality, 'peaceful' signals are more likely to be interpreted as a trap. This problem may be circumvented by assuming the presence of uncertain beliefs and a random distribution which accommodates the probability of the right initial move being made and being 'correctly' interpreted. Yet there is no reason why the appropriate conditional beliefs should typically be the case, and the optimal move may be hard to come upon by accident (while we may not want to have to wait for it to come upon us). If it is true that humans are characterized by a lack of fine-tuning and a tendency to go to extremes (Elster 1983), the assumption that trust will emerge naturally is singularly unjustified.

Nor would a unilateral belief in blind trust be less damaging, for to protract trusting moves in the face of another's defection could lead to disaster rather than cooperation. In other words, if one inputs into Axelrods experiments either unilateral blind trust or blind distrust – whether unilateral or bilateral – the game will not culminate in a cooperative solution: the latter depends on the absence of these two lexicographic inclinations and the presence of a basic disposition towards *conditional* trust. The optimality of tit for tat as a strategy in playing a repeated Prisoner's Dilemma and generating a cooperative outcome also suggests that distrust should not be allowed to congeal after defection from the other side. It would be best to have no memory,[16] to forget that past defections may be repeated in subsequent moves. But in the case of individuals who *do* have some (finite) amount of memory, this is to prescribe as rational the avoidance of unconditional distrust even *after* the evidence would suggest it to be advisable. One inflicted 'wound', in this argument, should not be considered a sufficient reason for prolonged retaliation once the other side has been tamed by the first retaliatory response. Some degree of revealed preference for defection, in short, does not mean the absence of an interest in cooperation.

Cooperation is conditional on the belief that the other party is not a sucker (is not disposed to grant trust blindly), but also on the belief that he will be well disposed towards us if we make the right move. Thus tit for tat can be an equilibrium only if both players believe the other will abide by it, otherwise other equilibria are just as possible and self-confirming. To show that trust is really not at stake, Axelrod should have shown that *whatever* the initial move and the succession of further moves, the game tends to converge on tit for tat. What he does do is express a powerful set of reasons why – under certain conditions and even in the absence of trust generated by friendship, say, or religious identity – a basic predisposition *to trust* can be perceived and adopted as a rational pursuit even by moderately forward-looking egoists. We learn that, tentatively and conditionally, we can trust trust and distrust distrust, that it can be rewarding to behave *as if* we trusted even in unpromising situations.[17]

We might, of course, conceive of different moves – cooperative or defective – as simply appearing in random succession until the optimal blend is found and spreads through generations selected on that basis.

[16] Strictly speaking, to have one-period memory and act only in response to the other player's last move.
[17] For an excellent example see the collection of essays edited by Kenneth Oye (1986).

We might even agree that, in a certain number of billion years, the universe is likely to contain only those planets – or underdeveloped countries – whose inhabitants happened to hit on the right sequence of cooperative moves and to behave, to just the right extent, *as if* they trusted each other. On the other hand, we would also like Earth – and *our* children – to be among them. Evolution has bestowed upon us the mixed blessing of being able to generate intentionally the *as if* behaviour. Knowing this, we can hardly avoid the responsibility of considering trust a choice rather than a fortunate by-product of evolution.

IV

The strategy of economizing on trust does not of course imply that we should wait for cooperation to evolve by itself; it just claims that we should set our sights on cooperation rather than trust. We should, in other words, promote the right conditions for cooperation, relying above all on constraint and interest, without assuming that the prior level of trust will eventually be high enough to bring about cooperation on its own account. In a 'dissenter's confession', Hirschman (1984b) – although he disagrees with taking the strategy of economizing on trust too far (1984a) – makes an important case for breaking vicious circles in underdeveloped countries by implementing systems with technologically severe constraints capable of generating, rather than merely presupposing, trust: 'According to my way of thinking the very attitudes alleged to be preconditions of industrialization could be generated on the job and "on the way", by certain characteristics of the industrialization process' (p. 99).[18]

However, attractive as this strategy may be, it begs the crucial question of what is to be done either when p is so low that conditions suitable for cooperation are not available in the first place, or when p is not high enough to sustain potentially beneficial cooperation where those conditions are too complex, costly, or unpleasant to be a conceivable alternative to trust. The arms race might fall under the latter heading (see Hinde 1986), and most underdevelped countries under the former (see Arrow 1972: 'Virtually every commercial transaction has within itself an element of trust, certainly any transaction conducted over a period of time. It can be plausibly argued that much of the economic backwardness in the world can be explained by the lack of mutual confidence').[19]

[18] See also Hirschman (1967 and 1977). Hawthorn discusses the limits of this approach in this volume.

[19] On the relevance of trust for economic development see also Banfield (1958) and Mathias (1979).

What is at issue is not the importance of exploring in greater depth the causality of those forms of cooperation which are independent of trust, but the fact that *economizing on trust* is not as generalizable a strategy as might at first appear, and that, if it is risky to bank on trust, it is just as risky to fail to understand how it works, what forces other than successful cooperation bring it about, and how it relates to the conditions of cooperation. Considering the extremely limited literature on this crucial subject it seems that economizing on trust and economizing on understanding it have been unjustifiably conflated.

Motives for cooperation and factors other than trust that render those motives effective must be taken into account, and further research in line with Axelrod's study is likely to prove fruitful in the very near future.[20] Good, in this volume, considers experimental evidence which suggests the fundamental importance of long-term arrangements, of the absence of potentially aggressive devices, of the lack of ambiguity in what people cooperate about, and of a step by step increase in the risk involved in cooperation. Each of these conditions, by affecting constraints and interests, can also affect cooperation irrespective of a given level of trust, and when successful can serve to reinforce trust itself. Yet as Williams shows (this volume), such conditions cannot be assumed: formal structures and social reality have a distressing tendency to diverge, sometimes sharply. It is in the space of this divergence that trust must be wedged, and if *la fortuna* does not help, then intentionality based on the *as if* game must be brought into play. The issue now is the extent to which intentionality *can* be invoked.

Prima facie, trust would seem to be one of those states that cannot be induced at will, with respect either to oneself or to others. In the former case this is because rational individuals cannot simply decide to believe that they trust someone if they do not (Williams 1973); in the latter because they cannot easily set out intentionally to impress someone of their trustworthiness (see Elster 1983: 43: '[They are states which] appear to have the property that they can only come about as the by-product of actions undertaken for other ends. They can never, that is, be brought about intelligently or intentionally, because the very attempt to do so precludes the state one is trying to bring about'). There is a sense in which trust may be a by-product, typically of familiarity and friendship, both of which imply that those involved have some knowledge of each other and some respect for each other's welfare. Similarly, trust may emerge as a by-product of moral and religious values which prescribe honesty and mutual love.

---

[20] In his more recent work Axelrod stresses much more forcibly the crucial importance of beliefs and of the interpretations of situations that actors entertain (see Axelrod and Keohane 1986).

Personal bonds and moral values can only function as encouragements to action and cooperation if they are concepts in which we believe. Motive and belief belong together here: they are part of a person's identity, they arise out of his passions and feelings. It is constituent of the definition of personal bonds that – within the limits of character and skill – one trusts one's friends more deeply than strangers (see Hart and Hawthorn).[21] If it were not, the motive for acting on the basis of personal bonds would vanish. A similar argument applies to values: one can hardly act, say, out of fear of God, if one does not have faith in his existence.

Furthermore, neither of these potential sources of trust can be brought about at will: I cannot will myself to believe that X is my friend, I can only believe that he is. Nor can they easily be manipulated *in order to* bring about mutual trust and fruitful cooperation: if X detects instrumentality behind my manifestations of friendship, he is more likely to reject me and, if anything, trust me even less (Elster 1983). Thus we may explain the genesis of trust as an effect of moral and religious feelings – a point Weber notoriously pursued – or we may invoke the bonds of friendship as its prime source. But as rational individuals we cannot expect to induce these feelings simply because they may be useful, nor can we build our lives on the expectation of fooling ourselves or others systematically or for any length of time. It would seem to be a matter of social luck should such feelings happen to exist, and we cannot trust to luck. Moreover, personal bonds and values cannot be trusted as the foundation of cooperation in complex societies, not just because they cannot be wilfully generated, but also because of their fragility in a disenchanted world, and because they necessarily operate on a limited scale: I may believe in God, but I can still have my doubts as to whether you do too; even in Iran religious faith is backed by massive coercion, just to remind those who misbehave, by way of appetizer, what God's punishment will be like.

Yet at one extreme this view clashes with the rich historical and anthropological catalogue of cases where the bonds of friendship and familiarity have been extended in ritualized and codified forms – sometimes far beyond the socially narrow limits of 'true' friends and believers (Eisenstadt and Roniger 1984) – and where people, relying on limited and even truly scarce resources of familiar bonds, have acted on the fiction of

21 Trust in friends very much depends on what we need to trust them about. In pre-modern societies trust and friendship belonged together much more extensively. To the extent to which modern society has relaxed our dependence on friends for acquiring and maintaining resources, and has diffused and 'specialized' our relationships beyond localized familiarity, it has also given us a greater freedom to include among our friends some highly unreliable persons. The point though is that we are free not to depend on them. With respect to certain actions, we may actually trust others much more than our *friends*. For an extensive discussion of friendship and trust see Silver (1985).

the *as if* behaviour to the point where skilful and intentional pursuit can hardly be told from the random appearance of more or less fortunate practices (see Gellner, Hart, Hawthorn, and Lorenz, this volume). This applies equally to the 'good guys' and the 'bad', to the Florentine bankers of the late Middle Ages (Becker 1981) and to the mafia networks of 'friends of friends'. Fragile as these 'aristocracies' – as Hawthorn calls them – may be, always in need of external reinforcement both by sanctions and by success (in satisfying at least some people's interests), they often represent the only means of instigating a cooperative relationship that would otherwise fail because of uncertainty or frozen distrust. Among the rotating credit associations of Mexicans, studied by Velez-Ibanez (1983), there is an explicit 'cultural construct' known as *confianza en confianza*, trust in mutual trust: within the boundaries of 'aristocracies', trust is set to a value which is high enough for tentative cooperation not to be inhibited by paralysing suspicion.[22]

Conceptual and theoretical arguments likewise suggest that the maintenance of trust via the extension of associations based on personal bonds might be seen to involve an element of rational pursuit. Trust, although a potential spin-off of familiarity, friendship, and moral values, must not be confused with them, for it has quite different properties (Luhmann, this volume). It is perhaps such confusion which has led to the conclusion that we should treat it as both an eminently scarce resource and purely a by-product. This does not take adequate account of our ability to act, to simulate, try out, learn, apply and codify signals and practices which may initially be predicated on unintentional states, but which could be duplicated in the *as if* behaviour form far beyond their source. Trust, of course, can take on the connotations of a passion (Dunn, this volume; Mutti 1987), reinforced or undermined by feelings of affection, dislike, and irrational or intuitive belief (none of which can be induced at will). To economize on the latter – to assume that the right set of feelings and beliefs may simply not obtain – may be justified. But even in the absence of that set and of the 'thick' trust which may accompany it, and even if we do not believe in the social viability or in the moral desirability of those 'aristocracies' which bank on them (cf. Williams, this volume), it still does not follow that we should economize on trust or relegate it to the status of by-product.

The limits of this approach are probably more interesting than the approach itself. There is a wide range of anecdotal, historical, and socio-psychological evidence to suggest that our capacity for self-delusion far exceeds rational optimistic expectations, and that we can indeed make ourselves and others 'believe'. Trust is of historical interest to us

---

[22] See also Coleman (1984) who refers to similar associations in South-East Asia and Japan.

precisely in those cases where it is misplaced: it could not exist without the betrayal (Shklar 1984), deception, and disappointment our foolishness sustains. But let us start from the charitable assumption that the typical case is that of persons who tentatively adopt rational strategies in the formation of their beliefs and who present a degree of healthy resistance to fooling themselves and others. Fundamentally, we expect rational persons to seek evidence for their beliefs and to offer that evidence to others. Within limits (Williams, Lorenz, this volume), we can increase (or decrease) our p by gathering information about the characteristics and past record of others, and whenever the gaps left by asymmetric information and uncertainty appear detrimental to us, we can try to bridge them by rationally enhancing our reputation for trustworthiness, pre-commiting ourselves, and making promises. A reputation for trustworthiness is not just tangential to a good economic system: it is a commodity intentionally sought by – and a constant concern of – anyone who aims at such (see Dasgupta, this volume; Akerlof 1984). Interest may generate the pressure to behave honestly, but reputation and commitment are the means by which others are assured of the effectiveness of that pressure: 'A dealer is afraid of losing his character, and is scrupulous in observing every engagement. When a person makes perhaps 20 contracts in a day, he cannot gain so much by endeavouring to impose on his neighbour, as the *very appearance* of a cheat would make him lose' (Smith [1723] 1978: 538–9, my italics).[23] Conditions favourable to honesty and cooperation –that is, a healthy economy – *and* the reputation for trustworthiness must reinforce each other for a 'concert of interests' to be played. It may be hard to bank on altruism, but it is much harder to avoid banking on a reputation for trustworthiness: as all bankers (and used-car dealers) know, a good reputation is their best asset.

However, if evidence could solve the problem of trust, then trust would not be a problem at all. It is not only that the gathering and exchange of information may be costly, difficult, or even impossible to achieve. Nor is it just that past evidence does not fully eliminate the risk of future deviance. The point is that trust itself affects the evidence we are looking for. While it is never that difficult to find evidence of untrustworthy behaviour, it is virtually impossible to prove its positive mirror image (Luhmann 1979). As Tony Tanner has suggested (personal communication), this aspect of the nature of trust is implicit in Shakespeare's *Othello*. Othello asks Iago for 'ocular proof' of Desdemona's unfaithfulness. He could not conceivably have asked for direct evidence of her fidelity: the only ocular proof of (at least future) fidelity is a dead body. And given Othello's expectations, it is all too easy

---

23 I am grateful to Eduardo da Fonseca for bringing this passage to my attention.

for Iago to 'find' the evidence required. Doubt is far more insidious than certainty, and distrust may become the source of its own evidence.

Trust is a peculiar belief predicated not on evidence but on the lack of *contrary* evidence – a feature that (as Pagden (this volume) shows) makes it vulnerable to deliberate destruction. In contrast, deep distrust is very difficult to invalidate through experience, for either it prevents people from engaging in the appropriate kind of social experiment or, worse, it leads to behaviour which bolsters the validity of distrust itself (see my paper on the mafia, this volume). Once distrust has set in it soon becomes impossible to know if it was ever in fact justified, for it has the capacity to be *self-fulfilling*, to generate a reality consistent with itself. It then becomes individually 'rational' to behave accordingly, even for those previously prepared to act on more optimistic expectations. Only accident or a third party may set up the right kind of 'experiment' to prove distrust unfounded (and even so, as Good argues in this volume, cognitive inertia may prevent people from changing their beliefs).

These properties indicate two general reasons why – even in the absence of 'thick' trust – it may be rational to trust trust and distrust distrust, that is, to choose deliberately a testing value of p which is both high enough for us to engage in tentative action, and small enough to set the risk and scale of possible disappointment acceptably low. The first is that if we do not, we shall never find out: trust begins with keeping oneself open to evidence, acting *as if* one trusted, at least until more stable beliefs can be established on the basis of further information.[24] The second is that trust is not a resource that is depleted through use; on the contrary, the more there is the more there is likely to be (see Dasgupta for a demonstration, this volume; also Bateson 1986). As Hirschman suggests (1984a; also Hirsch 1977), trust is depleted through *not* being used.

The latter can be taken to mean different things. Firstly, trust may increase through use, for if it is not unconditionally bestowed it may generate a greater sense of responsibility at the receiving end. When we say to someone: 'I trust you', we express both a belief in and an encouragement to commitment by the trust we place in the relationship (Mutti 1987). The concession of trust, that is, can generate the very behaviour which might logically seem to be its precondition.[25] Secondly, if behaviour spreads through learning and imitation, then sustained distrust can only lead to further distrust. Trust, even if *always* misplaced, can never do worse than that, and the expectation that it might do at least marginally better is therefore plausible. However, while the previous reasons

---

[24] On the importance of acting *as if* for a solution of the Prisoner's Dilemma and related games cf. Sen (1974). On the 'suspension of distrust' see also Silver 1987.

[25] On the self-fulfilling nature of beliefs cf. Schelling (1978).

can motivate rational individuals to trust – at least to trust trust – this reason alone cannot, for though everyone may concede it, if the risk of misplacing trust is reputed to be high, no one wants to be the first to take it. It *is* enough, however, to motivate the search for social arrangements that may provide incentives for people to take risks.

More generally, trust uncovers dormant preferences for cooperation tucked under the seemingly safer blankets of defensive–aggressive revealed preferences. True, there are cases – such as in Sicily – where these preferences, if they were ever awake, have been sleeping so long that they may well be dead, reduced to the ashes of a historical reduction of cognitive dissonance. If this were the case, we might just as well give up, abandoning the place to its fate or simply trusting to collective disaster to generate the reasons for change. But the point is that if we are not prepared to bank on trust, then the alternatives in many cases will be so drastic, painful, and possibly immoral that they can never be lightly entertained. Being wrong is an inevitable part of the wager, of the learning process strung between success and disappointment, where only if we are prepared to endure the latter can we hope to enjoy the former. Asking too little of trust is just as ill advised as asking to much.

REFERENCES

Akerlof, G. 1984: *An Economic Theorist's Book of Tales*. Cambridge: Cambridge University Press.

Arrow, K. J. 1972: Gift and exchanges. *Philosophy and Public Affairs* 1, 4, 343–62.

Arrow, K. J. 1978: Uncertainty and the welfare economics of medical care. In P. Diamond and M. Rothschild (eds), *Uncertainty in Economics*, New York: Academic Press.

Axelrod, R. 1984: *The Evolution of Cooperation*. New York: Basic Books.

Axelrod, R. and Keohane, R. O. 1986: Achieving cooperation under anarchy: strategies and institutions. In K. Oye (ed.), *Cooperation under Anarchy*, Princeton: Princeton University Press.

Banfield, E. C. 1958: *The Moral Basis of a Backward Society*. Glencoe: Free Press.

Barber, B. 1983: *The Logic and Limits of Trust*. New Brunswick: Rutgers University Press.

Bateson, P. P. G. 1986: Sociobiology and human politics. In S. Rose and L. Appignanesi (eds), *Science and Beyond*, Oxford: Basil Blackwell.

Becker, M. 1981: *Medieval Italy*. Bloomington: Indiana University Press.

Binmore, K. and Dasgupta, P. 1986: Game theory: a survey. In K. Binmore and P. Dasgupta (eds), *Economic Organizations as Games*, Oxford: Basil Blackwell.

Brenner, R. 1986: The social basis of economic development. In J. Roemer (ed.), *Analytical Marxism*, Cambridge: Cambridge University Press.

Coleman, J. S. 1984: Introducing social structure into economic analysis. *American Economic Review* Proceedings, 74, 84–8.

Dunn, J. 1984: The concept of trust in the politics of John Locke. In R. Rorty, J. B. Schneewind, and Q. Skinner (eds), *Philosophy in History*, Cambridge: Cambridge University Press.

Eisenstadt, S. N. and Roniger, L. 1984: *Patrons, Clients and Friends: interpersonel relations and the structure of trust in society*. Cambridge: Cambridge University Press.

Elster, J. 1979: *Ulysses and the Sirens: studies in rationality and irrationality*. Cambridge: Cambridge University Press.

Elster, J. 1983: *Sour Grapes: studies in the subversion of rationality*. Cambridge: Cambridge University Press.

Elster, J. 1986: The norm of fairness. Chicago: unpublished paper.

Elster, J. and Moene, K. (eds) 1988: *Alternatives to Capitalism*. Cambridge: Cambridge University Press.

Hayek, F. A. 1978: The three sources of human values. L.T. Hobhouse Memorial Trust Lecture, The London School of Economics and Political Science.

Hinde, R. A. 1986: Trust, cooperation, commitment and international relationships. Paper given at the meeting of Psychologists for Peace, Helsinki, August.

Hirsch, F. 1977: *Social Limits to Growth*. London: Routledge and Kegan Paul.

Hirschman, A. O. 1967: *Development Projects Observed*. Washington: Brookings Institution.

Hirschman, A. O. 1977: *The Passions and the Interests: political arguments for capitalism before its triumph*. Princeton: Princeton University Press.

Hirschman, A. O. 1984a: Against parsimony: three easy ways of complicating some categories of economic discourse. *American Economic Review* Proceedings, 74, 88–96.

Hirschman, A. O. 1984b: A dissenter's confession. In G. M. Meier and D. Seers (eds), *Pioneers of Development*, New York, Oxford University Press for the World Bank.

Hont, I. and Ignatieff, M. 1983: Needs and justice in the *Wealth of Nations: an introductory essay*. In I. Hont and M. Ignatieff (eds), *Wealth and Virtue: the shaping of political economy in the Scottish Enlightenment*, Cambridge: Cambridge University Press.

Hume, D. [1740] 1969: *A Treatise of Human Nature*. Harmondsworth, Middlesex: Penguin Books.

Luhmann, N. 1979: *Trust and Power*. Chichester: Wiley.

Mathias, P. 1979: Capital, credit and enterprise in the Industrial Revolution. In P. Mathias (ed.), *The Transformation of England*, London: Methuen, 88–115.

McKean, R. N. 1975: Economics of trust, altruism and corporate responsibility. In E. S. Phelps (ed.), *Altruism, Morality and Economic Theory*, New York: Russell Sage Foundation.

Mutti, A. 1987: La fiducia. *Rassegna Italiana di Sociologia*, 2.

Nelson, R. and Winter, S. 1982: *An Evolutionary Theory of Economic Change*. Cambridge, Mass.: Harvard University Press.

Oye, K. (ed.) 1986: *Cooperation under Anarchy*. Princeton: Princeton University Press.

Sen, A. 1974: Choice orderings and morality. In S. Koerner (ed.), *Practical Reason*, Oxford: Basil Blackwell.

Schelling, T. C. 1978: *Micromotives and Macrobehaviour*. New York: Norton.

Schelling, T. C. 1984: Strategic analysis and social problems. In *Choice and Consequence*, Cambridge, Mass.: Harvard University Press.

Shklar, J. N. 1984: *Ordinary Vices*. Harvard: The Belknap Press.

Silver, A. 1985: Friendship and trust as moral ideals: a historical approach. Unpublished paper, American Sociological Association meeting, Washington DC, 26–30 August.

Silver, A. 1987: Friendship in social theory: personal relations in classic liberalism. Unpublished paper, New York: Columbia University.

Smith, A. [1723] 1978: *Lectures on Jurisprudence*. Oxford: Oxford University Press.

Smith, A. [1759] 1976: *The Theory of Moral Sentiments*. Oxford: Clarendon Press.

Velez-Ibanez, G. 1983: *Bonds of Mutual Trust*. New Brunswick: Rutgers University Press.

Veyne, P. 1976: *Le Pain et le cirque*. Paris: Editions du Seuil.

Weber, M. 1970: *The Protestant Ethic*. London: George Allen and Unwin.

Weil, F. D. 1986: The stranger, prudence, and trust in Hobbes's theory. *Theory and Society*, 5, 759–788.

Williams, B. A. O. 1973: Deciding to believe. In *Problems of the Self*. Cambridge: Cambridge University Press.

Index

240 *Index*